PAVIE IN THE BORDERLANDS

PAVIE IN THE BORDERLANDS

The Journey of THÉODORE PAVIE

to Louisiana and Texas,

1829–1830,

Including Portions of His

Souvenirs atlantiques

BETJE BLACK KLIER

Louisiana State University Press / Baton Rouge MM

Copyright © 2000 by Louisiana State University Press
All rights reserved
Manufactured in the United States of America
First printing
09 08 07 06 05 04 03 02 01 00
5 4 3 2 1

Designer: Amanda McDonald Scallan
Typeface: Sabon
Typesetter: Coghill Composition
Printer and binder: Thomson-Shore, Inc.

Library of Congress Cataloging-in-Publication Data

Klier, Betje Black.
    Pavie in the borderlands : the journey of Théodore Pavie to Louisiana and Texas,
1829–1830, including portions of his Souvenirs atlantiques / Betje Black Klier.
        p.   cm.
    Includes bibliographical references (p.) and index.
    ISBN 0-8071-2414-1 (cloth : alk. paper)—ISBN 0-8071-2530-X (pbk. : alk. paper)
    1. Louisiana—Description and travel. 2. Texas—Description and travel. 3. Frontier and
pioneer life—Louisiana. 4. Frontier and pioneer life—Texas. 5. Pavie family. 6. Pavie,
Thâódore—Journeys—Louisiana. 7. Pavie, Thâódore—Journeys—Texas. 8. Visitors,
Foreign—Biography. 9. Travelers' writings, French. I. Pavie, Théodore. Souvenirs
atlantiques. Selections. II. Title.

    F374.P38 K57   2000
    917.6304′5—dc21   00-028729

Unless otherwise noted, all illustrations are reproduced courtesy of the Chasle Pavie Collection, with the
photographs of them taken by Betje Klier and Yves Pavie.

The paper in this book meets the guidelines for permanence and durability of the Committee on
Production Guidelines for Book Longevity of the Council on Library Resources. ∞

CONTENTS

ILLUSTRATIONS

PREFACE

T HIS BOOK BRINGS to light the story of the remarkable Pavie family, whose lives reflected and influenced the history of four countries—France, Spain, the United States, and Mexico. The Pavie experience recounted here is of epic proportions, spanning sixteen decades (1733 to 1896). From their settlement in the Louisiana frontier outpost nearest the Mexican frontier, they witnessed the creation of the U.S. and its territorial expansion through the Louisiana Purchase. They saw Mexico achieve its independence from Spain, and personally helped Texas rise to autonomy.

All of the Pavie men who chose to come to America were educated *haute bourgeoisie*. Though they received inheritances from their families, all worked to support themselves and the families they created in the New World. They worked as traders, plantation owners, entrepreneurs, real estate investors, and priests. Their story relates the clashes and intermingling of races and ethnic groups and reflects the extreme social contrasts typical of frontier America. One family member was murdered. Several became wealthy. One made an illegal liaison with an African American and sired at least two mixed-race offspring, and in the egalitarian spirit of the time, his brother hobnobbed with the brother-in-law of the duc d'Orléans, whose son would be the last French king. Yet another contributed extensively to the records that document the times by faithfully tending his tedious administrative duties as village priest. The successive generations of the Pavie family embody the political, social, economic, and cultural flux of westward expansion, even though they never resided west of the Louisiana trading post where the first member settled. Their history thus provides a microcosm through which to view and understand the evolution of the American experience.

The Pavie adventurers created a tangible, physical world which enabled one of their progeny, Théodore Pavie (1811–1896) to benefit from his ancestors' endeavors and to capture and perpetuate some of that world for us today. Théodore Pavie visited Louisiana and Texas in 1829–1830, kept a journal, and made sketches of his journey. Upon his return home, his father published twenty copies of a travel book that Pavie prepared from his notes, and a Parisian publisher issued five hundred copies of a two-volume edition the following year. But the death without issue in 1838 of the most important Pavie family member to have settled in Louisiana sundered the French family from its American story. Thereafter, the Americanization of Louisiana and the extinction of the French language in Natchitoches completed the separation. A century and a half later, a sign in downtown Natchitoches proclaiming "Pavie Street" stood like a grave marker to one of the leading families of northwestern Louisiana when one day in the summer of 1988 I pulled *Souvenirs atlantiques* from a shelf in the library of the University of Texas at Austin where it had languished untouched since its acquisition for $8.70 in 1954. (Several years passed before I learned that this was one of only two bound original copies of the first edition of *Souvenirs atlantiques* known to exist in the United States, the other being held by the New York Public Library.) In 1988, when I couldn't afford to air-condition my large house during the merciless heat of a Texas summer, I spent much time in the library indulging my passion for nineteenth-century utopians and Romantic travelers who explored Texas, by systematically reading my way down the shelf marked 917, Travelers in America: French. In the table of contents of *Souvenirs atlantiques* I discovered a chapter entitled "Nacogdoches." When I also came upon "Natchitoches," I thought it was a typographical error, as I had never heard of the village that has since become *la patrie* of my intellectual life. It was some time before I discovered the letters from Victor Pavie to Victor Hugo in the Artine Artinian Collection of the Humanities Research Center at the University of Texas. With the help of the published Victor Hugo correspondence, I came to understand that the story of *Souvenirs atlantiques* tapped into the larger story of the major figures of French Romanticism as well as the history of the Louisiana Territory and Mexican Texas.

After I recognized the connection between the book in one building at the university and the manuscripts in another just a few hundred yards away, several more years passed before I was able to locate the writer Geneviève Chouan's [sic] (1908–1994), the matriarch of the Chasle branch of the Pavie family, who still held many of Théodore Pavie's letters and sketches.

A prize-winning poet herself, Mme Chouan's had founded a literary group, "Le Cercle d'Amis," and a literary journal, *Les Cahiers de Littérature et de Poésie, Les poètes et leurs amis,* which she edited for nearly thirty years. Geneviève Chasle Voisin had taken her nom de plume in honor of the servant Manette, who came to work for the grandmother of Théodore Pavie and cared for three generations of Pavie children. (A *Chouan* was a faithful follower of the Catholic Church and the King, Louis XVI, living in the Anjou region of France during the uprisings against the Revolution. She had added " 's" to the name to give it what she thought was an English spelling configuration.) When I wrote to her from America to express my admiration for her great-great-uncle's book, she responded, "Come to France; I have many letters to share with you." Somewhat invalid, and unable to travel or speak English, she welcomed the Louisiana I took to her parlor. We shared photos, documents, letters, and stories, as well as sketches, books, and laughter. Though Mme Chouan's had always intended to write the story of her ancestor Théodore Pavie's journey to America, at 86 she understood that she had waited too long to start. Many times she said I was "completing her destiny." After her death, in the auction for the dispersal of her estate, the "Vente Pavie," many literary documents of the notable Pavie companions and the extensive collection of medallions and sculptures by David d'Angers were purchased by the Musée David d'Angers and the Louvre.

This book presents for the first time the story of the Pavies, reconnecting the French and American narratives for a comprehensive view such as was known only by Charles Pavie and Théodore Pavie. It marks the first publication in book form of an English translation of the eighteen-year-old's interpretation of the Sabine borderlands of 1829–1830. Pavie's descriptions are unique in the history of the region because he was the most educated visitor who sojourned there without a political or reli-

gious agenda. His goals were to see and feel, and to record what he saw
and describe how he felt. The year that evokes revolution in France—
1830—was, in the Louisiana-Texas borderlands, a brief interlude of relative peace in the rush for conquest and empire. Texas historians will note
that Pavie's journey occurred between the Fredonian Rebellion (1826–
1827) and the Battle of Nacogdoches (1832). When the young Frenchman crossed the Sabine River, he situated himself culturally as being in
an "England, reproduced by Americans, giving way to Spain, now the
Republic of Mexico."

In order to understand the significance of the Pavie family and the significance of Pavie's journal to American history and literature, I have
framed their stories within a multicultural context. My narrative opens
with an account of the family's early experience in North America, followed by an examination of Pavie's youth and the cultural context
thereof, including the turbulence generated by the destruction of the Revolution and of Napoleon's empire and the temporary reconstruction of
French society under the Bourbons. Bored with his tedious life working
in a provincial print shop, the seventeen-year-old yearned to follow the
voyage of the seductive Chateaubriand—a genius as a writer and a failure
as a politician—to the American wilderness. Once there, Pavie used his
knowledge of Chateaubriand's writings as a tool for processing what he
encountered; in several passages beyond youthful idolatry and imitation,
the young traveler considered his own experiences and confirmed or disa-
bused himself of ideas garnered from the elder's work.

Following translations of Pavie's correspondence from America, "The
Historical Moment" analyses how Pavie's travels transformed his imagination and propelled him, in his later writings, to reclaim France's empire
which had been lost to the English in the eighteenth century. Part II presents the final third of *Souvenirs atlantiques,* wherein its author describes
his descent of the Mississippi and his winter in Louisiana and Texas.
Pavie created—or, more accurately, reinvented—an intellectual world of
proportions just as significant and far more enduring than that of his
forebears. One of his short stories, "Le Lazo" (appended to the second
edition of *Souvenirs atlantiques*) is a founding text of Texas literature by
virtue of its uniting Mexican and American western themes.

Appendices include (A) a family genealogy extending from the marriage of Joseph Pavie in 1733 to the death of Théodore Pavie in 1896,

with notes on the prominent Pavy family of Louisiana; (B) the passage from John Murel's own account of a murder that Théodore seemingly corroborates; and (C) a brief account of the important connection between the Pavies on one hand and Athanase de Mézières and Madame de Genlis on the other. In addition to the Geneviève Chouan's collection of Pavie's letters and sketchbooks, other descendants of his brother Victor Pavie have generously shared documents from their private collections to complement *Souvenirs atlantiques* and my own archival research in Natchitoches, Louisiana. This broad array of documents enables us to penetrate the adolescent mind of a future scholar while reconstructing the cultural contexts of his French and Louisiana milieus and building a better notion of the borderlands east and west of the Sabine River, from Natchitoches to Nacogdoches. With this firm foundation, *Pavie in the Borderlands* explores the psychological, intellectual, and geographic spaces that Théodore Pavie encountered in 1829–1830.

This project, in all its incarnations including the finished book, owes a great deal to the support I have received in Texas, Alabama, and California, where I lived while I wrote it, and Louisiana and France, where the story took place and where most of the materials are found. In Natchitoches, Louisiana, Conna Cloutier told me stories that brought the town's past to life, and helped sustain my enthusiasm by providing information and Creole hospitality. The narrative could not have been written without the support of the descendants of Victor Pavie, particularly Yves Pavie and the late Geneviève Chouan's, who furnished many of the materials and encouraged and assisted me at every step. Pascale Voisin and Serge and Gilles Pavie and their families also supported the extended project with information and hospitality.

I wish to thank several people for making possible the three separate tasks of composing this book: Diane North, who edited the discussions of history and literature; Claude Baudoin and Yves Pavie, who patiently assisted in the transcription and translation of the letters; Mary Ellen Foley and Alexandra Wettlaufer, who offered numerous helpful suggestions on the translation of *Souvenirs atlantiques*. When I was teaching at Auburn University, Dan Latimer encouraged me, "his fellow Longhorn", to translate the Texas chapters and edited them for the *Southern Humanities Review*, where they were first published in the summer of 1992.

I would like to thank three professors at the University of Louisiana in Lafayette: Carl Brasseaux, at the Center for Louisiana Studies, and Louisiana literature specialist Franz Amelinckx, for their help in providing information on various southern Louisianians encountered by Théodore Pavie; and William Dean (Bill) Reese, who edited the material on flora and fauna throughout the book. Felix O. Pavy, of Opelousas, held a family meeting for me that led to a productive discussion of the family's history, and artist Francis X. Pavy delighted my eyes with his Cajun creations and contributed additional documents on the Pavy-Pavie puzzle.

The genealogical and historical tools provided by Elizabeth Shown Mills and Gary Mills, quintessential to studies of the Natchitoches region, were generously augmented by personal correspondence. Natchitoches historians Carol Wells and Bobby DeBlieux, as well as Northwestern University archivist Mary Linn Wernet, provided much useful information. Judge R. B. Williams and the late Lucille Prud'homme graciously engaged in oral interviews. Marie Norris Wise provided a photo of Marianne Pavie's portrait as well as a guided foray into the photos of Eliza Bloodworth Blanchard's other descendants who lived in Evergreen Lodge, today the gracious home of Jack and Connie Curtis. Connie's mother, Carolyn Perot, and her husband, Joe, own the Ile aux Vâches plantation land today (between Natchitoches and Campti), a consolidation of the former plantations of Charles Pavie and Théodore's Aunt Helen (Hélène Pavie Poissot), who was Joe's ancestor. Although the plantation houses sadly no longer exist, I enjoyed the Perots' gracious tour of the Pavie-Poissot-Perot holdings, where one can easily imagine the steamboat dock at the bend of the river.

The entire manuscript in a longer version was meticulously read and helpfully criticized by devoted friends Jeff Gorrell, Agnes Peterson, and the beloved professor who introduced me to nineteenth-century France, Roger Shattuck. Portions of the manuscript were also critiqued by Jonathan Beecher, Gordon Bond, Frances Burkhart, Charles Cronin, Sheila Gaudon, Jack Jackson, Frances Karttunen, Archie McDonald, Mary Fae McKay, Karen Offen, Paul Robinson, Josine Smits, Phillip Stewart, Margaret Waller, Georgia Wright, and several infinitely patient French colleagues who were undaunted by Théodore Pavie's handwriting: Claude Baudoin, Mark Bertrand, Annie Berthier, Georges Cesbron, Cathérine Pavie, and Jean Soublin.

The best testimonial to the necessity of Franco-American cooperation on a project like this is the transcription of the first letter Pavie sent from Louisiana across the Atlantic Ocean to his family and friends in Angers. A copy of this missive, which was written on December 28, 1829, crossed the Atlantic Ocean in the opposite direction among my papers some 160 years later. Difficult handwriting and the inch the copier sliced off the *verso* forced me to send my tentative efforts back to France for assistance. The letter was returned to me neatly typed, almost complete, except for a few gaping holes where the vocabulary was indecipherable even by my French friend. It was again my turn. In red ink I added the missing words, which had become very clear to me after the other mysteries were solved. My final contribution was the names of five Indian tribes plus that of one dish from the evening meal, which Pavie described as a "delicious stew made with rice and Chateaubriand's sassafras" called *gambaud d'écureau*. (Théodore Pavie was enjoying *squirrel gumbo*.)

The other family I would like to thank, in addition to the Pavie descendants, is my own. My son sent e-mail messages to help me regain my focus when new endeavors distracted me and, as the years passed, my daughter never doubted that this book would be in your hands today. My husband Paul handled all the electronic questions and pushed, pulled, prodded, and propped me up through it all. The completion of this work owes more than I could express to his patient and affectionate support.

NOTE ON EDITORIAL METHOD

T HE TRANSLATION PROVIDED here begins in Part III of the 1832 one-volume edition of *Souvenirs atlantiques*. The English translation follows the French text closely. Regarding the use of ellipsis points, especially in Part II, please note that no text has been elided, except of course in the rare instances where a name or word was illegible; therefore, ellipses—whether present in the original French or added by me—indicate the trailing off of thought. Although I occasionally edited out conversational phrases devoid of content, such as "there are" and "As I was saying," I did not bowdlerize the text. The English version respects almost every paragraph separation in the original, but for two reasons does not always keep the nineteenth-century punctuation. First, most sentences would be too long for the modern reader, and second, as some of the letters containing similar phrasing demonstrate, Pavie most likely did not punctuate the book himself. Two generations after it was published, his brother's grandson, André Pavie, established the modern precedent of dividing his ancestors' lengthy sentences when he published some of Théodore's and Victor's correspondence early in this century. Several words used by Pavie whose meanings differed in the nineteenth century or in Louisiana are defined in the footnotes.

All of Pavie's prolix and effusive descriptions are nonetheless kept intact, despite the fact that his juvenile style became less enthusiastic—although retaining its vividness—as he learned to prune his texts in the years after the publication of *Souvenirs atlantiques*. The book in its overblown affect captures the heightened emotions of the splendor-in-the-grass moment of youth considered by British Romantics like Words-worth to be life's zenith. Please remember, also, that this book was written in a time when a writer could secure eternal fame with a few perfect lines. Théodore Pavie's place in Texas letters should have been secured when he crossed the Sabine in 1830 and wrote, "Texas is a whole other country"!

PART I

PAVIE IN THE BORDERLANDS

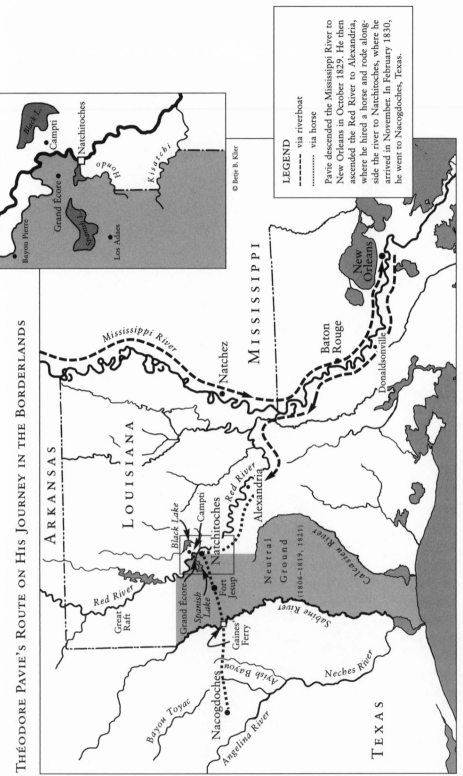

THÉODORE PAVIE'S ROUTE ON HIS JOURNEY IN THE BORDERLANDS

LEGEND

– – – via riverboat
· · · · · · via horse

Pavie descended the Mississippi River to New Orleans in October 1829. He then ascended the Red River to Alexandria, where he hired a horse and rode alongside the river to Natchitoches, where he arrived in November. In February 1830, he went to Nacogdoches, Texas.

© Betje B. Klier

Note: Neutral Ground boundaries based on Judge John C. Carr's description of January 2, 1809, to Governor William C. C. Claiborne. (Carr was Charles Pavie's brother-in-law.) My thanks to historian-cartographer Jack Jackson.

1

FRENCH PREDECESSORS OF THE PAVIES IN
LOUISIANA AND TEXAS

FRANCE'S CLAIM TO THE LOUISIANA Territory stems from the
expedition of René Robert Cavelier, Sieur de La Salle, who explored the
Mississippi River from Canada to the Gulf of Mexico in 1682. He
claimed half of the North American continent for Louis XIV and inserted
a French wedge between Spain's colonies in Mexico and Florida, which
until 1819 extended westward to the Mississippi. La Salle then returned
to France to garner the king's enthusiasm and support, and in 1684 he
sailed back from La Rochelle—soon to become the Pavie family's home-
town—to the forbidden Spanish Gulf with four ships and some three
hundred colonists bound for the mouth of the Mississippi. After being
blown off course in a storm, they unwittingly landed in Texas, where La
Salle was forced to establish his colony, Fort Saint Louis. "Fevers" and
cannibalistic Karankawas on the coast of Texas killed most of the colonists, and in 1687 La Salle was murdered by two of his own men, who
left his body without Christian burial, exposed to the wolves and vultures.

One hundred years later, Théodore Pavie's great-uncle Étienne Pavie
also sailed from La Rochelle and, like his countryman La Salle, was mur-

dered in the New World. Although illnesses claimed the lives of many members of the extended Pavie family in Louisiana, the European-born Pavie men who went to America as adults seem to have largely resisted at least the fatal effects. Nonetheless, fear of the "fevers" controlled the young French visitor's schedule in 1829; moreover, when he left Natchitoches, Louisiana, for Nacogdoches, Texas, he confided to his brother about the weapons he would take with him as a precaution for going to Texas: "Day after tomorrow I'm leaving with several people to take a four-day trek into Mexico, mounted on a big mule with a carbine and two loaded pistols, without forgetting my dagger. I ask you not to tell the parents for fear they would be worried. This journey offers almost no danger, however, and the anthropophagic savages holed up more than ten days from here, and we're arming only as a precaution."[1]

Pavie's mention of the "anthropophagic savages" alluded to a widespread French belief about the Texas coast derived first from the reports of La Salle's chronicler, Joutel. The idea of cannibalistic Indians was reinforced not only by the popular map of Guillaume Délisle but more recently by published accounts of the brutal deaths of two exiles who had followed Bonapartist general Charles Lallemand to the Texas coast in 1818.[2]

Another of Pavie's countrymen succeeded—where his predecessors had failed—at extending the long arm of France into New Spain to gar-

1. Théodore Pavie to Victor Pavie, reproduced in full on pp. 99–101 herein. Some of the Pavie correspondence has been published in the collections of Victor Hugo, Sainte-Beuve, David d'Angers, and other public figures. A small collection of the letters of Théodore Pavie's brother Victor (primarily correspondence with Adèle [Mrs. Victor] Hugo) is in the Artine Artinian collection at the Harry Ransom Humanities Research Center at the University of Texas at Austin. Most of the family correspondence is dispersed in private French collections.

2. Guillaume Délisle published his map in Paris in 1718. In letters larger than those of the villages or tribal names, he proclaims "Indiens errans et Antropophages," literally, "wandering anthropophagic [flesh-eating or cannibalistic] Indians." The most significant account of the anthropophagic Indians near Champ d'Asile is L. Hartmann and Millard, Le Texas, ou Notice historique sur le Champ d'Asile (Paris, 1819), a book that would certainly have been in Charles Pavie's library since he served in the Saint Domingue campaign with the colony's founder, Charles Lallemand, and the two belonged to the same Masonic lodge in New Orleans.

ner some of the riches coveted by Louis XIV by opening up French trade in Texas just before the monarch's death. The grandson of the Sun King had become king of Spain in 1700, precipitating the Wars of Spanish Succession which lasted from 1701 until 1713. Then for one glorious year, 1714, a year of peace in the kingdom and health for the king, Louis XIV ruled France and his grandson Anjou ruled Spain as Philip V. At that time, the Canadian Louis Juchereau de Saint-Denis established the first trading post in Louisiana, the "Poste des Natchitoches," which opened up European trade in the area. Using as his pretext a letter from Padre Hidalgo requesting French help evangelizing the east Texas tribes, Saint-Denis traversed the forbidden Spanish Texas and arranged to trade with Indians in east Texas and Spaniards at the revived Presidio de Los Adaes,[3] which became the administrative center and de facto capital of Texas. Without naming Saint-Denis, Pavie acknowledges his achievement by stating that "the village of Natchitoches is the oldest settlement in Louisiana and the farthest [French] point in the immense wilderness which extends to the Pacific Ocean." Apparently he found it more important to affirm that Natchitoches predates New Orleans than to add to his family pride by naming its founder, whose descendant married into the Pavie family.

Before leaving for New Spain, Saint-Denis had helped three tribes of the Caddo confederacy—the Kadohadachos, the Yatasis, and the Doustionis—establish themselves at a previous dwelling site of the original Natchitoches Indians on the Red River in Louisiana. In 1713, the tribes, accompanied by twenty-four Frenchmen and five boatloads of merchandise, journeyed up the river to the site, where they built living quarters and a warehouse. Subsequently, the French helped protect their Caddo allies from the Chickasaws, allies of the English, in exchange for food,

3. The modern English spelling of the village is "Adaes," but in French, an accent is required—Adaës—to indicate that the word has three syllables, as it has in Spanish (Adais). See Robert S. Weddle (*The French Thorn: Rival Explorers in the Spanish Sea* [College Station: Texas A&M Press, 1968]) for the stories of the expeditions of La Salle and Saint-Denis. Interest in La Salle has been greatly stimulated by Barto Arnold's 1995 discovery of the explorer's sunken ship, *La Belle*, in Matagorda Bay. "Spanish Texas" existed prior to 1821; Pavie was quite familiar with it from the writings of Lafiteau, Humboldt, and Volney, all of whom he mentions in *Souvenirs atlantiques*.

furs, and horses.[4] Pavie describes the remnants of those tribes and others who joined them in the flight from the encroaching United States.

After Saint-Denis and a handful of his men crossed Texas, they arrived at San Juan Bautista, the Spanish presidio near the Rio Grande. The ease with which they had entered and crossed Texas alarmed the Spanish officials, who reacted by establishing a barrier against further French penetration into Texas, ordering reoccupation of their east Texas missions, including the one fourteen miles west of the trading post at Natchitoches at Los Adaes, to which they added a presidio. The French complained that they had only agreed to a mission, and that the new Spanish fort intruded on the land between two of their licensed trading partners.[5] Despite official grumbling, gradually, the French and Spanish settlers became accustomed to coveting one another's assets—the French had better-cultivated land, the Spanish better livestock—as their interdependency grew imperceptibly. Midway between the two establishments, the creek known as the Arroyo Hondo became the de facto border between Spain and France in the colonial Southwest. More than a century later, Pavie and his fellow travelers watered their horses in the Hondo, which he called "a delicious stream that for a long time served as the boundary of two powers."

Though the Spanish government considered all other trade items "contraband," the Spanish fort at Los Adaes always depended upon the nearby French post for food. The French at the Natchitoches post were traders first, and military men second. Although they served as soldiers to protect French trade, they regarded the nearby Spanish soldiers more as a market for their goods than as a military threat. The two remote outposts continually reinvented and renegotiated their relationship.

In 1762 and 1763, France lost all of her colonies in North America and India. Louisiana came under Spanish rule when Louis XV turned it over to his Spanish relatives to prevent it from falling into English hands. Shortly afterward, Los Adaes ceased to be the administrative center of Spanish Texas. The boundary between French and Spanish colonial hold-

---

4. F. Todd Smith, *The Caddo Indians: Tribes at the Convergence of Empires, 1542–1854* (College Station: Texas A & M University Press, 1996), 39–41; 87.

5. A Spanish mission is a settlement with a religious, i.e. Catholic, purpose. A French mission is a religious or civil journey for the purpose of either gaining converts to the Catholic Church or gathering cultural information for the French government.

ings no longer needed to be enforced after western Louisiana fell under Spanish rule and Texas became an interior province of New Spain. Spain's holdings extended east across western Louisiana to the Mississippi River, whose waters separated New Spain from the English Floridas on the opposite bank. Trying to consolidate its administration of Texas, the Spanish government ordered the people of Los Adaes to abandon their homes and move to San Antonio. The order was not well accepted, and eventually their natural leader, Antonio Gil y Barbo, led the Adaesaños back to the piney woods. They reestablished a settlement in 1779, but this time west of the Sabine River at Nacogdoches. Gil y Barbo built a large stone house at the intersection of the trade route to La Bahía on the Gulf of Mexico and El Camino Real, which led east to Natchitoches and west to San Antonio. From this location, Gil y Barbo took charge of trade with the east Texas tribes.[6] Variously called the Old Stone House, the Stone House, or the Stone Fort, after a quarter of a century this edifice came to embody the idea of Texas's independence from Mexico, and serves as the western setting of our story.[7]

When the Spanish took control of the post at Natchitoches, they arranged for French administrators in the Louisiana-Texas borderlands to continue working for the Bourbons, but to switch from the French branch of the family to the Spanish branch.[8] This was a wise precaution,

6. The name of Mateo Antonio Gil y Barbo, one of the major characters in the colonization of east Texas and the founder of modern Nacogdoches, has at least four additional spellings: Ybarvo, Ybarbo, Ibarvo, and Ibarbo, enumerated by Elizabeth A. H. John (*Southern Historical Quarterly* 98, pp. 31–2, n. 1). Even though she cites "Ibarvo" as the modern standardization, I have retained a nineteenth-century spelling in this book because it reflects the family genealogy. In *With the Makers of San Antonio* (San Antonio: privately published, 1937), Frederick C. Chabot alphabetizes "Gil Ybarbo" under "G" (216–18).

7. Numerous historians have attempted to objectively relate the story of Texas independence. See, for example, the *Puelles Report* (*Louisiana History* 19 [1978]: 133–82). I find most interesting the heated exchanges between the lawyer-diplomats John Quincy Adams and Luís de Onís before they concluded their treaty. Adams adopted the French point of view in order to gain more land for the U.S.

8. As referred to by Herbert Eugene Bolton, the "Spanish Borderlands" is a mobile area that shifts with the frontier. Sometimes, but not always, the Spanish Borderlands, which he calls simply "the borderlands," is equivalent to the Sabine Borderlands, i.e., the land about 50 miles east and west of the Sabine River between Natchitoches, Louisiana, and Nacogdoches, Texas. The reference here is always to the Sabine Borderlands.

since the Native American tribes generally disdained the Spaniards and respected the French, with whom they preferred to trade. This may have been partially a reaction to monolingual, arrogant, domineering Spanish administrators; the three primary French figures—La Salle, Saint-Denis, and Athanase de Mézières—all had spent brief periods living among Native American tribes learning their customs and languages.

After Saint-Denis, the most successful French administrator in Spanish Louisiana was his son-in-law, de Mézières, an "undesirable" in France who had been exiled to the colonies by his own mother. (According to the memoirs of his niece, Mme de Genlis [see Appendix C], when his widowed mother sought to remarry, her son's presence in France made it impossible for her to keep her age a secret from suitors, so she had him banished to improve her marriage prospects.) By the time the Pavie brothers and their friend Pierre Metoyer arrived from La Rochelle seeking economic opportunities, de Mézières had taken charge of borderlands trading.

The story of the Pavies and Metoyer begins in the mid-eighteenth century, when it took a month to six weeks to sail from a French port on the Atlantic to La Balise, the God-forsaken island in the shifting sand estuary at the mouth of the Mississippi River that had eluded La Salle when he approached it from the Gulf of Mexico. By the middle of this next century, great sailing ships regularly hired pilots at La Balise to help them negotiate the notoriously shallow bar and treacherous waters of the Mississippi up to the port of New Orleans, where each ship deposited exiles and adventurers in exchange for products of the New World. Among the exiles had been de Mézières; among the adventurers were the Pavie brothers, Étienne and Joseph, the younger sons of Joseph and Marie-Jeanne Pavie of La Rochelle. (Since by French law the father's business would be inherited by the oldest son, younger sons had few choices and frequently set out for "the colonies.")

When Étienne and Joseph landed in New Orleans, they struggled up the Mississippi with one or two friends from La Rochelle and headed west on the Red River until they were stopped by the logjam that blocked the river at Natchitoches. Théodore Pavie later described and sketched the "Great Raft," which by the time his great-uncles arrived had provided Natchitoches its strategic position for fifty years, as the western-most French trading post in North America accessible by water. From this intersection in the Louisiana-Texas borderlands, the young Pavie brothers could receive goods like precious furs or bear grease from Canada or western Indians, and then allow their merchandise to float downriver to "the city," as they called New Orleans, to be shipped either to prosperous Saint Domingue or to France. Later their brother Jean-Baptiste established himself as a furrier in Bordeaux on the west coast of France and received their American furs.

Their father, Louis Joseph François Marie Pavie, worked successfully as a printer in La Rochelle, where he had founded a three-generation book-centered dynasty. He printed multicolored playing cards, convened a literary salon in his bookstore, Au Temple de Minerve, and served as a judge magistrate in La Rochelle. Joseph Pavie had married Marie-Jeanne Coasse in 1733. Beginning eleven months after the wedding, Mme Pavie gave birth to at least eighteen, and possibly twenty, children in twenty-eight years, and then, not surprisingly, she died. The surviving sons were born between 1739 (Guillaume, the heir) and 1752 (Louis-Victor, the youngest male). Ironically, not a single one of her daughters ever married; all six became nuns, devoting their dowries to the church. Guillaume assisted his father in the print shop and bookstore in La Rochelle, his destiny fixed by both custom and law. Under the *Ancien Régime* the other brothers could serve the church, join the military, move to the colonies, or marry well. Upon their mother's death, her dowry by law went to her offspring instead of her husband, thus expanding their possibilities.

The heir Guillaume was tethered to the Temple de Minerve, but Étienne, the second oldest son (b. 1740), was free to sail for Louisiana around 1765 to become a trader at the post at Natchitoches and join the militia of Louis XVI, soon to be turned over to Spain. Étienne's name became Esteban the following year when the Spanish took control of western Louisiana. His younger brother Joseph (b. 1746), who had accompanied him to Natchitoches, later moved to New Orleans. At least three other Pavie brothers stayed in France. Besides the furrier Jean-Baptiste (b. 1742), Pierre, a priest, lived in France about twenty years before fleeing to Natchitoches to escape the Revolution. Thirteen-year-old Louis-Victor became a printer, settling in the Loire Valley's largest city, Angers. The latter's unfulfilled desire to go to Louisiana may have been reborn in his grandson, Théodore, who heard the stories of his great-uncles' adventures in the family's colonial outpost.

The 1766 census of Natchitoches is the first to include information about the Pavies in western Louisiana. "Estevan Pavia" [variation: Esteban] was listed as "one man bearing arms having three horses, two hogs and sheep, but no land, woman, children, slaves or cattle." His first trading contract is dated January 14, 1766: merchant Étienne Pavie contracted with Antoine Ollivier to purchase all that he produced for a period of two years. The document sealing the agreement illustrates the anachronism of using noble language in the wilderness: "The gentlemen Antoine Ollivier and Étienne Pavie, both merchants, the former of New Orleans and the latter of this post . . . agree to form a commercial enterprise together for this post for two consecutive years . . . at the risk of loss during transport of said merchandise sending to New Orleans all he produces be it silver, hides, bear grease, or other products."[9]

Four years later, de Mézières made note of the trading activities of Étienne Pavie, who seems to have been in his favor. In January 1770, de Mézières seized and sold at auction a herd of horses and mules which had been purchased among the Indians by Pavie and two Frenchmen named Duchesne and Poeyfarré. He further prosecuted only Poeyfarré, however, expelling him from Natchitoches, apparently for illegal trading. During the summer, de Mézières settled a dispute over furs between Antoine Charbonet and Esteban Pavie, deciding in favor of Pavie because Charbonet had monopolized trade.[10] (Under Spanish rule, French merchants were forbidden to monopolize trade in the respective villages within which they were licensed to operate.)

In 1773, de Mézières traveled to Europe to visit the Spanish and French courts and garner honors. In Paris he went to the Palais Royal, the family seat of the duc d'Orléans, where he was welcomed by his niece, Mme de Genlis, and his half-sister, Mme de Montesson. He also met his new brother-in-law, the duc d'Orléans, who had recently contracted a morganatic marriage (without hereditary rights to title) with Mme de Montesson.

Mme de Genlis, a noteworthy political and literary figure in her own

9. The contract between Antoine Ollivier and Étienne Pavie is document 410 (1766) in the Natchitoches Parish Courthouse. Bear grease was used as both butter and a beauty product, as well as to grease wooden carriage wheels.

10. Herbert Eugene Bolton, *Athanase de Mézières and the Louisiana-Texas Frontier, 1768–1780,* vol. 1 (1914; reprint, New York: Kraus Reprint, 1970), 89–90.

right, gave voice to the curiosity of untraveled Europeans toward the
flamboyant New World adventurers when she described her uncle's appearance in Paris: "Through his silk stockings could be seen the snakes
painted by the savages that he had irremediably engraved [tattooed] on
his legs. He showed me his chest also covered with large painted flowers;
the colors were very vivid."[11] Athanase de Mézières returned to New Orleans by February 1774. No evidence has been found of subsequent European visits by the fascinating de Mézières, whose new brother-in-law
would meet a tragic end twenty years later when he tried to exploit the
Revolution as a useful vehicle for eliminating his family rivals. He took
the radical name "Philippe Égalité," then voted to behead his cousins,
Louis XVI and Marie Antoinette. Unfortunately, the revolutionary ax
swung full circle and he, too, lost his head. Madame de Genlis fled with
her children and his, one of whom succeeded him as duc d'Orléans. In
1830, this son—tutored and rescued by de Mézières's niece, would become King of the French (quite distinct from King of France) as Louis-
Philippe, and conduct his government's relations with Texas in a highly
friendly manner.

Looking at the Natchitoches to which de Mézières returned from the
European courts, the village where Joseph and Étienne Pavie and Pierre
Metoyer had settled, one sees that interpersonal relationships were often
more difficult to regulate than commerce. Soon after the La Rochelle
group's arrival, Metoyer began a concubine relationship with an African
slave named Coincoin or Marie-Thérèse (hereafter called Marie-Thérèse-
Coincoin). Her pure African parents had belonged to the late Saint-
Denis, whose daughter, Mme de Soto, now owned Marie-Thérèse-
Coincoin and leased her to Metoyer. By law, Mme de Soto owned all of
the offspring born to her slave. After an initial difficult struggle with local
religious officials, the Franco-African children born to Pierre Metoyer
and Marie-Thérèse-Coincoin over the next twenty years grew into a dynasty referred to today as the Cane River Creoles of Color.[12]

11. Madame la Comtesse de Genlis, *Mémoires . . . sur le dixhuitième siècle et la Révolution française depuis 1756 jusqu'à nos jours*, vol. 1 (Paris: Ladvocat, 1825), 115–6.

12. In the 1830s when Pavie wrote *Souvenirs atlantiques*, a Creole was a white person
of European—Spanish or French—parents, born in America, although the term is broader
today. Acadians, who were in Nova Scotia for several generations before coming to Louisiana, were not called Creoles in Louisiana, but "Cajuns." In Natchitoches, Louisiana, today,
"Creoles of color" often refers specifically to the descendants of Pierre Metoyer.

Between 1768 and 1776 Metoyer and Marie-Thérèse-Coincoin had six children. All were baptized in the Catholic church, despite the strong protestations of the Spanish priest who listed the father in the registry as "unknown." The priest also filed a formal complaint with Commandant de Mézières denouncing Coincoin as a "public concubine," and insisting that she be forbidden to go into Metoyer's house. The commandant issued an order for Metoyer to expel Coincoin from his home and service, never to buy her, and to affirm that he had no desire to cause further scandal or disgrace. Metoyer reluctantly complied.[13]

Despite de Mézières's grief over the loss of his wife, son, and daughter in an epidemic the previous fall, his duties as lieutenant governor of Louisiana and acting governor of Texas called him to San Antonio de Béjar in January 1778. En route, de Mézières and Gil y Barbo led an expedition to unite the friendly east Texas tribes against the fierce Lipan Apaches during which de Mézières took a bad fall from his horse while fording a rocky stream and died at San Antonio in November 1779.[14] In his absence, Coincoin and Metoyer reestablished their household and, in July 1778, Metoyer arranged to buy his beloved and their infant child from her owner, the late commandant's sister-in-law. To avoid the consequences specified in the Code Noir for fathering children by one's own slave—sale of both slave and child for the benefit of the hospital and permanent denial of freedom—Metoyer privately called in witnesses and manumitted thirty-eight-year-old Marie-Thérèse-Coincoin and their last child, Joseph. A document, witnessed by his friends, declared them free. Athanase de Mézières—who was about to be installed as the only Frenchman to govern Texas—was survived by several children including his namesake, Athanase de Mézières fils, who remained legally unmarried

13. According to Gary B. Mills (The Forgotten People: Cane River's Creoles of Color [Baton Rouge: Louisiana State University Press, 1977]), marriage would not have been possible for Metoyer and Coincoin as long as they resided in Louisiana (21). Article 6 of the Code Noir states, "It must be absolutely prohibited to all white subjects of either sex to contract marriage with any blacks or mulattos, upon pain of being dishonorably expelled from the colony."

14. Bolton, de Mézières, vol. 1, p. 84; Mills, The Forgotten People, 21. According to Al McGraw and Patti Lemée, the stench of decomposing bodies made it necessary to remove a number of them from the grounds of San Fernando Cathedral, where de Mézières was buried. His gravesite is currently unknown because the church burial records were subsequently destroyed by fire.

throughout his life in deference to his enduring relationship with Coin-coin's sister, Marie-Jeanne. That son's inheritance—a source of numerous legal woes—would pass to the Pavie family.

Étienne Pavie married twenty-seven-year-old Marie-Thérèze Eugénie Buard (b. 1752) on December 1, 1779. She was one of seven daughters of Jean-Baptiste Gabriel Buard, a Swiss soldier in French service who remained in the colonies after he was discharged in Natchitoches in 1725. As the post distiller, he brewed tafia rum from sugar cane, today known as "moonshine," and his large family provided wives for Étienne Pavie and many of his friends.

Étienne brought to the union the sum of "18,000 livres minted in Tours, in good specie, coming from the succession of his parents." The bride's dowry included Marie-Louise, a "small mulatresse aged twelve, creole of this post, valued at 1250 livres," and "500 livres minted at Tours, coming from the succession of her father; 1240 piastres, and four mother-cows valued at 60 piastres."[15]

Nine months and two weeks after the wedding, the first of three children, a daughter, was born to the couple. She lived only four years. A second daughter, Marie Louise Hélène Euphrosine, called Hélène, was born to the Pavies in August 1782. She was still living in 1829–1830 when her nephew Théodore visited Natchitoches, although she died before the end of the year. Their third child and first and only son was born in 1786 and baptized as Juan Bautista Estevan Pavia.[16]

Etienne and Marie-Thérèze acquired a small plantation and a "vâch-erie" [pasture or ranch] for Marie-Thérèze's dowry of four cows to graze. The young Pavie family enjoyed all of the elements of success until May 27, 1787, when Etienne Pavie along with two of his slaves, was shot on his own plantation. Two days later, as he lay dying, Étienne prepared his last will and testament in the presence of a handful of witnesses. He designated Pierre Metoyer and another friend to carry out his last wishes.

---

15. Winston de Ville, *Marriage Contracts of Natchitoches, 1739–1803* (Nashville, Benson Printing Company, 1961), 62. "Livres minted in Tours" is probably a mistranslation of "livres tournois," which was purely a money of account, according to noted British historian Robin Briggs, because there was no coin worth a livre.

16. Elizabeth Shown Mills, *Natchitoches: Abstracts of the Catholic Church Registers of the French and Spanish Post of St. Jean-Baptiste des Natchitoches in Louisiana, 1729–1803*, Vol. 2 of the Cane River Creole Series (New Orleans: Polyanthos, 1977), 223.

Marie-Thérèze Buard Pavie, fulfilling the terms of her husband's will, inherited a plantation on both sides of the Red River where she subsequently lived and maintained custody of their two children.[17] The murder was never solved.

No one can know the conversations between the dying Étienne and his longtime friend Metoyer, but soon after Pavie's death Metoyer dissolved his relationship of more than twenty years with Marie-Thérèse-Coincoin, then a free person of color, and married the white Marie-Thérèze Pavie in 1788. Though the Pavie-Metoyer contract is missing from the archives at the Natchitoches Court House, the marriage of October 13, 1788, is listed in the abstracts of the Church Register. Eleven months later, Marie-Thérèze Pavie Metoyer presented Claude Thomas Pierre Metoyer—father of eight Franco-African offspring born over some twenty-three years in Natchitoches—his first "legitimate" son. They had another son and a daughter. Far from repudiating the children he had fathered with Coincoin, Metoyer purchased their freedom and gave them his name. He may also have contributed to their education and travel, and he certainly offered financial help and advice to their mother, Coincoin, whose remarkable life and implausible success demonstrate the power of the human spirit in a way that mere fiction could not.

Metoyer provided Coincoin a small cabin on sixty-eight acres where she and their children cultivated tobacco so successfully that in 1792 she sent her own barge with 9,900 rolls of tobacco and 300 hides to New Orleans along with his. Family tradition says that Coincoin and her brood also produced herbal medicines and indigo dyes for the uniforms of the Napoleonic Wars. In 1794 she received an additional land grant of eight hundred acres on the west bank of the Old River branch of the Red River from the local Spanish colonial government in the name of the king, a gesture extended to deserving heads of households to increase local productivity. "Maria Teresa Metoyer" then had to meet numerous conditions of clearing, fencing, and road building. In 1795 Augustin, Pierre's oldest son, moved the locus of family properties to Ile Brevelle

17. Will of Étienne Pavie, Melrose Folder 665, Eugene P. Watson Memorial Library, Northwestern State University, Natchitoches, La. According to the census count of August 17, 1787, the thirty-four-year-old widow Pavie owned a tract of land, six slaves, and four cows. She had two children: Hélène, age five, and Étienne, age one, and one employee whose function is not mentioned, Jean de La Haye, age forty-five.

where he and the other children received separate land concessions, including the site of Melrose plantation. Marie-Thérèse-Coincoin and her family's holdings eventually extended from Grande Écore south to Cloutierville. The matriarch died in 1816, a year after "the fever" claimed Pierre Metoyer. At the time of her death she owned twelve thousand acres and at least ninety-nine slaves. Marie-Thérèse-Coincoin and her children and grandchildren were the wealthiest slave-owning free family of color in the nation in 1830.[18] The Metoyer children were half-brothers and half-sisters to the half-brothers and half-sister of Hélène Pavie. Théodore Pavie understood that among his French relations there were African American stepchildren, not an unusual arrangement among the educated upper classes who settled on the frontier. When he visited Louisiana in 1829, he spoke of Natchitoches as "a country where almost all of the inhabitants were known to me by name and were attached to me by all sorts of liaisons to the names of my own family which came to establish itself on the banks of the Red River." The Pavie family letters and the Natchitoches archives illuminate the phrase, "all sorts of liaisons," which summarizes, without detail, the intriguing fate of Étienne and his two brothers, who lived in Natchitoches and New Orleans.

Joseph Pavie had been promoted to ensign in the post militia in 1780 when the Natchitoches Militia was eager to help the Americans fight the British. Sometime before 1790, he moved to New Orleans and worked as a merchant. He apparently never married legally, but documents mention a quadroon "mujer" or female consort and two children called simply "niñas" (daughters) in the Spanish warrant for his arrest for embezzlement of the funds, i.e. import duties, of Real Aduana of Tepeaca dating from May 1, 1803.[19]

The fate of Pierre Pavie, the priest, is emblematic of the French-U.S.

---

18. Mills, *The Forgotten People*, 30–1; Francis J. Smith, *A Brief History of Ile Brevelle and St. Augustine Church* (Natchitoches, La.: n.p., ca. 1981), 9. At Melrose plantation today a film financed by the National Endowment for the Humanities examines three local women who were "major cultural transfer agents": Marie-Thérèse-Coincoin, artist Clementine Hunter, and Kate Chopin, the author of *The Awakening*. The narrator claims that the French-African descendants of Metoyer and Coincoin number approximately ten thousand.

19. Note in Spanish from the Bexar Archives CHI, E. 5/1/1803. Photocopy from filmstrip in the Barker American History Center at the University of Texas at Austin.

experience. When the revolutionary government in France demanded that all Catholic priests swear fidelity to the civil constitution, he objected, instead fleeing to Spanish Louisiana, where priests were both needed and welcomed and where he could live by the principles he refused to compromise. He arrived in New Orleans where he was never just another solitary exile, because he was received by his brother Joseph. The Catholic hierarchy sent him "upriver" where he settled into the Natchitoches community as parish priest at the church of St. Francis of Assissi (St. François d'Assissi des Natchitoches). For over a decade he guided the spiritual life of the community and tended its records while he participated in the lives of the small family left behind by Étienne's murder as the godfather of his brother's grandson.[20] Sometime after 1808, Pierre Pavie retired to New Orleans and lived with Joseph after administrative changes (resulting from the transfer of Louisiana to the United States) pushed him out of his parish.

When Joseph Pavie died in 1814, Pierre took charge of selling the properties in Louisiana, giving Hélène her father's portion. Joseph had bequeathed "2,000 piastres to two of his children" and the same amount "to a quarteroon named Chouteau, daughter of Marie-Jeanne." The family members in France received the remainder of the cash and the proceeds from the real estate (which by law returned to them as part of their parents' estate since Joseph had no legal heirs). In a letter to his family in France, Pierre related this distribution matter-of-factly, but he did lament having wasted money just prior to Joseph's death. "Our brother Joseph, deceased the 22nd of last month after an illness of several years' duration, which worsened continuously. He must have believed that his health would come back because he had a boat built to go take the waters of the Wichita, for someone told him that the waters would be beneficial to his health. They are sixty leagues farther than Wichita. The day before his death he sent me to look at his boat and to make the purchases necessary for his trip. To satisfy him I was obliged to make a lot of useless purchases."[21]

20. Pierre Étienne Poissot, son of Hélène Pavie Poissot and Athanase Poissot, a descendant of Saint-Denis. (The mother seems to have named the baby after frocked uncle Pierre and her murdered father instead of turning to his illustrious paternal ancestry.)

21. Pierre Pavie to the Pavie family in France, April 4, 1814, in private collection.

The process of settling Joseph Pavie's estate coincided with the restoration of the Catholic royalist Bourbons to the throne of France, after the fifteen-year rule of Napoleon Bonaparte, during which it became legal for nonjuring priests (who had not sworn allegiance to the revolutionary government) to return to their homeland where they would be tolerated. Around 1815, therefore, Pierre Pavie was welcomed back to France where he received recognition for his faithful service to the church and the monarchy. He was installed as Canon at the Cathedral of La Rochelle, and died in 1820 at the age of seventy-nine at the family home. He left his nontransferable possessions in Louisiana to his nephew, Charles.

The last Pavie who came to settle at Natchitoches, Charles Roque Pavie (1777–1838), inherited his uncle Pierre's slaves and Texas real estate, including a site for a Catholic church at Nacogdoches. Charles was the sixth of thirteen children born to the Bordeaux furrier Jean-Baptiste Pavie and Anne Bernard and was sent by his parents to Angers to live with his aunt and uncle, Marie Fabre Pavie and Louis-Victor Pavie. Charles was to serve as an apprentice to his uncle, the youngest of the La Rochelle men, who had stayed behind in France to assist his father and the future heir at the Pavie press when his brothers first set out for Louisiana, and who now owned a print shop in Angers.

It so happened, however, that widespread political unrest disrupted Charles's plans. In January 1793, French revolutionary leaders guillotined Louis XVI, who had made an unsuccessful attempt to escape France as an *émigré* (the official term designating an illegally missing counterrevolutionary). Shortly after Charles arrived in Angers, his apprenticeship was interrupted by the actions of the counterrevolutionary troops, the Catholic Royalists—priests, peasants, and nobles in western France— who rose up against the Revolution under the white banner of the king. The counterrevolutionaries forced the Pavie press to print their proclamations, paying for them in worthless scrip. When the revolutionary army subsequently occupied Angers, they smashed Louis-Victor's presses and arrested and imprisoned him, leaving his wife and fourteen-year-old Charles at home. Because Louis-Victor was an influential community leader and the editor of a local newspaper, the revolutionary leaders planned to transfer him to Paris to be judged by the harsh Revolutionary Tribunal of Fouquier-Tinville. Through the negligence (or possibly the complicity) of a guard, however, who averted his eyes while the prisoner supposedly urinated, Louis-Victor escaped to Spain. Unable to find him, the revolutionaries declared him *émigré*.

Nine months after the revolutionaries guillotined the king, they turned their malevolent attention to his wife. After beheading Marie Antoinette in October 1793, provincial radicals repeated the measure against women throughout France. They declared Charles' aunt Marie an *émigrée* (a designated enemy of the Revolution, even though she had not actually emigrated) and arrested and imprisoned her in the Chateau of Amboise to await execution.

Marie's mother took care of Marie's ten-year-old Louis, Charles went to live with another family member. From prison, Marie Pavie wrote her son a touching letter which, in spite of her dignity and restraint, conveys both her anguish and hope manifested in a single geography book that, for the young mother, had the power to transcend political realities and unite the three of them in spirit.

> How long it seems to me since I have been able, my dear child, to embrace you. . . . I want to believe that you are not neglecting anything. I would like, my son, for you to learn geography during your moments of recreation. At your grandfather's, there is a geography book divided by departments; ask him to lend it to you, and take good care of it because it is the only one left from the book shop. It was printed by your father, and you should think about the author. Good-bye, my dear friend. Think about acquiring virtues and developing talents and, to fortify your courage, think of your unfortunate mother. I love you with all my soul and I am your tender mother.
>
> Marie Fabre, wife of Pavie.[22]

Three months after she was imprisoned, ignorant of her husband's fate, Marie Pavie wrote a letter from Amboise on January 27, 1794, to her parents in Angers, in which she expressed guilt, remorse, and loneliness. The Revolution (and apparently Marie's father as well) demanded that women keep out of politics. Her letter would not have gone uncensored:

22. Marie Pavie to Louis Pavie, January 27, 1794, in private collection.

In my solitude, isolated far from all that could help me bear the excess of my sorrows . . . may I at least delude myself into believing that my exile will not be of long duration and that I will soon be returned to my family. Three months have gone by since they snatched me from your arms and separated me from my dear little one in spite of his supplications to follow his unfortunate mother. How much pain have I suffered; I shall spare you the details. . . . It is not that I disdain meddling in political matters, my father, but confessing my ignorance in this regard, I leave it to men to take care of the laws for us. Teaching my son to know and respect them would have been the task that I would have imposed on myself. I had summoned him back from the *collège* with this intention; but too soon separated from him, it was necessary for me to abandon him to your care; satisfied in that regard, I nonetheless feel deprived of the pleasure of seeing him; but you are opposed to having him sent to me. I concede, albeit regretfully, to the rationale behind your refusal and will not speak of this to you again. . . . I have also written to Charles.[23]

After Robespierre was guillotined, prison doors opened throughout France. Marie Pavie left her prison in Amboise and Louis-Victor left his hideout in northern Spain. They returned home to rue St. Laud where their son Louis joined them. Even today, the Pavie family tells the story of the fatal chagrin that Louis-Victor Pavie suffered at the sight of his presses, smashed by the Republicans. Broken in spirit and unable to start over, he died the following year on April 12, 1796. The hero of this generation is thus the brave young widow Marie Pavie, who returned from prison and successfully rebuilt the family press to pass on to her son Louis, who would later publish his son Théodore's *Souvenirs atlantiques*.

Nephew Charles returned to Marie's home at the end of the Reign of Terror. He resumed his apprenticeship at the press, making it possible for Louis to complete his education at the École Centrale, where the student became friends with future chemist and color theorist Chevreul and sculptor David d'Angers, who plays a major role in chapter two of this

23. Marie Pavie to her parents, January 27, 1794, in private collection.

book.[24] These two friends of Louis Pavie made profound impressions on his future offspring as well as on the cultural life of France and Europe.

After Napoleon's astonishing 1797 victories in Italy, Charles Pavie left Angers, abandoning the printing trade to join the navy. A document from the "Commission for conducting his Majesty's Transport Service," housed at the Ministry of the Marine in Paris, provides most of the information available regarding his naval experience. He may have been among the earliest conscripts, his literacy (exceptional among an age group whose education had been interrupted by the Revolution) lending great promise to his military career. Sometime in 1799 or 1800, the twenty-two-year-old was serving as a midshipman aboard the *Vengeance* when he was captured by the English navy at Guadeloupe. His English captors described him as "5 feet 7 inches tall with an oval face, dark complexion, hair, and eyes; having no marks or wounds." They held him for a time at Chatham on a *ponton,* a disabled "hulk" vessel moored in the mud, one of many used by the English as low-cost prisons, then arranged to discharge him through a prisoner exchange.

The British released Charles and allowed him to return to France, in their words, "upon having entered into an Engagement not to serve against *Great Britain,* or any of its Allies, until he shall be regularly exchanged for a British Prisoner of War, of equal Rank." They further stipulated that "immediately after his Arrival in France, he shall make known the Place of his Residence there to the British Agent for Prisoners in Paris, and shall not change the same, on any Account, without first intimating his Intention to the said Agent; and, moreover, that at the Expiration of every Two Months until his exchange shall be effected, he shall regularly and punctually transmit to the said Agent a Certificate of his Residence, signed by the Magistrate or Municipal officer of the Place." The pass permitted this return home "provided he leave this Kingdom within *five* Days" after September 26, 1800, or be subject to arrest.[25] Shortly after pledging his word as an officer, he must have de-

---

24. Michel Eugène Chevreul (1786–1889), director of the Gobelins tapestry workshop, performed experiments on how the observer's eye mixes colors and authored the influential work *De la Loi du contraste simultané des couleurs,* still studied today by artists as well as art historians. For Chevreul's influence on literature, see Roger Shattuck's succinct explanation in his *The Innocent Eye* (New York: Farrar, Straus, Giroux, 1984), 143.

25. Copy in possession of author.

cided that he had no economic future in France, because he set out to search for his three uncles in Louisiana, with whom communication had been severed by the disruption on the high seas from continuous warfare—the American and French Revolutions and the Napoleonic Wars. Unfortunately, Charles Pavie's whereabouts between his stint in an English prison in 1800 and his resurfacing in Natchitoches in 1805 cannot be determined.

Even before the United States acquired the Louisiana Territory, the uneasy seam between Louisiana and Texas—temporarily maintained by the Bourbon kings in Spain and France for the purpose of thwarting British encroachment—began to unravel. In the region between Natchitoches and Nacogdoches, the United States and Spain played out their contest for empire, and local problems escalated into matters of national and international significance.

Around 1800, Natchitoches assumed its role as the staging ground for a series of failed "filibustering expeditions," attempts by foreigners (usually from the United States) to wrest Texas from Spain or Mexico. Filibuster operations east of the Sabine accelerated after the Louisiana Purchase because Natchitoches was the most westerly town indisputably situated within the jurisdiction of the United States. West of the Sabine, Nacogdoches, second in size only to San Antonio among Texas towns, became the center of revolutionary activity that justifiably troubled the Spanish government. Naturally this activity was concentrated within the Stone House, the only permanent building to survive from the eighteenth century into the twentieth. Each failed rebellion brought retaliatory measures from the Spanish government, which over the years destroyed every other building in town while intensifying the desire for Texas's independence. In 1801, a hundred Spanish soldiers hunted down and shot the first of the filibusters from Louisiana, Philip Nolan, who was thought to be plotting against the government.

Around the same time, Napoleon took back the share of Louisiana that had been held by Spain since 1763. He then sold it to the United States in 1803 without a precise western boundary. The unknown lands west of Natchitoches tantalized Americans, including President Jefferson, who initiated a boundary inquiry. Jefferson wanted the Rio Bravo or Rio Grande del Norte for his border, but he anticipated that the people of Louisiana would say that the boundary between Louisiana and Texas was the Sabine River, fifty miles west of Natchitoches. But not a single longtime resident placed the boundary any farther west than the Arroyo Hondo, midway between Natchitoches and Los Adaes, whose residents had been forcibly removed by the Spanish and were now resettled in Nacogdoches. That ephemeral boundary served as the border between the United States and Mexico for almost two decades.

Not surprisingly, the Spanish colonial government claimed the land up to the Hondo, including the Los Adaes and Bayou Pierre settlements, and used this area for spying headquarters. (Bayou Pierre was where Charles Pavie later owned land on which he and his nephew Théodore hunted.) Indian factor Dr. John Sibley correctly reported the century-old understanding to Jefferson's newly appointed Governor Claiborne. Sibley also advised Claiborne that the jurisdiction even east of the Sabine properly belonged to the governor general of the Interior Provinces, under Spanish authority, yet he advised, even encouraged Claiborne and his mentor President Jefferson to violate the locally accepted status quo. Said Sibley, "it is Clearly my opinion that the United States Should immediately Establish a Post on the East Bank of the Sabine, the Country is Open no Hostile Interpretation can be put upon it." Having acknowledged the local tradition and the Spanish jurisdiction, he cavalierly dismissed their authority as "only an arrangement between two commandants."[26] Jefferson seized Sibley's pretext—open land without a binding treaty—which aroused some of the president's latent ambitions, as well as the ambitions of many other observers. In violation of the agreement between the commandants, Spanish, French, and American settlers and outlaws moved into the disputed territory between the Sabine and Nat-

26. Autographed letter from John Sibley to Governor Claiborne, in the Jefferson Papers in the Library of Congress. Copy in Charles Edwin Carter, ed., *The Territory of Orleans 1803–1812*, vol. 9 of *The Territorial Papers of the U.S.* (Washington, D.C.: U.S. Government Printing Office, 1940), 72–8. Dr. Sibley (1757–1837), a Massachusetts physician, went to live in Natchitoches in 1802. Ascending the Red River in 1803, he became an authority on the Native Americans of the region. Sibley befriended Governor Claiborne and, through him, his fellow Virginian Thomas Jefferson, who appointed him contract surgeon to the U.S. Army at Natchitoches, and later Indian Agent for the Orleans territory. Sibley held that post from 1804 to 1814. After participating in the failed Long Expedition of 1819, he turned to local and state politics. His private correspondence and official reports helped shape the views easterners held of Louisiana and the West early in the nineteenth century, and enrich our knowledge of the region today.

chitoches, but neither Spain nor the United States wanted a military showdown that might ignite an international conflagration; therefore, they only patrolled the land by mutual consent of the military leaders.

The Arroyo Hondo had endured as the traditional boundary between the French traders and the Spanish soldiers since the days of St. Denis nine decades earlier. Natchitoches and Nacogdoches, the amiable trading partners sharing priests in 1800 (that is, sharing Pierre Pavie, who purchased a site to build a Catholic church) underwent dramatic political and—surprisingly—geographic transformations in the next half-century before they were again reunited under the same government. In 1803, upon learning of the retrocession of Louisiana to France, the Spanish began to be leery of the loyalties of east Texans. They transferred the New Orleans archives to Cuba, leaving untouched the Natchitoches archives, and moved large numbers of Spanish troops to Nacogdoches to protect it against "foreign aggression." In 1804, the United States took command of the Poste Saint Jean-Baptiste des Natchitoches, as well as the Natchitoches archives from 1732 to 1804. As a special concession to the citizens of Natchitoches, the French flag was flown for one hour between the lowering of the Spanish flag and the raising of the American flag.[27]

Charles Pavie arrived in the Louisiana Territory some time before mid-March, 1805, and was welcomed warmly in Natchitoches by his uncle Pierre and by Étienne's daughter, Hélène (Mme Athanase Poissot). The baptismal record of Marie Victoire Poissot from March 15, 1805, when Charles stood godfather to his uncle's granddaughter, is the earliest known documentation of Charles in Louisiana.

Ten months later Spanish troops entered the parish of Natchitoches. Whereas the local citizens remained cordial to them, the U.S. military troops garrisoned at Natchitoches were incensed. The friendly relations between the remote French and Spanish outposts, worked out over a century, had ended with this watershed moment in the Americanization of Natchitoches, a process that would not be complete until the close of the

27. The American troops were under the command of Lt. Edward G. Turner. See Powell A. Casey, *Encyclopedia of Forts, Posts, Named Camps and Other Military Installations in Louisiana, 1700–1981* (Baton Rouge: Claitor's, 1983), for information concerning all relevant forts. Information in this paragraph is taken from p. 46.

U.S. Civil War. In the summer of 1806, Natchitoches was a tinder box of wrangling, bluffing, and accusing. The United States, Spain, England, and Napoleon—who had just invaded Spain—were all poised to grab for territorial spoils at the first sign of war in the borderlands. On September 26, Dr. Sibley, now officially Jefferson's representative in charge of Indian affairs in the new territory, wrote a letter to his son from Natchitoches describing the borderland chaos that greeted Charles Pavie.

The movements of the Spaniards on this frontier has affected the Indian Chiefs in a manner that I cannot get them away. . . . The Spaniards, resenting being removed over the River Sabine by the Officer commanding here last winter, have returned, taken their old ground in force—about 1200, under the command of two officers of rank and experience, equipt with cannon, etc. They have with them about four thousand horses, and they frequently patrol within five or six miles of Natchitoches, have turned back an exploring party ascending Red River by Order of the President, have captured and taken away prisoners three American citizens, and two other made their escape from them, have cut down and carried away the flag of the United States, that with other insults and outrages not to be borne with. . . . We shall drive the Spaniards (if we can) over the Sabine again, but capture as many as we can. . . . Whether this will bring on a general war or not is uncertain, but the probability is that it will. We are however in doubt whether their taking these new positions and advancing upon us is by the order of the King of Spain, or only by the authority of the Viceroy and Council of Mexico—The territory they had lately taken possession of is beyond all doubt part of the country the United States have purchased and paid for, and we ought to defend it or perish in the attempt.[28]

28. John Sibley to Saml. H. Sibley, A. L. S. from Sibley Manuscript Book, vol. 4, Missouri Historial Society, published in *Louisiana Historical Quarterly* 10 (1927). Neither of Sibley's letters was corrected for spelling and punctuation in order that the reader may perceive the level of education of the best-known American observer in the borderlands. I am indebted to Elizabeth Shown Mills for sending Sibley's letters to me.

The postscript added by the bellicose Sibley would become relevant to Charles Pavie, who later married the sister of this "French girl" (and to Théodore Pavie, who would fall in love with the new couple's daughter): "James Bludworth was married to a French girl last Sunday. He cannot be accused of marrying for beauty or for riches by those who know his Bride."[29]

In November 1806, armed and mounted Spanish and American troops faced one another in the same region where French and Spanish traders had exchanged goods for nearly a century. War seemed inevitable. Fortunately, however, the Spanish leader, Simón de Herrera, was a prudent man with instructions to avoid war. Colonel Herrera and General James Wilkinson (1757–1825) reached an agreement through their interpreter Juan Cortés to declare a neutral zone, traditionally referred to as the Neutral Ground.[30] The Americans agreed to retreat east of the Hondo if and when the Spanish retreated west of the Sabine, thereby dampening the spark that would have ignited a general war.[31] Interestingly, many doubted Wilkinson's loyalty at the time, and documents now prove the general's treachery, the blame for which he managed to deflect onto his relatively innocent partner, Aaron Burr.

Throughout the time of this conflict, Charles Pavie supported himself as a trader, probably a *caboteur* who traveled the Mississippi and Red Rivers peddling merchandise purchased in Natchez or New Orleans to settlers or soldiers. Such is at least the supposition suggested by the

29. The "French girl" whom James Bludworth married on September 9, 1806, was Aimée Rouquier, the sister of Marianne Rouquier, who would marry Charles Pavie the next year. James Bloodworth was born in 1779 in New Hanover County, North Carolina. He went to Natchitoches in 1805, changed the spelling of his name to Bludworth, married Aimée Rouquier in 1806, and died in 1852. See Marie Norris Wise, *Norris-Jones-Crockett-Payne-Blanchard: The Heritage of Marie Norris Wise* (Sulphur, La.: Wise Publications, 1994), 126–9 for the Bloodworth/Bludworth genealogy.

30. Juan Cortés (1734–1829) was a Frenchman in Spanish service living in Natchitoches, soon to become Charles Pavie's brother-in-law.

31. Charles Pavie joined the international land grab in the Neutral Ground, also known as the Neutral Strip or the Free State of Sabine, but by some kind of poetic historical justice, the Arroyo Hondo land would be the least successful of his investments. Fifty years after his death, his estate was incorrectly declared a vacant succession, and a court-appointed curator took over the property in 1889.

manuscript of an unfinished story by Théodore Pavie, in which only the last name of Charles and Marianne has been changed.[32] On March 17, 1807, Charles Pavie paid $4,000 for the property in Natchitoches at the corner of Washington Street and the street which, in 1825, became Pavie Street.[33] According to his deed, he purchased "houses, mill and powder magazine of brick."[34] Nearing thirty when he made this real estate investment, Charles Pavie was one of the best educated men in the borderlands, highly literate by virtue of an excellent Ancien Régime Catholic education on the eve of the Revolution, and also familiar with contracts from his apprenticeship as a typographer in Angers. Having learned English during his detention at Chatham, he was fluent in at least two languages, and probably understood Spanish as well. Economically astute and sensitive to the financial opportunities inherent in military shifts, Charles would have certainly profited from the military buildup taking place literally in his back yard on Washington Street. The time was right to take a bride to this house, today known as the Magnolias.[35]

His marriage to Marie-Anne (Marianne) Rouquier on August 8,

32. See also Théodore Pavie's description of *caboteurs* in "La Peau d'ours," a short story with characters loosely based on the widowed Charles Pavie and Elisa Bludworth, in my *Tales of the Sabine Borderlands: Early Louisiana and Texas Fiction by Théodore Pavie* (College Station: Texas A&M University Press, 1998), 26–59. The vivid descriptions of the caboteur and his sales techniques likely come directly from Charles.

33. Evidently Charles Pavie officially gave the family name to Pavie Street—at the edge of today's downtown Natchitoches—in 1825 when he administered the estate of his neighbor Mme Fontenau-Grappe and partitioned her property into lots, one of which he purchased from her son-in-law Bartholomew Fleming.

34. Whether the grand three-story (two floors plus attic and basement) house with 13-foot ceilings that stands today at the corner of Pavie and Washington is this house is uncertain. Dr. Charles Chauncey Carroll, the previous owner, who died in 1950, printed a history of the house which is in the vertical file at Northwestern State University Library, but that version is contradicted in the 1989 guide, *Natchitoches: A Walking Tour of the Historic District,* by Robert B. "Bobby" DeBlieux, published by the *Natchitoches Times.* DeBlieux says that the "sales price certainly indicates a house had been built on the property. However, architectural details indicate it was not the house you now see." Nonetheless, he judged it "the most significant Greek Revival house in Natchitoches" (8).

35. The Magnolias acquired its name after Charles Pavie sold the three-story house to Tauzin, who planted the four trees for which it became known; the legal description, however, will always include the Pavie ownership, so perhaps the house might someday regain the name of its historic proprietor.

1807, joined him to the extensive Prudhomme and Rouquier family networks.[36] Marianne's father, François Rouquier, a major presence in colonial Natchitoches, provided the couple land from which they fashioned a working plantation through long years of hard work. Marianne's brother François (Juan Francisco) Rouquier became Charles Pavie's brother-in-law, friend, and hunting companion. In Creole fashion, Charles was considered "beau-frère" (brother-in-law) to all of the Creole Marianne's sisters' husbands, none of whom were Creole men. Instead the daughters of this prominent Creole family married the border makers—men from France, the United States, England, and Ireland who played major roles in the expansion of the U.S. frontier. Henriette married Judge John C. Carr of Liverpool, Joséphine Aimée, the "neither rich nor beautiful French girl" mentioned by Sibley, married Col. James Bludworth, Jr. ("Santiago Bludwirth" in Spanish documents), of North Carolina, and Marcelite married J. Cartes d'Artheits from the Basses Pyrénées, whose name hispanicized into "Juan Cortés." Cortés was the French interpreter at the Neutral Ground negotiation, who also served as a Spanish spy, then as Mexican consul in Natchitoches, dying just before Théodore Pavie's arrival in Louisiana. This intermingling of nationalities, cultures, languages, and religions formed a microcosm of the assimilation process that created the American citizen and extinguished the French language in Natchitoches' leading families within two generations after the Louisiana Purchase.

Between 1807 and 1812, while Charles Pavie was building up his plantation and holdings, trouble threatened Spanish Texas from all sides. Mexican revolutionaries attempted a revolt from Spain, and several filibustering expeditions from Natchitoches again failed to separate Texas from Mexico. The Gutiérrez-Magee attempt in 1812–1813 angered the Spanish government, which was bent on executing all the participants, or at least emptying Nacogdoches of all its Anglo settlers. Temporary exiles included Charles Pavie's friend John Durst, who returned to Natchitoches at that time.[37]

---

36. Record preserved in Natchitoches, Louisiana, at the Immaculate Conception Church; copy provided to me by Shelby M. Nealy, Secretary/Archivist.

37. Brothers John (1797–1851) and Joseph (ca. 1789–1843) Durst were friends of Charles Pavie and were his property-holding, cotton-trading counterparts farther west in Louisiana and west of the Sabine. Born at the Arkansas post, they moved to Natchitoches

In January 1812, Charles Pavie joined other local businessmen to lodge an official complaint with his relatively new American government against lawlessness in the Neutral Ground. Surely it fell on deaf ears at such an ominous moment in international relations: "The commission of robberies on the Territory West of the Arroyo Hondo, and East of the Sabine River, and as your memorialists believe within the limits of your Excellency's Government, has become so frequent, that it is no longer safe to travel on the highways & roads through which the commerce of this Parish with the adjoining Mexican provinces have hitherto been carried on . . . on the second of January last a Company of Spaniards, whilst travelling on the highway leading from the Sabine to Bayou Pierre, were attacked by a party of Said Banditti about thirty in number, with their faces blacked, and otherwise disfigured, who fired upon them, killed one man, wounded several, one it is supposed mortally so, and robbed them of all their horses, mules, baggage and about six thousand dollars in specie."[38]

The Neutral Ground also became an irresistible temptation to those slaves hoping to reach freedom in Mexico since that country would not extradite runaway slaves to the United States. Spaniards chased from Mexico fled across the Sabine in the crosscurrent. Under the leadership of General Charles Lallemand, a member of Charles Pavie's Masonic

---

in 1803 with their father, then to Nacogdoches in 1806 where John was taken into the home of P. Samuel Davenport, variously described as his godfather, natural father, and guardian. Davenport taught him to manage a mercantile firm and to speak several languages, notably Spanish and Cherokee. The firm of Barr and Davenport occupied the Old Stone House (or Fort), which also served as the center of political activities. Along with other American participants in the Gutiérrez-Magee and Long expeditions—failed filibuster attempts to free Texas—Davenport and Durst returned to Natchitoches several years before Davenport's death in 1824. In 1829 Durst reestablished residence in the Stone House, at which time the title was transferred to him. He was living there when Théodore and Charles Pavie stayed there in February 1830. See "Davenport" and "Durst" in the *New Handbook of Texas* (ed. Ron Tyler [Austin: Texas State Historical Association, 1996]) and Archie P. McDonald, *The Old Stone Fort* (Austin: Texas State Historical Association, 1980).

38. The complaint was signed Compère & Hertzog, Vienne & Landray, C. Pavie & Ce. Jos. Tauzin, A. Sompyrac, Jn. Cortés, Ambse Duval & Ete. Lauve. *The Territorial Papers of the United States*, vol. 60, *The Orleans Territory*, 976–7. Théodore Pavie captured the grief and confusion surrounding the dissolution of New Spain in a short story titled "El Cachupin." See the translation by Alexandra K. Wettlaufer in my *Tales*.

lodge in New Orleans with whom Pavie may have served in the West Indies before his ship was captured by the British, between 250 and 400 veterans of the defeated Grande Armée and refugees from colonial slave uprisings in the Caribbean arrived on the Gulf Coast of Texas in 1818. (This may have been at a time when Charles and Marianne Pavie were in France.) Taking advantage of the Louisiana Purchase boundary confusion, they established a colony called Champ d'Asile on the banks of the Trinity River near present-day Moss Bluff or Liberty. Their presence in the disputed territory further distressed both Spain and the United States, particularly because their nearest neighbor, who actively assisted them with supplies and transportation, was the Galveston piratical establishment of Pierre and Jean Laffite, whose members played havoc with American and Spanish shipping in the Gulf of Mexico. Unable to tolerate these arrangements which served to rivet the world's attention on the long-disputed boundary problem, now enmeshed with the Florida question, in 1819 American diplomat John Quincy Adams and the Spanish ambassador, don Luís de Onís, finally concluded the agreement which today bears their name.

France's defeat in Russia in 1812 had emboldened England to attempt to resubjugate its American colonies and seize the port at the mouth of the Mississippi. Charles Pavie fought in the Battle of New Orleans on January 8, 1815, after the American troops received the blessing of his uncle Pierre Pavie, who was retired and living in New Orleans. Jean Laffite and his pirates and future filibusters Dr. James Long, Samuel Davenport, and young John Durst also participated. Though General Andrew Jackson ordered Col. James Bludworth, Jr. (Charles' brother-in-law) and his Eighteenth Regiment of the Louisiana Militia to proceed immediately to New Orleans from Natchitoches, they did not arrive until after the fight was over. Recounting the battle story to Théodore on the Plains of Chalmette in May 1830, quite possibly in the presence of Eliza Bloodworth, who had accompanied them to New Orleans, Charles said: "We did not follow the English at all as they got away on their ships, evacuating the lakes. . . . That night the Militia from the Red River arrived." Bludworth claimed that Jackson did not specify what day to arrive.[39]

39. This did not keep him from presenting the document he received when he set out forty days later to "obtain the land to which he may be entitled under the Act granting

Théodore Pavie added Charles's version of the story of the Battle of New Orleans to the second edition of *Souvenirs atlantiques.*

The War of 1812 had ended in a U.S. victory in international diplomatic circles even before the astonishing American victory at New Orleans in 1815, a year that vindicated the choice of Napoleonic veteran Charles Pavie to emigrate to Louisiana. His participation in the January victory over the British contrasts starkly with the tragic June defeat at Waterloo by the British of his brothers-in-arms in Napoleon's Grande Armée. After the departure of British troops from Louisiana, tension mounted between the Americans and the Spanish. In 1819, the Neutral Ground Agreement pertaining to the land between Natchitoches and Nacogdoches was dissolved by the Adams-Onís Treaty establishing the Louisiana-Texas border.[40]

Not everyone in the U.S. was satisfied with the Sabine River as the boundary, however. One of the dissatisfied, James Long, initiated yet another American invasion of Texas in 1819 with about three hundred men, again including John Durst. Long established the Supreme Council of the New Provincial Government of Texas in the Stone Fort in Nacogdoches and declared independence from Spain. Mexican authorities responded by sending troops from San Antonio to sweep the invaders back across the Sabine. Soon afterwards, Long was murdered in Mexico, but his expedition encouraged even more Americans to covet Texas. In 1821, Mexico formally gained its independence from Spain, precipitating a change in the government in San Antonio. This time the Nacogdochians crossed the Sabine to return home, and the town grew from a handful of settlers to about seven hundred citizens in 1827. It was not yet the picture of a peaceful, growing community, however; of those seven hundred citizens, six hundred were male.

Competition for east Texas land generated tensions that erupted in bi-

---

Bounty Land to Certain Officers and Soldiers who have been Engaged in the Military Service of the United States." Wise, *Norris-Jones-Crockett*, 128.

40. This was also the border between the United States and Spanish Mexico. Though not ratified until 1821, it is important for the history of northwestern Louisiana to consider the treaty as dating from 1819, because all the U.S. property certifications for Louisiana are predicated on an occupancy date of February 22, 1819. For details on the treaty, see Philip Coolidge Brooks, *Diplomacy in the Borderlands: The Adams-Onís Treaty of 1819* (Berkeley: University of California Press, 1939).

zarre ways. For example, Castañeda attributes the makings of an international incident to a Natchitoches priest, Abbé Aristide Anduze, who arrived in Nacogdoches in the company of the brothers-in-law Juan Cortés and "Carlos Pavi" [Charles Pavie] on October 3, 1826. Anduze delivered mass without first appearing before Alcalde Samuel Norris. Reporting the incident to Saucedo, the political chief in San Antonio, Norris added that the priest had not rung the bell before saying Mass, and he wanted to know how to make Anduze show him proper respect. Saucedo promptly replied that the priest should present his credentials to the alcalde and that the cleric was in fact acting without proper authority. According to Saucedo, if the priest persisted in refusing to comply with the law, he should be expelled as provided by the orders of the Supreme Government of March 18 and June 5 concerning the exercise of professions or trades by foreigners without express permission. Fortunately, the incident died down when Anduze, Cortés, and Pavie returned to Natchitoches, but such a serious reaction to the minor infraction of not ringing a church bell demonstrates the tension now felt between Natchitoches and Nacogdoches.[41]

By the end of that year, sparks flew through Nacogdoches again over more serious concerns: land titles and Texas independence. An argument between the young Mexican government and its grant holders in Texas resulted in a series of events referred to collectively as the Fredonian Re-

---

41. Carlos E. Castañeda, *Our Catholic Heritage in Texas, 1519–1936*, vol. 6, *The Fight for Freedom* (Austin: Von Boeckmann-Jones, 1950), 334. In 1839 the same Abbé Anduze rankled the pride of the French chargé d'affaires for the Republic of Texas, Alphonse de Saligny, who wrote to Molé (April 20, 1839) in a jealous rage that "a French plenipotentiary," Anduze, the chaplain of the French fleet blockading the port of Vera Cruz, had been "sent by Admiral Baudin to conclude a treaty of alliance with Texas against the Mexicans that very morning." Nancy Nichols Barker, *The French Legation in Texas* (Austin: Texas State Historical Association, 1973), vol. 1, p. 82.

It is easy to imagine the discomfort caused in Mexican Nacogdoches by the trio of "foreigners," especially Juan Cortés, the former captain for the cavalry at La Bahía, who before serving as the interpreter in the Neutral Ground conference had been sent to Nacogdoches by Spanish officials in 1792 to issue valid land title claims but who, by the time the mass was said without proper church bells, had completely cut his ties to Spain or Mexico and worked for the aggressive Dr. Sibley. Cortes's spotted career on the Louisiana-Texas frontier is briefly summarized by Adán Benavides, Jr. in his *Béxar Archives (1717–1836): A Name Guide* (Austin: University of Texas Press, 1989).

bellion, which was initiated by the posting of a red and white flag proclaiming "Independence, Liberty, Justice" in front of the Stone House. Empresario (land grantee) Hayden Edwards and his brother Benjamin angered old and new settlers alike. They threatened to take land away from the old settlers unless they could prove ownership of a valid title. Edwards angered the new settlers as well by trying to charge them fees. But they complained to the political chief at San Antonio, and government officials in Mexico canceled Edwards's grant. Having invested his fortune in starting the colony, he gathered the support of a few friends, and on December 16, 1826, declared Texas independent of Mexico, under the name of the Republic of Fredonia.[42] For a while the Cherokees aided him. Austin and his colonists refused to help, though, and Peter Ellis Bean persuaded the Cherokees to put down their arms when Mexican soldiers began advancing from San Antonio. Realizing the hopelessness of their situation, the Edwards brothers fled to the United States on January 31, 1827.

The Fredonian Rebellion prompted another buildup of the Nacogdoches presidio under Colonel José de las Piedras, an impeccably mannered and extremely well educated Creole from a village near Veracruz. Finding no place to quarter his troops and having no budget to remedy the deficit, Piedras converted the parish church into barracks; religious services were conducted in a house.[43] John Durst was buying and inheriting Nacogdoches properties at this time, and in 1828 Charles Pavie sold Durst the property in Nacogdoches that he had inherited from his priest-uncle Pierre Pavie, who had purchased it as a church site, presumably with

42. "Fredonia" was the name proposed by Thomas Jefferson's friend Samuel Lathan Mitchill (1763–1831) for the United States of America, a name Mitchill considered ambiguous. Like Jefferson, he shared the prevailing Romantic view that America's destiny was to create the most nearly perfect society possible, and like Hugo, he liked to invent new words for new situations. Mitchill offered several similar explanations for his term "Fredonia," all of them indicating that he was trying to get across the idea that liberty had been accomplished. Thus he combined "free" with "done" and appended "ia" to mean "the place where." See Alan D. Aberbach, "A Search for an American Identity," *Canadian Review of American Studies* 7 (Fall 1971): 77–78. Two decades after he returned to France, Pavie wrote a short story titled "La Peau d'ours" that reflects the tension of the Fredonian Rebellion, which he missed. See the translation in my *Tales of the Sabine Borderlands*.

43. According to Castañeda, this was the former home of Nathaniel Norris, moved to the site of the Stone Fort National Bank in October 1829.

money inherited from his parents. After their paths converged in Nacogdoches, Durst and Piedras worked together congenially for several years.
The Dursts moved into the Stone Fort in 1829, where they were living,
of course, when Théodore Pavie visited the following year.[44]

According to Pavie in *Souvenirs atlantiques,* no Mexicans owned mercantile establishments and few occupied prominent professional status.[45]
But what concerned the presidio commander most, and what Piedras
warned his superiors about repeatedly in his letters, was the flood of An-
glos who would soon outnumber the Mexicans in Texas. In addition to
detailed descriptions of the town of Nacogdoches, the young Frenchman
gives an eyewitness account of a rodeo one mile outside of town, and
seems in the portion of his book written between February and April
1830 to admire Piedras. But sometime after the passage of the Law of
Sixth April—Mexico's belated and inflammatory attempt to stem the
Anglo tide by forbidding further immigration into Texas from the United
States—Pavie penned a fictional ending to "Le Lazo," in which he has
Piedras die a violent death. (The commander did indeed die a violent
death, but it was at the hands of his political enemy, Santa Anna, who
had him assassinated in 1839.)[46]

Thus three generations of Pavies journeyed, with varying motivations,
to the rugged, often tumultuous Louisiana-Texas borderlands between
1765 and 1838. They came seeking refuge, adventure, or economic gain.

44. Copy of Bill of Sale from Villalpando to Pavie in vol. 4, p. 224 of the R. B. Blake
Collection, Nacogdoches Archives, Barker Center for American History, University of
Texas at Austin. See Archie P. McDonald, *Nacogdoches: Wilderness Outpost to Modern
City, 1779–1979* (Burnet, Texas: Eakin Press, 1980), 26–32, for a description of the devel-
opment of the pueblo from available materials prior to the installation of a water-powered
saw mill in the late 1820s. For a description of the events leading to the Fredonian Rebel-
lion, see Théodore Pavie's short story "Le Lazo" and the accompanying notes. (*Tales of the
Sabine Borderlands,* 10–25)

45. Mexico was under Spanish rule until 1821. Pavie carefully calls Piedras "a Creole
from Mexico," meaning that he was born in Mexico of European (in his case, Spanish) par-
entage.

46. Robert Bruce Blake, "Piedras," in *The New Handbook of Texas,* ed. Ron Tyler (6
vols.; Texas State Historical Association, 1996). Hubert Howe Bancroft gives a fuller description of the political confrontations leading to the tragic end of Piedras in *The Works
of Hubert Howe Bancroft,* vol. 13, *History of Mexico: Vol. V, 1824–1861* (1885; reprint,
Arno Press for McGraw-Hill, n.d.), 206–226.

Each migration, moreover, reflected the current political and economic climate in France. Several Pavies went on to amass considerable fortunes. Two of the seven men married Creole women born in Natchitoches, but not a single male heir survived to perpetuate the name. One was murdered, just as his countryman La Salle had been, and his name-bearing son died suddenly of "the fevers" at sixteen. All of the Pavies remained in Louisiana a quarter century except Théodore, who arrived in the United States in 1829 and returned to France in the summer of 1830. The story of his trip connects the family history with over 150 years of French colonial expansion and contraction and the concurrent development of Louisiana, Texas, and Mexico.

2

THE PAVIE BROTHERS IN ANGERS AND PARIS

THROUGH LITERATURE AND HISTORY, both written and oral, Théodore Pavie's French predecessors to Louisiana and Texas sparked his desire to visit the borderlands. Whether merely fellow western Frenchmen like La Salle and Chateaubriand, or family members like Étienne, Joseph, Pierre, and Charles Pavie, they framed his expectations of what he would find and informed his record of it. Also, his absorption of the Pavie household's dramatic stories about the French Revolution, his reading of works of travel literature, and his intense encounters with the geniuses of French Romanticism—particularly Victor Hugo and David d'Angers—prepared him to observe, appreciate, and, often, treasure details that would have disappeared from historical view had he not recorded them.

Théodore Pavie was born on August 16, 1811, to Louis and Marie-Marguerite Pavie, who had another son, Victor, born three years earlier. They lived in the family home in Angers and Louis worked at the family press, where he had joined his widowed mother when he completed his education. Twenty-two-year-old Marie-Marguerite died in 1813, and Théodore was later to describe his earliest memory as the afternoon of the 1814 memorial service for his young mother. Teary-eyed members of the household dressed in mourning clothes entered his room, leaned over his tiny bed, and sobbed as they kissed him. For the next twenty years, the late Mme Pavie's mother draped her daughter's portrait to spare the grieving father, who would bring his sons to visit their maternal grandmother. While servants and family members also avoided mentioning young Mme Pavie in front of the bereaved widower, various relatives told Théodore in secret that his mother had been "pious, sweet, simple in her tastes, orderly, and a little melancholic."[1] He fastened onto the last trait and, whenever he felt melancholy, he naturally ascribed those feelings to her.

Whether his melancholy was Romantic posturing, or real, or both, the Pavie boys' childhood was generally stable, full of gaiety and good humor. They were surrounded by attentive family and friends, including their father Louis, their grandmother Marie Pavie, whom they lovingly called "Bonnemaman," and household servants and employees of the Pavie Press who lived on the property and functioned as an extended family. Théodore Pavie remembered his grandmother as one who "spoke little, prayed much, and sometimes smiled—without ever laughing." Marie Pavie, the oldest of twelve children the rest of whom retained a certain fear of their sister, was the only family member imprisoned during the Reign of Terror. Her grandson would one day describe her legacy of the revolutionary years: "This imprint of terror that could be read in her calm, austere, but profoundly sad traits . . . she devoted herself for long years to patiently reconstituting, by dint of doing without and spending carefully, the little fortune whose early beginnings had been ruined by the Revolution. Volney, who lived in Angers on his return from the Orient, in full glory of his renown as a traveler and great writer, came to have supper with her frequently and took great pleasure in her conversation."[2]

---

1. In 1876, Pavie began a lengthy autobiographic letter addressed to his niece and nephews. It opens "Le plus lointain souvenir qui me reste de ma première enfance . . ." or, "The most distant memory of my early childhood. . . ." He mined this never-published work to write a biography of his brother shortly after the latter's death, *Victor Pavie: Sa Jeunesse, ses relations littéraires* (Angers: Lachèse et Dolbeau, 1887). The unpublished family story which, unfortunately, stops after Waterloo, will hereinafter be cited as "Lointains Souvenirs"; the present passage is from page 2.

2. Pavie, "Lointains Souvenirs," 4.

While Bonnemaman never spoke of the great misfortunes and trage-
dies she had witnessed, the two resident family servants were more forth-
coming about revolutionary events. As Pavie recounted, "These two
women invariably brought up scenes of the sinister days of the Revolution. Manette Dubois, who had followed the [Catholic royalist] army,
talked like a soldier about marches, retreats, routs, and massacres; Renée
Boulay chimed in with her episodes . . . [Manette] personified the region
of the Vendée, with its heroism, unshakable faith, and ancient ways; the
other [Renée], of less lively intelligence, less ardent in her convictions,
blended the fantastic with memories of the terrible realities that she had
witnessed."[3]

They entertained the boys with the recitations of heroic tales which
undoubtedly contributed significantly to the development of Théodore's
storytelling style as it begins to emerge in *Souvenirs atlantiques*. There,
the eighteen-year-old's observational processes frequently echo Manette's highly descriptive and action-filled manner or betray Renée's belief in the supernatural. (More seasoned intellectuals, in contrast, tend to
develop stories whose plots turn on the psychological depth of their characters.) Thus rooted in his childhood, Pavie's narrative approach fuses
the diverse influences of his education by tutors, his father's and grandmother's highly rational and cultivated conversation in the manner of the
Ancien régime, and the servants' peasant tales filled with action and the
supernatural.

To add to this diverse environment, Théodore's uncle Charles Pavie
and his wife Marianne came from Louisiana to visit the Pavies of Angers
in 1818. The childless couple invited their nephew to return to Louisiana
with them, but his father would not consent to being separated from his
young son. Nonetheless, the invitation planted a possibility in the child's
imagination. Much later he reminisced, "What they told me about the
forests of Louisiana and the life they led there produced such a strong
impression on me that I always dreamed of seeing these beautiful things
with my own eyes. The sight of the sea produced an ardent desire to
know what lay beyond. A profound melancholy resulted that little by little changed into a sort of nostalgia for these unknown regions that became the homeland of my dreams."[4]

3. Ibid., 3.
4. Pavie, *Victor Pavie,* p. 117.

Théodore Pavie also took family excursions to Saumur to visit his great-aunt Duval (complete name unknown). There, on the wall in her dining room, he viewed hand-blocked wallpaper depicting scenes from the explorations of Captain James Cook. "When we were children," Théodore recalled, "she had already lost her husband and was living across the street from the *collège* in a little house, now destroyed, decorated with wallpaper showing the voyages of Cook and curtained with red drapes which remarkably darkened the living room. . . . From time to time, we used to all go to her house for dinner; and I loved these dinners because I could feast my eyes on savages and their *pirogues,* on their huts, and Cook's great vessels moored in front of palm-covered islands."[5] The widowed sisters may have taken special pleasure in surrounding themselves with these scenes from the explorations of Captain Cook and La Pérouse, his French counterpart, who sailed on a voyage of discovery for Louis XVI. Their brother Alexandre Fabre participated in the official expedition launched in search of the missing vessels of La Pérouse, whose two frigates were shipwrecked in 1785 at Vanikoro (New Hebrides), and later was himself killed in a naval battle against Lord Nelson. It is easy to see how input from various sources in the family lore (the lure of the sea and exotic places, and the Anglophobia) could have fed the child's own inchoate world view and inspired him to set sail in search of adventure.

Some of Pavie's other early memories stem from the last days of the Napoleonic Empire, but he does not later recount them as heroic triumphs, as was typical of members of the older Romantic generation whose fathers had found glory by following the emperor. For them, heroism was retrospective, a memory of childhood. Théodore's father, Catholic royalist Vendéan Louis Pavie, tended instead to blame Napoleon for the problems of the Restoration (1814–1830). A significant generational difference separated the young Pavie brothers from the majority of the Romantics, like Hugo, with whom they later associated and identified.

5. Pavie, "Lointains Souvenirs," 5–6. Dufour's popular wallpaper depicted Cook among exotic savages who dwelled on lush islands. "Les Sauvages de la mer Pacifique" was the first great panoramic wallpaper introduced at the Exposition of Industrial Products in 1806. According to Odile Nouvel-Kammerer in *Papiers, Peints, Panoramiques* (Paris: Flammarion, 1990), the exotic theme was dictated by three goals: "the desire to surprise, instruct, and invite the spectator to escape" (16).

The nine years that lay between Hugo, leader of the Romantics, and Théodore Pavie were sufficient to explain a completely different experience with heroism, "la gloire." Hugo, whose father had been a general of the Grande Armée and who had witnessed grand parades featuring the emperor on his white stallion, nurtured intentions of being the voice of Napoleon, the preacher for his God. Théodore, in contrast, knew only the dénouement and dissolution of the Empire, moreover, his memories are childlike in content, filled with episodes involving animals and moments of heightened emotion. Pavie admired his father's judgment and recalled his courage during the Hundred Days: "Like everyone else, we had to lodge several soldiers. First it was a Prussian sergeant who distributed, in the courtyard, enormous rations of meat to his subordinates. Our father's dog Trumpet, who was bad tempered and, on top of that, had puppies at that time, attacked the sergeant and bit his leg. The soldier tore loose and drew his saber; my father arrived very angry and took the side of the courageous animal. The situation became difficult, but it was all settled. The sergeant, with his slabs of meat, had to leave to be lodged elsewhere."[6]

Although Pavie fondly recalled the memory of a horse from this era, it was not the symbolic white steed of Napoleon that he remembered from the imperial soldiers' stop in Angers on their way to Waterloo. Instead, he recalled that his family had lodged two Russian cannoneers, one named Filoff, who was completely deaf and accustomed to drinking eau-de-vie by the glassful from a jug. He remembered these colorful figures as kind: "They waltzed with Manette . . . and let us sit on their horses."[7]

Angers, located on the Loire River, stood at the intersection of two great trade routes, the shipping waterway from Paris to the Atlantic, and the roadway from Spain through Belgium to Holland. The city's location provided young Pavie with frequent lessons in political and cultural differences. The greedy Prussian sergeant and the kind Russian cannoneer,

6. Pavie, "Lointains Souvenirs," 15. Among the leading Romantics, Alfred de Vigny was born in 1797; Delacroix, 1798; Balzac, 1799; Hugo and Dumas *fils,* 1802; Sainte-Beuve and George Sand, 1804; Gérard de Nerval, 1808. The exceptions were Alfred de Musset, 1810, and Théophile Gautier, born the same year as Pavie, 1811. For a detailed description of the immediately preceding generation (born between 1792 and 1803), see Alan B. Spitzer, *The French Generation of 1820* (Princeton: Princeton University Press, 1987).

7. Pavie, "Lointains Souvenirs," 13–16.

for example, were both fighting for the same Grande Armée. Another anecdote from 1815 demonstrates that not even a three-year-old child could hide from politics during the Hundred Days that Napoleon spent in France, between his two periods of exile. The political discretion of the mature Théodore Pavie, rare among those with whom he associated, seems to date to these two incidents.

The events of 1814 that changed the face of Europe and the fall of Napoleon which left France in the hands of foreign powers, passed by me unperceived. I wasn't even three. I remember, however, in March 1815, as a soldier was passing in the rue Petit Prêtre, under the terrace of our house, I started repeating the cry I had so often heard shouted with enthusiasm: "Long live the Emperor!" as they said in those days. The soldier, who was wearing a white cockade [symbol of the Royalists]—which I had not noticed at all— responded by cursing so terribly that I ran away trembling. A short time later, during the Hundred Days, the Young Guard was garrisoned at Angers. Seeing in the street these handsome Grenadiers in fur hats, I thought I was doing well to cry out, "Long live the King." This time the soldier blurted out a hideous curse, accompanied by such threats that I went and hid in the kitchen, more dead than alive, and I have never again dared to demonstrate any opinion publicly.[8]

Pavie had far more pleasant memories of the soldiers who defected to Napoleon during the Hundred Days than he did of the belligerent Royalist. Many of the imperial soldiers had to postpone having children to serve Napoleon, and it was for Napoleon's son whom he had symbolically placed on the throne that they were fighting. Pavie, born the same year as that long-awaited son, recollected his encounter with two of Napoleon's men on their way to meet their destiny at Waterloo. "A few days later as I was crawling up the wood staircase of Grandmother Fabre, on Forge Street, two of the grenadiers lodged in the house lifted me gaily in their arms and one of them, brushing aside the blond hair dangling in curls over my face, hugged me and said to his comrade, 'Well, look how

8. Ibid., 13.

he looks like our little one!' . . . Their 'little one' was the son of Napoleon, the King of Rome [who was] the same age as me. Those people were fanatical over the Emperor."[9]

Théodore also described the tragic destiny of his new friends of the Elite Corps. "I saw from the third floor over Chaussée St. Pierre Street, parading by, musicians leading, preceded by their unbelievable drum major, this magnificent Young Guard who were going to die at Waterloo! . . . I have never forgotten their pants floating over their white gaiters, their long greatcoats, their tall fur hats whose fur hung down to their mustaches, and their determined faces that seemed to defy the entire world. This time, and for the last, the cries of 'Long live the Emperor!' resounded everywhere."[10]

As the former emperor went into exile on the island of Sainte Helena, three-year-old Théodore Pavie's education began. A few months after the Guard traversed Angers, his father and grandmother summoned him to his father's tiny office, and announced that the time had come for him to learn to read. Théodore burst into uncontrollable tears, just as two of his aunts arrived and joined the harangue, pronouncing that it was "quite objectionable to wish to remain like a donkey, not knowing how to read." So Théodore's and Victor's studies began unbrilliantly when their grandmother sent them on foot to the school of a distant relative whom Pavie was to describe as "an obese and cross-eyed old maid." She, in turn, characterized them as "poor children" with "such good intentions, but such limited potential."[11]

The boys were sent to a second school, but with no better luck. A teacher rapped Victor on the knuckles with his ruler and one of the older boys stole and ate his lunch; this was enough to prompt Louis Pavie to keep them at home and hire a tutor, a young man who worked for the Pavie Press named Henri Langlois. Henri was also related to their grandmother through his mother, so the boys considered him a close relative, "an older brother; we loved him tenderly," although they also respected his firm manner. After a few months, when Théodore, age four, knew how to read and write, the boys began to study Latin.[12]

9. Ibid.
10. Ibid.
11. Ibid., 25.
12. Ibid., 24.

Langlois and Monsieur Salio, a domestic, lived in a bedroom on the third floor of the business and home on the rue St. Laud. It became the boys' classroom. From the street below arose the sounds of Angevine life in the 1820s: "Who needs scissors sharpened?" "Who wants to buy lettuce?" and the neighbor's unhappy wife castigating him, "I told you, you disgust me!" mixed with the rhythmic background beat from the nearby forge, the lowing of cattle herded to the slaughterhouse around the corner, and the chirping of canaries, whose cage hung out a window on the side street. Others, often eccentrics, passed under the window—traveling musicians, players in theater troupes, and bear trainers. Apparently the boys worked diligently among these fleeting distractions, and Langlois proved to be a competent teacher, as both entered *collège* (roughly U.S. grades 6–8), as the youngest in their classes. Once there, they won many academic prizes.

When Langlois realized, however, that he did not have a future working in a family firm for a proprietor with two bright sons, he left the Pavie Press precipitously to work for a competitor, without so much as embracing the boys. That was the saddest day of Théodore's childhood, he later claimed, or the saddest two days, for that is how long he cried. Heartbroken along with his sons, Louis Pavie forebade them to mention Henri's name, but Théodore sneaked off to visit him secretly. No one reported the clandestine meeting, and eventually all hurts were mended. Salio replaced Henri at the Press and in the boys' lives, but not in their hearts. In 1829, Langlois and Théodore exchanged letters that show that the pupil had by then exceeded his tutor's language skills.

Not far from Angers was the hamlet of Feneu where, during the dispersal of Church properties during the Revolution, Marie and Louis-Victor Pavie, Théodore Pavie's grandparents, purchased a small priory and used part of it as a country home. Crudely constructed roads made travel difficult, thus allowing the countryside to remain largely unspoiled. In this picturesque natural setting, among peasants whose worlds were peopled by apparitions, Pavie acquired the lifelong sense of connectedness with nature evident in all of his writing, as well as the instinctive association between nature and stories. He described his primordial response to water, which he perceived as an invitation to dream of travel:

It is to Feneu that we owe enduring feelings for nature that the Loire surroundings [Angers] did not develop in us to such an ex-

tent. The breadth and expanse of the Loire's vistas please everyone, which is not bad, but the Loire lacks intimacy. At the very first
sight, it delights, enchants, and gives forth all its secrets. It is like
history which instructs, compared to legend, which causes one to
dream. In the land of Feneu, on the contrary . . . how many mysteries, how many gracious and troubling perspectives! At night this
forested land became populated with apparitions; from every
mouth would come strange tales one laughed at during daylight,
but whose recollection evoked terror when night fell.

In our early years, Feneu was our favorite place: it was the land
of sorcerers and apparitions, *par excellence*. Everyone believed in
them, our farmer more than anyone. Never did a man exist who
was more haunted by fear, more obsessed by ridiculous ideas that
tormented him night and day. As soon as it got dark, he began to
tremble. Once it was thirty-two weasels holding on to each other
by their tails and who, said he, had stopped a man to ask him for
some tobacco. "The passerby, being drunk, didn't hear the question, and they rolled him into a furrow and rolled him over, and
rolled him over, and rolled him over and over 'till they rolled him
sober."[13]

This anecdote, which mixes the supernatural with animal lore while
also teaching a moral lesson, is easy to remember because of its compel-
ling internal rhythm. It demonstrates Pavie's early facility for recognizing
and retaining linguistically interesting nibbles from different cultures,
which he recounts in a lucid and nonjudgmental fashion: "One could
have believed that the peasant was making fun of us and enjoyed telling
us stories that he did not believe himself, but that wasn't it at all; the unfortunate devil believed all of these fantasies. At night, when he heard a
noise in the courtyard, too cowardly to open the door, he had to content
himself with locking himself inside with an old gun that our father gave
him so he could defend his somewhat isolated farm; after midnight, however, he got braver, because, it was said, the Evil One (*le Malin*) loses his
strength as daylight approaches."[14] Such interactions with these country

13. Ibid., 31.
14. Ibid., 31.

people who believed in ghosts, sorcerers, and evil beings seem to have sensitized Pavie for the experiences he subsequently underwent in Louisiana.

Unfortunately for us, he abandoned writing his memoirs after recording the early years. A hiatus therefore exists in the details of the next few years. Encouraged by father and grandmother, and prepared by their tutors, the boys attended the local lycée, then called the Collège Royal. Victor eventually headed for Paris to complete the final year of lycée. Théodore, barely thirteen and beginning to express the resentments and moodiness typical of that age, continued his studies in Angers until he successfully completed his exams for a Bachelor's diploma in philosophy, which the family considered to be the termination of his schooling. Besides his academic training, Théodore was honing his observational skills with coaching from his grandmother, who had edited a book on the flora of Anjou; his father, who enjoyed a significant reputation in natural sciences and horticulture; and his father's very skilled yet illiterate gardener, who, in the sons words, demonstrated "the succinct and solid notions of natural science that a peasant acquires from listening and watching while living in the middle of the fields."[15] At this time, Théodore Pavie took his place beside Louis Pavie at the Press, since the rightful heir exhibited no interest in following in his father's footsteps.

A fortuitous chain of events began to unfold when Victor Pavie enrolled at the prestigious Charlemagne School in Paris in 1824. Escorted by his father, he arrived in the capital the morning after the death of Louis XVIII, the last king of France to die while reigning. Louis Pavie took his son to visit two close Angevin friends: the scientist Michel Eugène Chevreul and the sculptor David d'Angers. Both men, especially d'Angers, would fill the role of family surrogates and help the new student merge into the creative mainstream of Parisian society.

When Pierre-Jean David had arrived in Paris in 1808, he added "d'Angers" to his name to distinguish himself from Napoleon's famous painter, Jacques-Louis David, then at the height of his influence. David d'Angers was a child of the French Revolution and the wars in the

15. Ibid., 12; T. M. Batard. *Essai sur la flore du Département de Maine et Loire* (Angers: Veuve Pavie et Fils, 1809). I am grateful to Gilles and Odette Pavie who provided this reference and a copy of the title page.

Vendée. His father, a woodcarver, took the young child along when he fought in the revolutionary army. At the close of the Revolution, when Louis Pavie resumed his education at the École Centrale, he met the younger David at school sometime around the turn of the century by rescuing the frail little boy from some local bullies. As the schoolboys grew into manhood, they considered their friendship to be above politics (Republican versus Royalist) and religion (Deist versus Catholic), for both families valued tolerance and justice above partisanship and dogma. David d'Angers became a kind of honorary member of the Pavie family, and as it grew with additions of wives and children, the alliance extended to include the new growth. When Louis Pavie left his son Victor in Paris in 1824, then, he was very glad that his friend lived there. Still a bachelor, David also needed the companionship. Victor Pavie felt a mixture of homesickness and exhilaration when his father returned to Angers. He wrote to thirteen-year-old Théodore, "I am living only off my memories here. . . . Sometimes, I am depressed and pensive, other times I feel full of fire and energy."[16]

Any homesickness he felt did not last long, however, because he was swept into the vortex of Parisian romanticism in several arts, thanks to David d'Angers and his acquaintances, including the greatest men of his times who filed into the artist's studio to have their portraits prepared, first as sketches, then as bas-relief "medallions." Nonetheless, Victor's early disdain for the capital city, which he communicated to Théodore in letters, may have contributed to the latter's desire to go to America instead.

In Victor's letters home, he also reported whom and what he saw, and advised his young brother on what to read, including Victor Hugo and

16. Victor Pavie to Théodore Pavie, October 18, 1824, quoted in Alexis Crosnier, *Théodore Pavie, le voyageur, le professeur, l'ecrivain, l'homme et le chrétien* (Angers: Lachèse et Cie, 1897), 10. Jacques-Louis David (1748–1825) was the leader of the neoclassical school in France best known for *The Coronation of Napoleon*. He served as the emperor's court painter. David d'Angers (1788–1856) was the most important French sculptor for half a century although, in the United States the familiarity of Rodin's (1840–1917) abundant work has obscured the significance of the Angevin, whose "Médaillons" (bas-relief portraits) preserve the profiles of the luminaries of his era before photography. A winner of the coveted Prix de Rome, David produced a colossal marble cavalier, the "Grande Condé," for the Pont de la Concorde; it became the clarion call for future French Romanticism in sculpture.

Lamartine. On the subject of Lamartine, he confessed, "I think of him more than of you"—a bittersweet acknowledgment of his sibling's diminished importance as Victor's homesickness faded and was replaced by enthusiasm for the great adventure he was having among the Romantics. When he attended a session of the Academy of Beaux-Arts, a self-selected gathering of the male elites in several arts, he wrote to Théodore on September 23, 1824, "I saw Chateaubriand!"[17]

In Angers, Louis Pavie added a local newspaper to his printing business and published several of Victor Pavie's poems, written at age eighteen. In 1826, while Victor was in Angers at Christmastime, he took an action that changed his own life and would have quite an impact on Théodore Pavie as well, although it took several years to come to fruition. From Angers, Victor Pavie forwarded to Victor Hugo in Paris a flattering review he had written of *Les Odes,* signed simply "V.P." Hugo, poet and father of three, responded immediately (December 13, 1826) to the eighteen-year-old schoolboy, whom he addressed as "Mr. V. P., one of the Editors of the *Feuilleton des Affiches d'Angers.*" Their correspondence was mutually laudatory from its inception: Hugo opened that first letter with, "It is not because you praise me that I thank you. I would not esteem praise which is nothing but praise. What I appreciate in your article is the talent found there; what pleases me, what charms me, what enchants me is having found in so few lines the complete revelation of a noble soul, a strong intelligence in an elevated mind . . . I regret not being able to write you except under the initials V. P.; they sign an article that the first names of our literature could subscribe to; but whatever it may be, the name that they hide will not remain unknown for long."[18]

Of course, Victor Pavie was dazzled to receive any letter from his idol, particularly one so laden with praise. The surprisingly prompt mail service might be explained by the cities' locations on the network of waterways. At any rate, Victor Pavie replied immediately (December 18, 1826), making this tempting request of Hugo: "If I had one wish left for your glory, it would be that you put into writing a project at which you

17. Victor Pavie to Théodore Pavie, September 23, 1824, quoted in Crosnier, *Théodore Pavie,* 10.

18. Published in Victor Hugo, *Lettres à la fiancée/Correspondance,* ed. La Librarie Ollendorff (Paris: Albin Michel, 1947), 437.

hinted in your last volume: to establish the changeless doctrine of Romanticism." Along with his request, the young man revealed to Hugo in absolute sincerity what he believed to be the poet's role in society, that is, Hugo's role for France: "He has a mission from on high, and, just like the echo of a great voice, he transmits secrets to men that God reveals to him."

The author could not resist such idolatry, especially since Victor Pavie's beliefs resonated with Hugo's own self-assessment and goals. When Hugo replied on January 3, 1827, he expressed intrigue with Pavie's request for a Romantic doctrine, but the polite poet first deferred to the young Angevin by suggesting that Pavie could and should write such a doctrine himself. "Sir, follow freely your own path. Obey your demon. You have all that is necessary: the intelligence for creation and the imagination to fertilize it. The oak is in you; let it grow."[19]

The two Victors, kindred spirits, thus became friends through their mutually flattering correspondence. When Victor Pavie returned to Paris to study law, Victor Hugo and his wife extended the young man from Angers regular invitations to come to family dinners and poetry readings. His company particularly delighted Mme Hugo, now busy with three young children, especially since the pious and charming young man was near the age of her own brother, Paul Foucher, who also frequented the household.

Hugo did indeed write the Romantic manifesto. He inserted it before the text to *Cromwell,* which he had already written, as the preface to the volume. The *Préface de Cromwell* became the credo of Young France— the stylish, artistic Parisians—articulating as it did their belief in their generation's right and duty to redefine beauty and art in terms that were their own and that were appropriate to their times. Hugo's credo was adopted in all the arts: music, architecture, sculpture, painting, and poetry. Even those whose practices had already anticipated the developments put themselves under Hugo's banner.

In one letter from this period, in response to some of Victor Pavie's poems published by his father's provincial paper, Hugo suggests that he "be even more strict with the richness of rhyme. . . . He can change rhythm as often as he wishes within the same ode" and other technical

---

19. Hugo, *Lettres à la fiancée,* 438.

recommendations. While Victor was receiving technical advice from France's most promising young poet, Théodore Pavie continued to work at the family press. He frequently joined his friends in vigorous activities like sailing, swimming, fishing, horseback riding, and, in winter, ice skating on the frozen river. He also took flute lessons, studied drawing, and read adventures like *Robinson Crusoe* and scholarly travel accounts like those of Volney, Raynal, Humbolt, and Champollion. This voracious reader drew from a perpetual supply of the latest books that went directly to the Pavie Press or found their way there indirectly through the studio of David d'Angers, having been sent by authors who reciprocated some artistic tribute. Pavie thus gathered notions from the most popular books of the era, and concocted a mental itinerary of places, views, characters, experiences, and emotions described by James Fenimore Cooper and, particularly, Chateaubriand. Chateaubriand did not "invent" Romanticism, but he did contribute to its fruition when he created the forceful literary works that instilled the Romantic spirit inexorably in Théodore Pavie.

Romanticism was a European phenomenon whose branches grew in diverse forms and at different times in Germany, England, and France. At a time before the French Revolution, when people and ideas circulated freely among the courts and salons of Europe, Jean-Jacques Rousseau planted the seeds of the movement, which he had garnered from Neoplatonic Christian traditions. He articulated his love of nature to counteract his exasperation at the insufficiency of reality. Rousseau described *le mal du siècle,* or the soul sickness: "Were all of my dreams to have come true, they would not have satisfied me: I would have imagined, dreamed, desired still more. I found within myself an inexplicable void that nothing could have filled, a certain yearning of the heart for another kind of pleasure, I had no idea what, and of which I felt the need nevertheless. . . . Even this was a pleasure, because I found myself penetrated with a very intense feeling and a seductive sadness that I would not have wanted not to have."[20]

Early in the nineteenth century, Chateaubriand brought forward Rousseau's love of nature and this seductive sadness, proposing to rem-

20. Jean-Jacques Rousseau, "Troisiemè Lettre à Malherbes," in André Lagarde and Laurent Michard, *XVIIIième siècle* (Paris: Bordas, 1960), 317, 144–50.

edy—or at least treat—the pervasive ailment with a dose of American wilderness such as that found on the Mississippi River or in Louisiana. He prized solitude and, under his pen, nature became the projection of an interior landscape or the imaginary support for a personal adventure. Chateaubriand's popularity passed through several cycles as his books were republished; his seminal works consoled the French masses left alienated in the wake of each political upheaval.

From just before until at least three decades after the French Revolution, the melancholic young wanderer, bereft of heroes and models, was a European commonplace that found expression in the literature of England, Germany, and France. Lord Byron created Childe Harold; Goethe, Werther; and Chateaubriand, a semiautobiographical alter ego to whom he gave his own name, René. Several generations of young Frenchmen (and at least one woman, George Sand) revived the image and took it for a model. Chateaubriand eventually wrote in his memoirs that René "overran the minds of part of the young." He described a prolific family of "René-poets and René-prose writers," bemoaning (or bragging?) that "all one could hear was the droning of lamentable, disjointed sentences. It was nothing but storming winds, unknown woes delivered up to the clouds and to the dark of night; there was not a single callow youth leaving school who did not believe himself tormented by his genius, who in the emptiness of his thoughts did not give in to his passions, strike his pale, disheveled forehead, and astonish an amazed mankind with an illness that neither he nor they could name."[21]

In *The Male Malady,* Margaret Waller cites numerous examples of adolescent imitation of Chateaubriand and René, his "alienated but sublime protagonist." She also provides the modern reader with a mechanism for dealing with this pattern of behavior by labeling it a "rite of passage not only to Romanticism but also to adulthood and to writing itself."[22] No better instance could be found in France and French literature of Chateaubriand's having modeled the "rite of passage" than the documents stemming from Théodore Pavie's journey to Texas and Louisiana.

21. Chateaubriand, *Mémoires d'outre-tombe (1814–1815)*, 2 vols., ed. Pierre Clarac (Paris: Gallimard, 1946), 111–7.
22. Margaret Waller, *The Male Malady: Fictions of Importance in the French Romantic Novel* (New Brunswick, N.J.: Rutgers University Press, 1993).

Chateaubriand's personal financial distress prompted him to publish *Voyage en Amérique* in 1826, a quarter of a century after the trip he took to escape the Revolution, and to reissue *Atala* and *René* at that time, along with *Les Natchez,* which was being published for the first time. This effort coincided with the supposed conclusion of the fifteen-year-old Pavie's studies, which would have freed him for more leisure reading. It also coincided with the instigation of Victor's friendship with Victor Hugo, which most certainly created a vacuum in Théodore's social and emotional life. Recognizing many of his own feelings described in the plight of René, Théodore naturally expected Chateaubriand to demonstrate a solution also. What did René represent?

Chateaubriand believed that the pain of his generation was even greater than that of the generation of Rousseau (whose pain begat the French Revolution) because civilization had advanced farther, so that the proportion of experiences enjoyed vicariously had outstripped the opportunity for real-life applications of the knowledge gained therefrom. There was too much reading and too little action. "The more a people advances in civilization, the more this unsettled state of passions grows, for a very sad thing happens: the great number of examples one can see, the multitude of books that treat of man and all his sentiments, renders one skillful without experience. One loses one's illusions without having felt pleasure; desires still remain, but without the illusions that they might be fulfilled." René, a victim of strong passions who is unable to focus on a single task, expresses his discomfort during the time we now call adolescence: "One lives with a full heart in an empty world; without having tried anything, one is disappointed with everything." Théodore Pavie and his friends mimicked this antihero, believing his dictum that "a great soul should contain more suffering than a small one" and proving their greatness by exhibiting their melancholy.[23]

Energized by Romantic writing, the young chose to escape or rebel. For the French this meant a choice between escape in time or space: in time back to the chivalry of the Gothic Middle Ages, and in space to Greece, Spain, the Orient, Louisiana, and elsewhere. The geniuses of Young France who rebelled against the culture, the artists and writers of the end of the Restoration and early July Monarchy, were serious men

23. Chateaubriand, *Mémoires d'outre-tombe,* 111–7.

of action making known their discontent through their costumes, their art, and their lives. Their idea of "action" included such activities as feeling, contemplating, traveling, sketching, and jotting, because these exercises ran counter to the rational grain of outmoded classicism. They sought self-determination and influence in a new France that would conquer the world not militarily, but intellectually. A wide variety of acts leading to cultural self-determination would also contribute to completing the aims of the Revolution in the spirit of Voltaire and Rousseau. Thus a new French aristocracy of letters rose up alongside the moneyed old-world aristocrats and the imperial elite named for their military victories. Victor Pavie participated in the protracted birth pains of this new elite into which his brother would later work his way.

The amount of satisfaction the young Pavie men drew from their respective lives could hardly have been more disparate in the summer of 1827, when their busy father instructed fifteen-year-old Théodore to write a letter to his brother in Paris. "My dear Victor," the younger son began obediently on July 17th, "I am writing to you once more because Papa hasn't time to write even though I find myself embarrassed to write again since I have nothing new to tell you about a city where nothing different ever happens. It is quite depressing to contrast everything that you are experiencing that is so stimulating with nothing but boring sentences on white paper just because a response to you seems necessary."[24]

Théodore nonetheless filled two and a half pages, then the busy father added a message extolling the great pleasure he was getting from Victor's letters. First of all, he was finding them well written, and second, they painted the image of the pleasure Victor was experiencing in the middle of the "enchanting whirlwind" in which he was living in Paris and wanted to share with his family in Angers. Such vicarious, passive pleasure might well satisfy Victor's father and grandmother, but what about Théodore? How long could letters from the Romantic cauldron content a restless young man, on the verge of turning sixteen, marooned in Angers so that Victor, the first-born whose rightful place was beside his father at the Pavie Press, could study law in Paris instead? How long would it be before Théodore Pavie's growing dissatisfaction and melancholy impelled him from the family nest? Victor Pavie and his father had

24. Théodore Pavie to Victor Pavie, July 17, 1827, in private collection.

taken at least one previous journey with David d'Angers. Happily, in 1828, Louis stayed home and let both of his sons depart with the sculptor. It would be the first time Théodore Pavie left France.

Late in April 1828 Théodore joined his brother and David d'Angers in Paris where both lived. This seems to have been his first visit to the capital without his father. To keep him informed, Théodore commenced his lifelong habit of writing him long detailed letters whenever he traveled. Victor and David d'Angers now presented their Paris to Théodore, complete with artists' studios and poets' living rooms. The time had come for Théodore to experience firsthand the creative intimacy of the leading Romantics. On Tuesday morning, April 22, 1828, he visited David d'Angers's studio, where he found the sculptor sketching the composer Rossini. Reporting the encounter to his father, Pavie was apparently under-awed by the most popular musician in Europe. "I had just entered [David d'Angers's studio] when I heard in the garden a kind of Italian jargon mixed with the barking of a little Maltese dog. It was M. Rossini senior; he came to pose. For more than half an hour, I had the leisure to contemplate this head whose sublimely inspired eyes looked up occasionally toward the ceiling. It is unfortunate that this head be placed on top of such a powerful body which overflows the piano stool on which he is posing. He is so fat that he always spits when he breathes."[25]

In contrast to the ebullient Victor, the more timid Théodore remained detached in front of the great men he encountered. He observed intensely, perceiving their humanity with his painterly eye instead of Victor's lively sociability. Upon encountering James Fenimore Cooper in David d'Angers's studio, for example, Victor had reported, "There I was in front of the author. I began to stammer enthusiastically in front of him, and even though he seemed to understand me, respectfully nodding his head, I quickly regretted the extreme volubility with which I had delivered my compliment, because he speaks French as well as I speak English."[26]

Thus in April 1828, Victor Hugo and his Romantic circle, which had absorbed Victor Pavie the previous year, absorbed his quiet young brother also. Théodore Pavie fit right in among Hugo's brother-in-law

25. Théodore Pavie to Louis Pavie, April 22, 1828, in private collection.
26. Fragment published by Victor Pavie's grandson André Pavie in *Médaillons Romantiques* (Paris: Émile Paul, 1909), 229.

Paul Foucher and the other youthful guests of the author, who dressed in garb which announced their historic and political preferences. The heyday of Romanticism had elements of a perpetual costume party; in fact, "the perfect gentleman" Victor Hugo stood out among his audacious followers because, like his hero Napoleon, he dressed plainly. Pavie wrote to his father and grandmother about an afternoon in Paris and his first evening at the Hugos'. Young Romantics seeking to externalize their souls through their extravagant costumes produced a great effect on the young Angevin. He described the painter Eugène Devéria, whom he met walking in the Luxembourg gardens, "with his medieval face, his large wide-brimmed top hat, his handsome black mustache and goatee on a face of the most beautiful brown, with admirable eyes and a chiseled face like the face of Henri IV. To see him so bizarrely done up and dressed in a strange and old-fashioned costume, one would take him for a character from *The Birth of Henry Fourth* which, by the way, is perhaps the most beautiful painting of the Exposition." After the walk in the Luxembourg, the Pavie brothers visited Hugo, who invited them to dinner the next evening with Devéria and Louis Boulanger, another painter whose popularity has not endured as well as that of their mutual friend, Eugène Delacroix, who was not present that evening.[27] Pavie depicted the sociable male gathering:

> Boulanger was seated next to me at the table; he's an excellent young man. He has a mustache, a tunic frock coat and tight pants; he promised to give Victor and me a detailed showing of his studio. I was still filled with masterpieces that I had just seen at the Exposition and I could not refrain from paying him a poor compliment; he responded to me with great modesty and kindness. Devéria (Achille) has neither mustache nor tunic; he is dressed like other men, but he has more than other men a colossal talent for engraving, a superb forehead, a nose of noble length, and well-formed

27. André Pavie devotes a chapter to this salon in *Médaillons Romantiques*. Edmond Biré's list of Hugo's cénacle in 1829 includes Balzac, Vigny, Baron Taylor, Sainte-Beuve, A. Soumet, Émile & Anthony Deschamps, A. Dumas, C. Magnin, Eugène & Achille Devéria, Delacroix, Fréderic Soulié, Armand & Édouard Bertin, Musset, Mérimée, Villemain, and— the sole female—Mme Tastu. Edmond Biré, *Victor Hugo avant 1830* (Paris: Jules Gervais, 1883).

legs. During the entire dinner, these three geniuses were making witty puns, pantomimes, and grotesquely playing on words. After dinner, we went into Hugo's office and, after a long spell of jokes and wild hilarity, Hugo read us some wonderful verses which he is going to publish and which were received enthusiastically by the group. Sainte-Beuve was there also. Imagine how Victor tormented himself, and me, I was completely dazzled, and I expressed to Foucher the kind of thrill this excitement caused. I believe Hugo has improved another notch in these latest pieces; they will be entitled *Les Orientales,* and they deserve this beautiful title. Sainte-Beuve read something; Victor, not knowing anything by heart, couldn't say anything in spite of the insistence of Sainte-Beuve, Foucher, and Hugo, who didn't stop repeating *'c'étaient trois voyageurs'* and entire verses from his ballad that they know almost by heart. Poor Victor at least finds himself avenged for the ungrateful province where you and I alone understand him.[28]

David d'Angers and the Pavie brothers left Paris for London to visit the Exposition of the Royal Academy. The sculptor's notebook shows that they visited Rouen en route to Dieppe, then traveled to London, from where Théodore wrote the next available letter. He inventoried people, places, and things he saw.

Each day, each excursion has been marked by new marvels.

Friday morning, we went to see the magnificent, wonderful abbey of Westminster, miraculous masterpiece of Gothic architecture, decorated with all that Great Britain has produced that is illustrious in every field: from Edward the Confessor to George III, admirals, poets, philosophers, generals, kings, princes, etc. Each plaza is marked by a more or less strange monument. [In] the magnificent St. James Park, each day the royal guard comes to play music, take the flag into one of the palaces that surround it, and from there go to the narrow courtyard of the palace of the King, built in bricks and of a construction that is completely oriental and Gothic at the same time. There this band tranquilly plays its entire

28. Théodore Pavie to Louis Pavie, April 1828, in private collection.

repertoire of motifs of *Dame Blanche,* etc. etc. etc. The same day we then visited another exposition of paintings for sale where Victor saw again, with great pleasure bordering on delirium, the painting of the good Delacroix, *The Doge of Venice,* which pleased me more than I had expected it to, from the newspapers.

We also visited the Exposition—the purpose of the voyage.

Sunday morning all three of us went to mass in a little Catholic chapel. . . . We spent the evening with a man whom M. David knows. Monday we ate at Mr. [Jeremy] Bentham's, and Tuesday morning, big time!

M. David comes to find us in bed and announces that Walter Scott is in London, that he has to leave frequently, but that he has his address. We get up, and we're on our way. After having wandered around a long time in Regent's Park, surrounded by beautiful private houses more beautiful than palaces, we knock at number 22. "Mr. Walter Scott, is he here?" "Yes sir." And we enter boldly. "Be seated, here, my children," says the great man, and trembling, we group around him. "I know how to jabber French a little," he says, and he begins to talk to us with soul and kindness. After having contemplated him well, we left, each one respectfully shaking that right hand that had peopled the entire world. From there we go to a painter who takes us to see the leading English sculptor, Chantrey; he was not there. Another person leads us into the studio of Lawrence, the man of his century for portraits. We did see him. From there we were presented to the chief of the Athenaeum. You may think that we didn't understand anything, but there we saw all the sketches and paintings in all genres that obtained prizes. Yesterday we heard a religious concert in Saint Paul's, and from there we went to visit this miraculous Tower of London. . . . We have seen all the curious things in London; we're leaving Sunday—impatient to leave behind the London fog finally to see the beautiful sunshine of France.

After predicting that they would arrive in Paris by mid-May, the youthful Pavie closed his letter with a single question that betrays the boy at the center of the antiquarian traveler: "I had a squirrel; do I still have one?"[29]

29. Théodore Pavie to Louis Pavie, May 9, 1828, in private collection.

David d'Angers himself benefited from his friendship with the young men. While the brothers met many of the world's luminaries who posed for David, they also provided the shy man a forum. Based on the success of his art, the prestigious French Institute bestowed upon David a membership in 1825. At the time of the Pavies' London visit, he was teaching at the École de Beaux Arts, in addition to working in his personal studio. The boys functioned as a sounding board for him to articulate the new ideas emerging through his fingers and in his mind's eye. They facilitated mutual aesthetic expression. David's style of portrait busts was undergoing a transformation beginning around 1828 (the time of the London adventure) that James Holderbaum describes as increasingly exhibiting "a new, modern imagery of exploratory morphology, capable of both conveying and eliciting higher intensities of emotional and spiritual communication." Though the physiognomy of Lavater and the phrenology of Gall and others were David's points of departure, the expressive forms are his own, characterized by Holderbaum as "a systematic hyperbole of towering foreheads, often arbitrarily furrowed or frowning, vastly domed craniums, lengthened and ennobled noses and necks, visionary eyes (their blankness in Neoclassical sculpture yielding to the subtlest soft-focus approximation of iris and pupil), splendid Romantic coiffures often endowed with gesticulatory eloquence, and upward- or downward-tilted heads with a variety of unfamiliar results."[30]

The extended visit to London opened Théodore Pavie's eyes. On his return to Paris, he continued to encounter Europe's cultural luminaries, this time those clustered in the man-made marvels of the capital. Late in May, he was still in Paris, apparently waiting for Victor to complete the school year. Pavie's tourist activities differed little from those of tourists today: "Sunday we went . . . to see the wonderful waters of Versailles; I saw there all that an artificial and tortured nature can produce. The chateau and the garden of Versailles are the most beautiful thing I have ever seen."[31] On Tuesday he had visited the Père La Chaise Cemetery, noting the tomb of Heloise and Abelard, and taken a fiacre to Les Invalides where he explored everywhere, even the interior of the Dome. At the Li-

30. James Holderbam, "Pierre-Jean David d'Angers" in *The Romantics to Rodin* (Los Angeles: Los Angeles County Museum of Art and George Brazillier, 1980), 211–25.

31. Théodore Pavie to Louis Pavie, May 22, 1828, in private collection.

brary of the King (presumably the modern Bibliothèque nationale) they saw manuscripts and engravings. Pavie especially appreciated the "extraordinary opportunity which I will never again encounter," to see a three-day exposition of the paintings of Gros, citing the *Battle of Elau,* the *Battle of Nazareth,* the *Pest-house of Jaffa,* and the portraits of Murat. Besides the masterpieces on display to the public, the Angevin brothers were drawn continuously into Romanticism's sanctum sanctorium.

> This good Hugo overwhelms us with kindness. Monday we had dinner with him; he wants us to return again. He read us some wonderful verses that will be part of *Les Orientales.* . . . I can't tell you about our return yet, I don't know when it will take place, Victor has no firm idea on that subject, he floats among a dozen friends with whom he makes appointments, whom he awaits at the house or he goes to see. Wednesday Foucher took us to lunch at the Palais Royal, to reciprocate a lunch to which we invited him. From there we went to Hugo's, and since Victor had the "misfortune" to bring him some wonderful views of Westminster, he does not know what to do to express his appreciation to us. He wants us to have lunch or dinner at his place at least five times before our departure.

Pavie reported to his father that Hugo had asked them to perform a small service for him: "the task of finding for him in Anjou a beautiful small and very Gothic chateau with outbuildings where he can live in a relaxed fashion instead of always being crammed in" as the Hugos were in Paris. Pavie assured his father of the seriousness of this request: "He told us this quite seriously. Madame Hugo would prefer a beautiful box with painted shutters, but he wants Gothic."[32] It seems *Notre Dame de Paris (The Hunchback of Notre Dame)*, which virtually spawned a re-

---

32. In *Médaillons Romantiques,* André Pavie misattributes this letter to his grandfather, Victor Pavie. (I have a copy of the autographed letter in Théodore Pavie's handwriting.) This error has been perpetuated by Hugo scholars and architecture historians, in their attempts to reconstruct Hugo's interest in Gothic architecture, which manifests itself in *Notre Dame de Paris.* Théodore Pavie later describes the belfry at Nacogdoches as "half-Gothic, half-Moorish."

vival in Gothic architecture, was beginning to stir in the poet's imagination at this very moment. Perhaps encouraged by Victor Hugo's slight disdain for Paris, which Pavie shared, the young traveler dropped a hint to his father of the future turns his life would take:

> I am beginning to see some cherry trees here which make me want to be in the country. It is in the springtime that the countryside is beautiful, from one city to the next, the homeland seems more and more beautiful. Paris is too big for the provincial, too populous, too beautiful, too dazzling for one who likes to take solitary walks beside a river, to see the white sail of the fisherman gliding by the banks of the Loire, to hear the piercing cry of the halcyon cleaving the tranquil waters of a lake with his diaphanous wing, the shrill cry of great herons in the air, and the farewell salute from the cannon of a ship that is leaving the beach. When one has collected memories, nothing is more pleasant than to call them up in the shade of the great oaks; to remember the homeland under an old chestnut tree next to the continuous sound of a water mill or to dash on the back of a white steed across a land of memories. The lovely countryside of Feneu, how many times it troubled my sleep in the middle of the beautiful city of London, how many times it thrust visions of vast chestnut trees into the middle of the great oaks in the English parks.[33]

Alone in his brother's rooms, after writing the usual paragraphs detailing his experiences, sixteen-year-old Théodore Pavie expressed his growing discomfort with Parisian society. He wanted his father to know that whether in London or Paris, he longed for the countryside and the pleasures of nature. When the brothers returned to Angers for Victor's summer vacation, Théodore resumed his tasks at the Pavie Press, and Victor dabbled in poetry and corresponded with his friends in Paris. On June 10, Victor Pavie wrote to Hugo, "I bring back for good a brother who had been snatched from us for a long while by unsettled thoughts of isolation; and, among the benefits are shared emotions, so new between Théodore and me."[34]

33. Théodore Pavie to Louis Pavie, May 5, 1828, in private collection.
34. Victor Pavie to Victor Hugo, ALS, Artine Artinian Collection, Harry Ransom Humanities Research Center, University of Texas at Austin.

Later correspondence suggests that the brothers gradually got along less well, resettled in their provincial environment where Théodore worked while Victor nurtured his obsession with Hugo, and the situation worsened when the latter returned to Paris for law school in October 1828. The family environment that had nourished the boys as children became stultifying for the younger brother. At seventeen, he led a dull and unfulfilling life as his father's helper in a provincial print shop.

Later that winter, Louis Pavie combined business and pleasure in a trip to Paris. From Angers, Théodore wrote him in January 1829 a letter that shows the young man's heart not to be in Angers at the Pavie Press, and reveals the extent to which Chateaubriand had taken hold of his mind and emotions as well as his pen. After a detailed description of business transactions, Pavie expressed his heightened desire to please his father, whom he was temporarily replacing at the Press. He seems to have accompanied his father to Paris in spirit if not in body; his yearning for his friends and intellectual stimulation is palpable despite his denial that he is envious of his father's journey.

That's enough for business; it is sad to be pursued by business concerns even when you are with friends and amid such beautiful things. It had to be you to prevent me from being envious. You will have already seen Hugo, Devéria, Louvain, Boulanger, Paul, and all in the company of Victor, and Victor with my fine friends who followed him into exile; then Mr. David who will have embraced you and M. Leclerc with whom you find yourself in harmony even on Sunday. Enjoy yourself while you are there; rekindle yourself at the hearth of Genius and Inspiration in every genre. You deserve it so much, you who have said to everyone dear to you "Go, enjoy, spend happy days," and all that without accompanying them; you contented yourself with following them with your eyes, listening to their long recitations, watching the flame of their memories shine in their eyes. It's your turn to look; replenish yourself, if possible, on Poetry and Fine Arts. Your soul is so well made for feeling; it is so Romantic in spite of your obstinate belief that you belong to a century that all of your ideas belie and abjure. You belong entirely to the nineteenth century, and you can count on us to support and reinforce you. And this poor Victor who loves you so much. He loves you so much that your word is a decree for him. If he has followed others than you into the career of letters, it is because you did not want to rally to Romanticism. He has another career waiting for him, calling to him more strongly, and for that one, he has taken you for a model, and then the stormy urges have been becalmed more than one time. Embrace him well, just for me; I have hurt him so much! So many times I have pushed him away; that is because I did not feel worthy of his friendship or of yours, since I would not have had the strength to leave you.[35]

The final statement suggests that Théodore and his father have already decided that he will be leaving. Following the epistolary tradition of Rousseau and Chateaubriand, the son attempts to describe his passions to his absent father: "They are so biting, the passions of a seventeen-year-old. Ideas which were born at fifteen develop strongly along with the body. Oh! How tyrannical are the vague desires that circulate from vein to vein within agitated members like the shiver of a fever. Oh! How despotic are these desires, unendingly reborn, which nourish the soul with a flame, which seize the body under their control, agitate it in everything, exalt it, stimulate it, cause it to swell then, letting it faint in front of a sad reality, abandon it alone in the middle of objects one might call enemies, alone with memories of hopes and expectations that have been thwarted but perhaps not yet extinguished."[36]

Pavie paraphrases Chateaubriand, who speaks of "the bitterness spread over life by this state of soul . . . and the heart turns inside out and ties itself in a hundred knots to use the power that it can tell is useless."[37] The disparity between Pavie's dreams and his actions depressed him; his family and friends attributed his "vague inquiétude" to the fact that he did not seem to know what he wanted to do with his life. But Théodore Pavie knew exactly what he wanted to do, what he needed to do, what he was going to do. Soon he would follow Chateaubriand's path—and that of the author's alter ego René—and journey to North America.

In March, a year after their trip to London, he wrote to Victor in Paris

35. Théodore Pavie to Louis Pavie, January 13, 1829, in private collection.
36. Ibid.
37. Chateaubriand, *Mémoires d'outre-tombe,* 111–7.

to announce his intentions. He quoted Chateaubriand before breaking his news.

"It delights the soul to plunge into an ocean of forests, meditating on the banks of lakes and rivers, skimming above the abyss of waterfalls and, so to speak, to find oneself alone in the presence of God." My dear Victor, there you have the text of my conduct in the past, present, and for this year especially, the future. Nature alone speaks to my soul which, restricted and cold as it is, senses and devours things quite avidly. Paris rolled out her marvels in front of me; London showed off her regular streets, her parks. . . . All that slipped by in front of me. My sights are set on another place, where the dangling vine drapes from coconut palms without the help of man, where the alligator raises its golden head in the water of the Father of Rivers, where the bison slumbers without hearing shots whistle by his ears. There you have it, since I must finally confess, the places that will be my retreat in three months. . . . When my soul has been sated with the great spectacles of a virgin nature under the climate that burns men like leaves; when I have seen flowing under me the waters of this antique Nile, whose length can hardly be measured by 900 leagues, when I have seen this river crowned with flowers and tiny boats, and then impetuous torrents overturning the forests and animals; then when I am satisfied and as avid for the homeland as I was beforehand for faraway lands, I shall return. But at least I will have collected memories, and I will have had some consolations *on this firm earth where I am having so much trouble taking root.* . . . You will treat me as a crazy fool, you will insult what I find beautiful. I have feelings; and I know what pleases me. Paris did not please me; one can not breathe there, the air is thick, and I would not know how to live there. Our tastes are different; but nonetheless, they can have the same result.[38]

All three of the young men to whom he announced his plans—his brother and his two close friends Henri de Nerbonne and Léon Cosnier—

38. Théodore Pavie to Victor Pavie, March 11, 1829, in private collection. See preceding note for location of Chateaubriand quote.

responded immediately. Nerbonne, who studied law in Paris with Victor Pavie, questioned the younger man's sanity before attempting to dissuade him with an impressive array of arguments, primarily that the trip would be unrealistic and dangerous, and that Pavie had responsibilities to his family: "I am surprised by so sudden a resolution . . . I believed I was seeing that your letters were not marked with a spirit of reality, but that you recognized the past as the only time during which your dreams could be fulfilled. . . . I am sure that the charms of frothy virgin beaches on the other side of deserts lose much of their attractiveness when one possesses them. . . . Emotions concentrated in you alone and not fixed by expressing them to another will be a little unsettled and will be extinguished easily, I believe that you will return confused over not having found what you were searching for." Beneath his persuasive rhetoric, however, flowed the aristocratic notion that the younger son has nonnegotiable obligations to the firstborn, that is, that Pavie might be compromising Victor's dreams. "Your brother is far away from your father and you may be forcing him to abandon his studies and leave us to replace you beside your father."[39]

After Pavie's friends had thus tried to dissuade him, his brother acquiesced grudgingly to the daring plan. But neither Nerbonne nor Victor failed to point out the element of fantasy and the potential for disappointment inherent in Théodore's model: Chateaubriand was a dreamer, his trip to America took place long ago, and America would have changed. Victor Pavie finally wrote on March 25, 1829, telling his brother to "Go forth. . . . May the sea be gentle to you: may it take you thirsting from our hands like a nursemaid, and bring you back weaned, safe and sound!" Victor, whose pride was hurt, could not resist attacking Théodore's dream—now a plan—one last time: "I wanted therefore to tell you that if I never smiled at the idea—very comprehensible to me—of a journey, it is because we never once discussed it, and I had to hear from the mouth of a friend, of a stranger, sometimes even on a street corner, about plans in which I had never been involved, not even as a spectator, nor as a witness." Victor Pavie's language is often inexplicably elaborate, but on this occasion he succinctly articulates his objections to Théodore's decision: "And also, but it is now a moot point: a country seen fifty years

39. Henri de Nerbonne to Théodore Pavie, March 13, 1829, in private collection.

ago through the imagination of a dreamy young man might no longer be recognizable by another in our time, and with fewer risks, one could find better!"

What has happened to Victor Pavie, who at age thirteen had written home to announce, "I saw Chateaubriand!"? How is it that his Chateaubriand has been reduced to "a dreamy young man"? For one thing, Victor Pavie's having outgrown his adolescent taste reflects the changed relationship between Victor Hugo and his own former idol. When Hugo was young, he had been known for his desire to become "Chateaubriand or nothing"; but now, in 1828, Hugo expected to surpass his idol and become the undisputed leader of the intellectual nobility.[40] Victor Pavie was committed to following Hugo, wherever that might lead him, while Théodore Pavie chose to follow Chateaubriand on the path the adventurer had taken fifty years before to the Mississippi valley, determined to recognize "the country seen by a dreamy young man." Although it was too late to influence Théodore's decision, Victor ultimately accepted the plan, and he closes with his blessing for the journey: "The only thing left for me to do is to place [the future] in the hands of God, who will fashion you in such a clay and such a shape as it pleases Him to do, to the greater submission of all. I embrace you and I commend you to Him."

Théodore Pavie was accompanied to Le Havre by his brother and their two friends. The day before he sailed, the traveler wrote to Bonnemaman in a final attempt to reassure her. "The fine season, the solidity and abundant provisions of the ships, everything contributes to making this voyage a pleasure cruise. For the present, all goes well: beautiful weather and no clouds among all of us; I could not have believed I would be departing under such happy auspices." He described his accommodations to his grandmother so that she might envision him as he crossed the ocean: "I have reserved my little room on board: an elevated bed on a kind of box of superb wood, with a beautiful white linen cabinet, a chest of drawers, a mirror, a water pitcher and the indispensable chamber pot, all this and another bed above, contained in four square meters—there's my cabin and that of the other passengers. Furthermore the luxury of

40. On July 10, 1816, fourteen-year-old Hugo wrote in his journal "Je veux être Chateaubriand ou rien." The story is a commonplace in the history of Romanticism; one source is Biré, *Victor Hugo avant 1830*, 10.

these rooms is surprising, and a cleanliness unknown in France reigns everywhere. The food is as abundant as it is healthy and varied, and an English and French library completes the lounge. There, my dear Bonnemaman, you have everything that I know about this voyage that frightened you so much." He then addresses the underlying issue of separation, the brevity of which he presents as essential to his emotional health: "My father is entirely reassured, and so it all comes down to the separation. Ten months, that's very short, when one knows that there is little danger or none at all; and then when one considers that this [voyage] returns life and strength to a sick and languishing mind!"[41]

Théodore Pavie sailed from Le Havre to New York at noon on April 15, 1829. Louis Pavie had written him a letter to open when he was in sight of America. He wished his son well in "this land which is the object of your desires and where our good wishes accompany you." Louis Pavie's vision of his son's destination is filled with familial and literary stories of Louisiana. The letter, which Pavie kept with him through two ocean crossings and a journey from Canada to Mexico on horseback, stagecoaches, and steamboats, also contained this advice:

> Enjoy in peace the marvels that will strike your eyes; free your soul, so noble and so pure, to the feelings that they will inspire in you. Troubling your happiness is far from my intentions! I share the idea of [your voyage] with you and congratulate myself on being able to provide you this, while awaiting the delight of your being able to share your story.
>
> However, my friend, beside these innocent pleasures, what dangers are going to surround you, about which I cannot think without trembling! In such a corrupt country where nothing will remind you of your religion, where no one will speak of its laws except to break them . . . you will keep yourself intact in the middle of the corruption whose forms are as varied and enticing in the burning climates, as the consequences are hideous.
>
> I will stop. To say more about this would insult your principles and your scruples.[42]

---

41. Théodore Pavie to Marie Pavie (Bonnemaman) April 20, 1829, in private collection.

42. Louis Pavie to Théodore Pavie, April 1829, qtd. in Crosnier, *Théodore Pavie*, 12.

3

THÉODORE PAVIE'S LETTERS
FROM THE BORDERLANDS

SEVENTEEN-YEAR-OLD THÉODORE PAVIE set sail from Le Havre that April day in 1829, on a paqueboat named *La France*, feeling the "secret joy of being free to see and feel in his own way." The crossing took thirty-three days, which he reported as the fastest time so far that spring. It was uneventful except one storm, which promised great misfortune but, to Pavie's disappointment, only ripped a few sails from the masts.[1] When he arrived in New York in late May, he rented a room near the home of the Peltier family, friends of his father with whom he dined regularly, and notified his uncle Charles in Natchitoches of his arrival. From Louisiana, Charles wrote Louis Pavie on June 24, 1829, to announce that he expected "Victor." (The mistake was not repeated.) Although the deadly fevers made it too dangerous for the younger nephew to proceed to Louisiana before late autumn, Charles extolled Théodore's presence as a source of consolation to his wife, Marianne, who had recently experienced numerous sorrows. According

---

1. Théodore Pavie, *Victor Pavie,* 118; Théodore Pavie to Marie Pavie (Bonnemaman), May 26, 1829, in private collection.

to church records, several members of her family had died in rapid succession, including her sister Aimée Bludworth, whose daughter Eliza now lived with them, and Juan Cortés, the husband of her sister Marcelite, whose insolvent estate was troubling Charles, the executor. As Charles explained in his letter, "I am writing him [your son] immediately to insist that he remain in the North until the month of November, the time when he will be able to come safely to Louisiana to spend the winter with us. I am also advising him to take some excursions in the country. He could not arrive at a more opportune time to soften the blows which have assailed us with a frightening rapidity. . . . I am tied up right now with selling off the properties of one of my brothers-in-law, whose estate is insolvent, leaving in misery a family that he raised in opulence."[2]

On the advice of both the Peltiers and his uncle, Théodore Pavie visited Canada and many northeastern states. That summer and fall, the seasonal yellow fever struck the Mississippi valley even more devastatingly than usual because Spanish refugees, fleeing an unsuccessful July attempt to reconquer Mexico, delivered tropical diseases to the port cities and deep into the forests. Pavie encountered many of the refugees, and took every precaution against contracting disease.[3] In his letters and poems, which begin in October 1829 as he departed for Louisiana, the details of the next nine months reveal his aunt Marianne and cousin Eliza to have replaced Chateaubriand and his fictional characters in the young man's emotional life. From a steamboat on the Ohio River, Théodore wrote to his father on October 26, 1829.

2. Charles Pavie to Louis Pavie, June 24, 1829, in private collection.

3. For a detailed description of both the politics and the biology of the ill-advised, ill-fated invasion of Barradas, which contributed to the illnesses in Louisiana and the rise of Santa Anna as well as to the French intervention in the Gulf of Mexico in 1838–1839, see my article "Peste, Tempestad, and Pâtisserie: The 'Pastry War,' France's Contribution to the Maintenance of Texas Independence" in the Gulf Coast Historical Review, vol. 12, no. 2 (Spring 1997), pp. 58–73. Pavie tapped his experience with the Spanish-Mexican conflict and his knowledge of the fate of the Spaniards trapped in Texas to write "El Capuchin," a short story published in La Revue des Deux Mondes in 1861. The English translation by Alexandra K. Wettlaufer is included in my Tales of the Sabine Borderlands.

On the Ohio River
on the right, the state of Indiana
on the left, Kentucky
  above, the sky
upon the water the one who loves you
    26 October 1829

Perhaps it will be impossible for me to stop at Louisville long enough to be able to write you, therefore I am taking advantage of the time that I have on board the steamboat to write you a few words that the continuous movement will render almost illegible. I left New York on the fifteenth, arrived at Philadelphia in the evening, and left the second morning for Pittsburgh after having painfully travelled five days and almost five nights in bad stages through beautiful mountains that made up for the fatigue of the journey. I left that very day, taking advantage of a boat small enough to go in spite of the very shallow water. I had the pleasure of finding some very educated and likable French people on board. We have already been on board five days, the boat stopping frequently and overnight. Tomorrow we will be at Louisville from where another boat will pick us up that evening to carry us to New Orleans . . . I will stop at Natchez on the Mississippi to go from there to Natchitoches; it [Natchez] is the point on my route closest to the latter place. My uncle, to whom I have written, should be there.

I have seen admirable things since my departure, but I have not had either the time nor the facility to tell you about it: sublime mountains where we traveled at night to the sound of wolves howling at the moon and the faraway roar of bears; then with snow, ice, and delicious sites. I have sketched as much as I could. The Ohio, which is conveying me right now, is the Loire plus plane trees, falcons, and cormorants, all decorated with a vegetation almost undisturbed everywhere and that autumn is gilding according to its fantasy. I draw furiously, I sketch, I daub. I struggle with a nature that it would take a genius to capture and I don't even know how to hold a pencil. At least it is devotion.

The climate is less rigorous here. It is mild and in eight days, I shall be too warm.

I had waited to leave New York for the arrival of the ship of September first. . . . Your last letters are from August fifteenth, from the day before my birthday. Soon it will be seven months since I left Angers. How many things I have seen from Quebec to New Orleans—what a panorama! It is too much at once. My imagination is exhausted. I ardently desire to arrive at my uncle's where I will replenish my ideas a little. Thank God all of this country lives up to my expectations. Nonetheless, I need some rest. The pilgrimage will be, I believe, quite honest and as much as I can see here. I do not say that from boredom or sadness, nor from regret, but with reflection. I shall leave New Orleans near the first of January to hurry into your arms at the end of February. I almost dare ask you not to write me anymore because I have decided not to remain beyond the first of January. Perhaps it will turn out otherwise. This time I had to draw from my uncle the last 200 piastres [dollars]. He offered and that will give you time and, kind Father, how I am scattering your harvest [i.e., spending your money]. May it not be scattered on a heart where it cannot bear fruit, on a stone where the birds of heaven would come eat them.

Pardon my scribbling, but this steamboat has a terrible thrust and shake. Now I know when I'll write from Natchitoches, but I don't know when will you receive my letter. At least, never worry. The same sun that lights you with its dawn sees me wander on the great rivers with my beard that has not been cut for eight days, my dagger and my wide shoulders, and then there is a God who is watching over me. May he also keep watch over those who are dear to me.[4]

When he arrived in New Orleans on November 9, 1829, an excited Théodore penned a letter to brother Victor. Anxious to share his own experiences, Théodore also yearns to hear how Victor has spent his time.

Where are you? What are you doing? Where do you live? What are the things that fill your days, alas! I would like to know these

4. Théodore Pavie to Louis Pavie, October 26, 1829, in private collection.

things to be able to empathize with you. I have just spent some beautiful moments, as beautiful as moments of happiness can be without being able to be shared. Be assured that there was something for you in each of these inexpressible sensations that capture the soul at the sight of a forest where one can say that man is not there, bucks and bears sleep there in peace; when above the dome of trees of a colossal height one sees vultures gliding peacefully, deer crossing the river without fear, herons and cranes descending the river on driftwood and passing in range of buckshot, flocks of pelicans fishing in silence on the point of a strand without even flapping a wing at the sound of two bullets shot at the wild bird. When the boat would stop in some isolated spot to get wood, I wandered under the shady vault of cypress trees entirely loaded down with "Spanish beard," moss three feet long that drapes from the branches of the catalpa trees, the pecan trees, the walnut trees, even the dangling vines and Virginia creepers, and makes the entire forest look like ghosts covered with shreds of shroud. Sometimes I sang songs that I learned from you, while balancing myself on these immense dangling vines that hang down more than 150 feet from the top of a magnolia and, among the enormous canes that I broke while walking, I chose one of those dwarf palms that roots in the shelter of tall weeds, and I amused myself by carving your name on it. Certainly all of these places are not just as Chateaubriand described them, but they are as beautiful as the imagination can divine them: twice we saw bucks cross the rivers and disappear behind the impenetrable willows that cover these immense islands, behind which the Mississippi turns and returns, submitting all these lands to the influence of its luxuriant vegetation. Dangling vines of all types attach themselves to each other; the catalpa is an exaggerated plane tree, where one hangs on each leaf a shred of poetry, one foot long; pecans, nuts of all kinds cover the land with their fruits, and one hears the crackling from squirrels devouring pecans under the branches of the cypress trees.[5] Cardinals spiral

---

5. Pavie seems to be calling the catalpa bean a "shred of poetry." It is a bean pod–like object that gets to be a foot or so long. My thanks to Bill Reese for identifying this particular "poem."

around the red jasmine and little green parrots, with their squawk so unique in these woods, flit through the moss. A few leagues from the city the cotton plantations begin, sugarcane, houses decorated with wisteria, orange and banana trees; but let's forget all that, this white man holds a whip in his hand; those black dots that come and go are slaves.

The yellow fever has ceased here. I'm not afraid, there is no longer any danger. Tomorrow I leave for Natchitoches where my uncle is. Here is my plan, not subject to change: I spend two or three weeks in Natchitoches at the longest, to collect a few birds, some seeds, see my relatives, continue sketching, and see the countryside. Then I return here to spend one more week, and finally to await a ship for some port in France on the Ocean, since the Mediterranean is not safe, and I embark for the beautiful country of France. I shall be at my father's at the beginning of February, I hope. If I go by Le Havre, I shall see you even before him. I have just travelled 800 leagues from New York: 140 by land, across the mountains of Pennsylvania, through forests where snow and ice had already set in. Since then, in 21 days I have done 660 leagues by river, and I find myself in a burning climate: it is warmer here now than ever in France in the month of June. I have continually sketched views, from New York to here. I have seen so much that I am tired from it, and all I desire is rest. When can I take my turn to hear the story of your pilgrimage to the doyen of Romantic literature [Goethe] with the one who feels so good [David d'Angers] in the middle of a country made for your soul?[6]

That evening, Pavie also wrote to his grandmother in Angers. Fearful of contracting a fever in New Orleans, he spent the night of November 9, 1829, on the boat instead of visiting the city.

The one who travels for long days in the middle of dark forests thickened by dangling red vines of impenetrable density; among romantic cypresses where the strange moss the French call Spanish beard hangs three feet long;

6. Théodore Pavie to Victor Pavie, November 9, 1829, in private collection.

The one who sees on the solemn banks of the Father of Rivers vultures by the thousands laying complete siege to the roof of an isolated cabin, eagles on the parched summit of the plane tree, hawks skimming across the tall grass untrammeled by the foot of man;

The one who, jumping to the fragrant bank as soon as the steamboat stopped, dangled from the yellow branch of the catalpa, was swinging to the piercing screeches of the green parrot in the magnolias;

The one who, wrapped in his coat, watched on the immense strand immobile cranes on one foot, blue ducks, red-headed grouse and, by chance, the two antlers of a swimming deer cleaving the waves and lying down sleepily on the golden sand where enormous pelicans from the wilderness were strolling;

The one who, descending from the cold mountains of Pennsylvania, crosses the states of Kentucky, Indiana, Illinois, Ohio, Missouri, Tennessee, and Arkansas, and finds finally on a burning soil where orange and lemon trees grow, on streets where banana palms decorate gardens graced by chinaberry trees, who for two days has seen the changed banks, white with cotton, greened by the impenetrable canebrake, here and there enormous palm trees . . .

That one, say I, rubs his eyes and dreams.

Barely three weeks ago he was in snow and ice, and then, all those things happened so rapidly. So quickly the orange of Louisiana replaced the orchards of New Jersey, the cedars of New York, the pines of Boston and La Tourmonte Mountain shining white in Quebec. And then, in the middle of the wilderness, his soul completely abandoned to the pure bliss of a sparkling nature, what did his heart say when a shaft of moonlight fell upon a blue heron descending the river on an enormous floating treetrunk, a heron that, voyager of the great rivers, strolled on its raft like a sailor on the deck of his ship? What I was saying, Bonnemaman, oh you already knew it all, I was saying, "Finally I see it, this land, the object of my desires, I see all of the objects of my dreams, of my sighs and it is as beautiful as the imagination can grasp," and then I prayed. As soon as these delicious sensations took hold of me I could not keep myself from thanking the One on high, He who created it all. But why am I then so happy? At my side I had a man whose talents elevated him to the highest rank in the American Judicial system, an author of very remarkable works, precisely on Louisiana [Barbé-Marbois?], in a word, who could be the most useful for me. What have I done to be so fortunate? Oh, you who spent your life suffering, pardoning, loving, you who persevered, righteous and persecuted and . . . fate knocks you down; your actions have stockpiled on high blessings that fall down on your children.

For the twenty-one days since I left Pittsburgh, I have lived on the steamboats. I saw some things that I could not describe in a hundred pages: 670 leagues by water across barely cultivated land to Louisville, even less to the Mississippi, completely untamed from there until near Baton Rouge. I could not stop at Baton Rouge, the yellow fever had not yet completely died down. . . . Here there isn't the least danger, let me assure you of that. Don't be afraid for me. It is as warm as the month of May in France, but all illness has ceased for a long time, and I am taking the additional precaution of living on board until tomorrow evening when I take off for Natchitoches, for I could not find along the route the place to await the steamboat going there. Natchez (on the Mississippi; don't confuse with Natchitoches) was too unhealthy, as were the neighboring places.

I still have quite enough money to go as far as the family. The boat for Nantes departs tomorrow. I embrace you all. Your grandson who loves you much. Th.P. [P.S.] I know positively that my uncle is in Natchitoches.[7]

One of Pavie's most important letters (because he would recycle the narrative into *Souvenirs atlantiques*) was penned to Salio at the Pavie Press from Natchitoches on November 20, 1829. He expected his letter to be shared with the entire group at work, and his expectation was apparently fulfilled.

---

7. Théodore Pavie to Marie Pavie (Bonnemaman), November 9, 1829, in private collection.

My good friend, I have gotten myself to these savage lands, the object of my desire 2000 leagues from you and everyone else in a very strange country, very new, where one lives solely from the deer that the Indians bring to the village; where one sees only immense forests and cotton fields. To get here I experienced the strangest things that I have seen in my life because I had thirty leagues to cross on horseback across marshes, cypress trees, cedars, dangling vines, catalpas, and magnolias. I was taken by surprise in the middle of the forest by a storm whose strength surpasses any European idea: uprooted trees, rain causing a frightening darkness, and thunder ripping the sky and tearing through the clouds, torrents of an enraged downpour, my horse trembling with each thunderbolt, and in the middle of all that, your friend arching his back under a canopy of tulip trees, more or less admiring the show, repeating with each lightning bolt the verse from the romance of Attala:

Great God, from your just furor

Spare the poor voyager!

Add to that that I had strayed completely from my route, and there was no one to point the way except a Choctaw Indian—painted, tattooed, and amusing himself by hunting on such a beautiful morning. I don't believe that I would have arrived here for at least ten years, had I not miraculously run into the postman, with whom I made the rest of the journey.

That was nothing yet. The streams were overflowing, and when night came it was impossible to advance. The mailman was even more loaded down than me, during a night that was even darker than the tunnels under the castle [the Chateau of Angers], we had to cross a cypress forest entangled in dangling vines that snagged and ripped us open with every step. *He* walked in front on a white horse, which served me as a guide and warned me of the brambles and thorns. Then twice we hurled our horses into the streams, wet to the waist. The third time, the water was over six feet wide. The mailman was overturned in the water when his horse bolted: Off with you! And with one thrust of the spur, I urged him on so violently that he reared back, bolted, and with one leap I was on the other side. Actually it was a miracle that I escaped: the current was horrible, the night hideous, and with all that I was singing and thanking the One who saved me from the danger. We slept in a cabin where the people made a fire to dry us out, and the next evening I arrived after having done 45 miles (15 leagues) on horseback without having anything else to eat besides a hunk of cornbread, my horse starving, worn-out, dead; me feeling good and _____ about all that.

Here the game is so abundant that it seems exaggerated. I fired some shots into seven alligators ten feet long sleeping in the sun; it is true that it was far from any houses, but I often saw twelve stretched out here and there in the sunshine. As I was coming up the river by steamboat I counted forty-two in one hour. Vultures are more common than chickens, no one ever shoots at them; they are useful for clearing this countryside of carrion and dead bodies. I often hit them with a stick when passing by on horseback. They puffed up and ran away abjectly, turning the crests of their crooked beaks red. Ducks litter the waterways. Monday my uncle is going fishing on a nearby lake. There will be three or four of us camping in the woods. Enormous cardinals, popes, and parrots are killed by the dozens.[8] Squirrels run through the cypress trees; wildcats, enormous black rabbits and deer, those are the usual fare; bears and tigers [Pavie's term for any wild feline] are rarer. Birds are often quite unafraid and in unheard-of abundance. The Indians are quite surprising, real children of nature, incessantly on horseback, completely striped in red, with silver plates suspended from their ears, their noses, from braids of hair, often almost black. They are abundant around here. They live in huts made of these picturesque palm trees, called *lataniers* here. In the woods one often encounters Spaniards from Mexico, wandering hunters in leather stockings, camped under the catalpas in their very strange costumes.

I was received here with tenderness by everyone; I am going to write Papa immediately; this letter will be of utmost importance

8. Pavie called these birds "pape," the French word for "pope." They were indigo buntings or painted buntings, called blue pop or red pop by Cajuns today. ("Pop" sounds like the French word "pape.") George Lowrey, *Louisiana Birds*, 2nd ed. (Baton Rouge: Louisiana State University Press, 1960), 561.

relative to my return. I was not even sick after all of my exhausting experiences. I get around on horseback. The one I ride is white, with a short tail, lively, Adonis [his horse in Angers?] minus a few years, little trained, and full of energy. Otherwise, my thoughts cross the distance: two-thousand leagues, the soul is immense and trifles with milestones. I would like to see here all those who love nature. It is more beautiful than one can say; in truth, Chateaubriand exaggerated very little; I have often seen alligators sleeping on natural rafts cemented with delicious flowers floating that way with herons and white cranes.

Farewell, love me as I love you. TP[9]

Pavie penned another carefully crafted letter to a group—this time the extended family—on December 18, 1829. He included a note from his aunt Marianne. Seemingly quite occupied with having fun, he designed this missive to catch everyone up on his adventures. Philosophically, he has replaced the "insufficiency of life" that he learned from Rousseau and Chateaubriand with effusive enthusiasm for reality. Perhaps love provided the antidote to the sickness afflicting his soul the previous spring?

Don't be angry with me!

My story since my arrival here:

When, completely exhausted from hardships, still completely soaked with the rain from heavens and from streams, I caught sight of the smoke rising slowly toward the clouds and, stopping my worn-out horse, I let the reins hang loose on his neck, a thousand thoughts seized my mind. The faraway voyages undertaken alone among a people whose language was foreign to me, the hardships of a year isolated in the middle of a new world—all that was finished; and this terrible struggle against a virgin nature was the last effort against almost insurmountable obstacles that held me so long far away from these places where so many dreams lured me. At my feet flowed this Red River of alligators, cayman,

---

9. Théodore Pavie to Salio, October 20, 1829, in private collection. (Salio ran the Pavie Press. After watching his proprietor's son grow up, Salio, who had replaced the tutor Henri Langlois, had more recently been Pavie's supervisor at work.)

and vultures. This group of houses, the last station of man in this isolated country, the advance guard of the European civilization in the middle of the American wilderness, the lost sentinel of civilization among the Pascagoulas, the Choctaws, the Caddos, the Apaches, and the Cherokees: there it was, this Natchitoches so yearned for, it was two thousand leagues from the paternal roof that I was going to find a language, a name, and hearts in harmony with mine. "Thus tossed by the tempest, the skiff wanders from rock to rock up to the distant towers where a friendly flag reflects its color."[10]

The stranger who might have seen me crossing the long veranda of the creole house would have thought me the ["prodigal"] child returned to the right side of his father. We didn't have enough of those made so dear to me by blood ties, and the first evening a family banquet took place during which the lively voices of several nephews of my uncle proposed a toast to the child-traveler; the calm voice of my aunt imposed silence. It was to you, the best of fathers, and to you, sweet Bonnemaman, that the first wishes were addressed; it would have taken very little for me to cry at this touching idea, for the soul of the traveler, while his body tans from the rays of the canicule ["dog days" of summer, July 22–August 22], is consumed by excursions across the forest, his soul is always open to these delicious impressions which are the only charm of a life on earth.

Nature offered me millions of new, original, and bizarre things completely particular to the country. The camping trip taken on the banks of Spanish Lake, formerly in the province of Texas, this side of the frontier, that canvas tent on the bank of a lake blackened by game, where in the evening one could see the pink wing of the woodstock gliding or where, to the plaintive hoot of the owl the lugubrious voice of the wildcat or the roar of the panther responds, where no one was living but us: there are some of these impressions that have surpassed all of my dreams of fifteen years. One evening, for example, after a stifling heat, I came back to the

---

10. The "tempest" quotation was apparently well known at the time, but is no longer identifiable.

campsite with some ducks, abundant squirrels, two falcons, and one of those black vultures. Voraciously hungry, I tore the thigh off a duck placed on a spit near the fire; I dried my moccasins—indispensable shoes in this kind of hunt. Everyone returned to the tent; I smoked a few cigars in the area, and then the horn sounded to call us all together: the uncle, his brother-in-law, me, and the two slaves who were accompanying us.

The weather was threatening from the North. Each one devoured some chunks of half-cooked duck, lots of squirrel gumbo, a delicious stew made with rice and Chateaubriand's sassafras, and drank a cup of briny water because the wine and milk were finished. We were living richly from our hunt. We were barely settled in, the uncle and I were all enjoying smoking, the guns were deep in the tent, arranged in a picket, the game strung between a cypress and a catalpa. Suddenly a tornado swept across the lake.[11] We were glad to have established our campsite in a place where the trees were low, for in two minutes it passed near us tearing, tearing loose everything in its path. The noise of willows and pines being uprooted was really frightening. A site with tall trees (the kind of site an imprudent European might have chosen) would have endangered our lives even more than a *chasse-marée breton* [three-masted ship] endangers a crew in the Channel. As for us, we were secure in our 6 foot square tent, watching a candle placed in the hollow of a bamboo pole burn without flickering, tranquil as during a "calm flat" at sea. Thus isolated in the middle of a wrathful nature, we spent part of the night talking about Feneu and all of you; then we fell asleep on our bear or bison skins, using logs as pillows.[12] The next day the sun was very high when we woke up. I

11. This region is periodically hit by the storms that follow when hurricanes in the Gulf of Mexico turn inland. They are so frequent in the autumn that Mexico had come to rely on the protection of its eastern coastline afforded by the "tempestad." The 1829–1830 hurricane season was particularly virulent. I have described the political consequences, a boost in the career of Santa Anna, in "Pesta, Tempestad, & Pâtisserie."

12. In this village (Feneu) in Anjou, Louis-Victor and Marie Fabre Pavie bought a priory (Bignon, with a history extending to the Gallo-Roman period) during the dispersal of church property early in the Revolution. Apparently Charles Pavie had also visited this spot to which Théodore Pavie attributed his poetic love of nature. Geneviève Chasle Voisin (*nom*

don't believe I have ever slept better, nor experienced more unusual feelings than during this frightful night, that we spent in such a tranquil manner.

Thus did I spend delicious days beside an uncle whose gruff kindness is boundless, with an aunt who has more affection for me and shows me more kindness than a son would receive from a mother. As for the cousin, she is attractive, I could call her pretty, very gay. She likes to laugh and gets along well with my strange character as well as being full of tenderness for her adoptive father and mother. In a word, I would never have been able to expect to find here friendship that surpasses all that you could believe and touches me deeply. Now listen to the dénouement. It is irrevocably decided that the whole family will be in France in June, unless extraordinary circumstances, like those that have been happening for two years, detain them further. No project has ever been more firmly set. It is an immense sacrifice that my aunt is making, leaving her whole family, especially two young nieces deprived of their mother and for whom she is everything. But the sacrifice is made, there is no turning back, all three of them are leaving in April. As for me, I had wanted to leave for France in two weeks having already collected a certain quantity of unusual things, a task at which I have been working relentlessly. But when I declared my intention, my aunt almost broke down in tears to have me stay at least until the first nice weather, wanting me to accompany them. (They are going by way of New York.) This disturbed me; I promised to spend at least the month of January here, not promising to wait that long. At the instant these words escaped me, Aunt held out her hand to me and she wanted to embrace me to thank me. Excuse me my poor father . . . such big storms in January in the Caribbean and in the Gulf of Mexico that I am delaying my time of arrival; but in truth, it would have been cruel to flatly refuse.

Nonetheless, regardless of all the pleasure that surrounds me here, I want and must leave in early February. In the end I don't

---

de plume: Chouan's) ceded the chapel on the property at Feneu back to the Catholic Church in the twentieth century. The rest of the property remained in the Chasle Pavie branch of the family until 1998.

dare promise anything. I beg you to forgive me and make my excuses with Victor.

Last night it was warm because, in spite of several nights cold enough to freeze the water inside the houses, it is warm when the sun comes out. I was strolling on the gallery with my aunt and Eliza, the sun was setting behind the tall cedar trees and some Indians (for they are both numerous and curious) were passing by on their little horses when my uncle handed me a letter with the postmark of Weimar. I read with unheard-of delight this delicious letter from him. It had been three months since I had heard from Victor—three months. The one from yesterday caused me a great emotional fever. I thought I was delirious; here they thought I was mad; today I took a sedative, it is nothing.

And [Victor] also was a traveler; three hundred leagues separated him from the fatherland; and this letter crossing Germany, France, the ocean, and all of North America bore a striking solemnity. What must be the thoughts of the father depriving himself of everyone, staying with the chain around his neck and not tiring of the happiness of his family. When I think of the immense debt of gratitude and devotion that I am taking on, it makes my poor head spin.

I wrote to Victor by way of M. Leclerc. I wanted to tell him myself about the extended delay that pushes off my return; my aunt was kind enough to write him some kind words where she places all the responsibility on our uncle and herself.

Say a thousand affectionate things to the people in Angers and Paris: Messrs. Leclerc, David, Hugo, Fouché, Mazure, Nerbonne, Cosnier.[13]

The young traveler waited a week before writing to his brother in Paris on December 26, 1829. In this letter he mentions, for the first time, their intention of going to Texas—a journey they evidently postponed.

The evening was delicious, for in these devouring climates, it is the springtime in Anjou that they call winter [here]. Some groups

13. Théodore Pavie to Louis Pavie, December 18, 1829, in private collection.

of Choctaws, so remarkable for the athletic form of their red-skinned limbs, and for the nobility of their demeanor, worthy of the chisel of a sculptor, were dancing the peace pipe around the sparkling fire, camped in the middle of the palmettos of the plain. I strolled around the gallery with my aunt and cousin, I was silent; since the fourth of August I had learned nothing about the one who is so dear to me, also a traveler, he in Germany with its black pines, his pilgrimage to the great manitou of literature was already finished when I heard about it (Sept. 20) and I knew nothing about his romantic sensations with the great man. Withdrawn to the confines of upper Louisiana in the middle of the forests where dangling vines of a thousand colors form three quarters of the nearly fabulous vegetation, where everything is grandiose, gigantic, I can hardly breathe, tired of being thus alone and deprived for so long of the outpouring of a brotherly soul. "Tomorrow, I'll dance at the ball," said I to our aunt, "if I should receive some letters from him." "So be it," says our aunt, and, at the same moment, a letter falls into my hands. The Weimar postmark tells me everything; it almost fell out of my hands I was trembling so much. I had hardly read this delicious letter, full of surprising things and ideas that they thought I was delirious; I was seized by fever and half the night I leapt around the room casting myself under the mosquito net of my bed, seizing my bow and my arrows from the Pascagoulas. At other times I remained profoundly sad thinking that the time of my return gets farther away day by day, then rereading "your mustache, your long German pipe and, especially, the little pipe of the friend" [David d'Angers] and all the rest about the beard, I laughed like a madman; then since day before yesterday, a day that will be solemn forever, I was attacked by a fever that knocked me down completely; but that will soon be cured; it would be difficult to imagine the extraordinary care, truly maternal, of the aunt for me. How could I express my gratitude? There is but one way, and unfortunately it is to delay my departure, which is killing me.

You can imagine that in these intimate conversations that hold so much charm two thousand leagues from the fatherland, your name comes up constantly; why do I not have with me some pieces of your poetry so that the people in America would have read them? What happiness I would have had to read them, full of glory upon adding at the end: "Victor, my brother, the one who opened my eyes to nature and taught me to love everything derived from it."

We went hunting in the woods, camped far from any human face, on the bank of Spanish Lake, which was formerly in Mexican territory. Imagine the evening, the pink-winged spoonbill skimming the pale surface of the lake, the cry of the deer at night frightened to see our fire sparkling, the long howling of the raging panther that I saw passing through the sassafras trees; then, in the evening, in a darkness worthy of Hell, the imposing solitude where we were alone, camped under a canvas tent, where the candle burned tranquilly, planted in a cane pole; we slept on bearskins and buffalo robes [blankets] and when I awoke at night the slaves who had accompanied us slept on their skins, outside the tent, camped around the fire like the guardians of Choctas. During these days we had a succession of curious incidents, hurricanes, storms, etc. As for me, I killed numerous teal ducks glistening all colors, hawks, and falcons, then four of those red-crested vultures which, mortally wounded at 200 feet tumble from limb to limb, bringing down enormous branches in their fall.[14] Before the first freeze I saw, by going upriver, 42 alligators within pistol-shot range, asleep on the strands, in less than one hour; but the enormous ones took lead from my rifle at twenty feet directly into their open mouths without accelerating their salamander stride. There are also pretty parrots, cardinals more numerous than swallow in France, immense quantities of mockingbirds, eagles, hawks, falcons, etc. Last night some Indians kept me from sleeping with their guttural cries, to which it amused me to respond, and they spent several hours dancing and howling, until midnight; there was something magical about hearing, in the middle of a terrible wind, the sweeter voices of these women savages blended with their war cries, and always in tune, this time up an octave, that time in harmony.

14. Louisiana naturalist William Dean Reese identifies Pavie's red-headed vulture as a turkey vulture. Black vultures (solid black with no red coloration) are also found in Louisiana.

I tried vainly to save a parrot that I wounded in flight, but it lived only a short while. I have some rather strange things, and when it is dryer, because sometimes the rains flood entire leagues in an hour, I will continue to pluck feathers from birds. In two weeks I am going to make an excursion into the prairies: the most curious things are found in the interior of Mexico which begins 10 leagues from here, but some tribes of cannibalistic Karankawas make these trips too dangerous: their poisoned arrows are shot with so much strength that they can kill two bisons with a single arrow.

Marianne Pavie appended this note to Théodore's letter to his brother: "My dear cousin, You will be surprised to learn that our dear Théodore is delaying his return two months. It is a sacrifice that he is making for me for which I am much obliged. It is God who sent him to me to give me more courage about leaving my family and to diminish my sorrow. Besides, I can no longer do without him, he is absolutely necessary for me for my journey: his friendliness and gaiety will reduce its length. Good-bye, my dear Victor, I am anxious to see you. I embrace you wholeheartedly. Your aunt and friend, A. Pavie[15]

Charles Pavie picked his own pen back up on January 8, 1830, to write to his cousin Louis to announce that Théodore Pavie had been there since November. He also wanted to warn him that the young man's return would be delayed because he and Marianne wanted him to stay with them.

Your son has been here with us since the month of November. When he arrived he announced his intention to leave soon; filial love, he said, making that a duty. I took on myself the responsibility of keeping him, reconciling my interests with his. However painful his absence might be for you, I would never seek to abrogate it by exposing him to the risks of a winter crossing. As for my own needs, I would find it impossible to allow him to leave. My wife had been expecting Théodore like the Messiah. He finally arrived. For three years a profound sadness had reigned in the house;

15. Théodore Pavie to Victor Pavie, December 26, 1829, in private collection.

he made it disappear and brought joy back into our home. He has captured the heart of my wife to such an extent that she can no longer do without him, that she considers him her own child. Do you really think that I owe it to you to send him back to you, just when the designated time is near for him to help me bear the shock I will receive at the moment of my departure next April? We will go through the northern United States and embark from New York to Le Havre.[16]

Neglecting his correspondence tasks, Théodore Pavie spent some time in Natchitoches "putting his notes in order," as well as enjoying Louisiana and his new family—especially his pretty young cousin. He wrote Bonnemaman in Angers on February 2, 1830, to catch her up on his winter activities.

I do not know how the time is passing at home, but here it is flying. I have already been in Natchitoches nearly three months and it seems as if I just arrived yesterday. Also they are spoiling me here, overwhelming me with care and consideration. They anticipate and satisfy my least whim, and if I fell ill, I believe they would die worrying about me. Thank God there is nothing to fear for me. It has not been any warmer in the last fifteen days than it is in Angers in the month of June and it often freezes at night. Never have I seen a weather more clear nor a sky more blue than have predominated all winter. There was hardly a day of rain. Regarding my social life, I am very happy because the loveliest young ladies in this place are my aunt's nieces and, without flattering her at all, Eliza is, if not the prettiest, at least the most remarkable. It is true that seven years in a row of dreadful illnesses have almost ruined her education, but natural intelligence can compensate for everything. As for me, I am placed in the most brilliant company in the place. Like the Savage who would find himself in the middle of the Hall of Mirrors [at Versailles], I often prefer the uncertain moonbeam on the reddened waters of the river to the most joyful gatherings. Often I leave behind the noisy laughter for my solitary strolls. In a

16. Charles Pavie to Louis Pavie, January 8, 1830, in private collection.

country where everybody is a friend, I must have seemed strange, but little by little they grew accustomed to it. Since my uncle is essentially in charge of all amusements, I contrast strangely with him. I cannot hide from you, you who love me, that it hurt him. When leaving for a ball where her daughter was the principal ornament my dear aunt complained about leaving the traveler alone to wander on the gallery, but, alas! such is my character. I am sick within my soul; I have the weariness of a life that is too happy, the fatigue of a heart searching for a struggle. At least, I am as kind as possible. Pardon these words but I must tell you what I am becoming here: my heart is speaking, it opens itself up entirely, that is to say that I am doing what I can to reciprocate the extraordinary kindness that has been shown to me here. Several times I have had the opportunity to witness all the tenderness my aunt has for me when I was deep in thoughts as profound as the ocean and she believed that she saw a tear in my eyes. She rushed to me for tears as tentative as the dew, she who has known so much real sorrow. Generally a solicitude has been expressed for me here that I do not know how to repay and I would be vain to think that I even half deserved. Here what is needed is essentially two things: crazy gaiety and boldness—one of which I lost years ago and the other I never had. Do not believe that I languish in boredom. Never, since I left the paternal roof, have I spent days that are gentler, more even, calmer, more beautiful. The horses of the plantation are offered to me at every occasion but I just cannot spend all of my days and all of my evenings in the company of other people, going to at least one ball every week, but I rarely decide to leave my room or rather to change the direction of my wandering thoughts; only I always accompany the members of the household to the homes of relatives. I stay home and keep people company at the house, but the days of balls I withdraw to the shore and from there, leaning against the trunk of a black locust or plane tree, I listen to the strains of the violin and the dancing of people for whom life is such a light burden.

Poor Uncle sometimes worries about my sadness and wants to permit me to leave; he believes that I am bored and unhappy unless

I am on a walk, off hunting or in a group; however I have explained my personality to him so thoroughly that he ends up laughing about it and feeling sorry for me. And also since my health is always perfect, and the time to leave coming so soon, I don't have time to get upset about it. It will be a terrible day for me—what tears will I see shed when I have to break such close ties. Will my aunt be able to take such a terrible thing? She still harbors a confused idea about returning here after 5 or 10 years' absence.

3 February. Yesterday the heat was unbearable; today the cold is atrocious and I am near a large fire writing to you. Large numbers of Savages still come and they always stop at the house because I buy as many things as possible. I have a rather good collection of bows and arrows for my friends. I know how to pluck a bird's feathers and hunting is one of my great pastimes. Unfortunately all of the birds that I have caught alive in traps ended up dying. I have already made six attempts to keep cardinals and mockingbirds, but they did not have any desire to come to France. I was more fortunate with a rattlesnake that I kept alive for six weeks, but he often escaped and his rattle was so frightening that I had it killed; he was six feet long. I have some little turtles the size of a *piastre* which will look good in the goldfish bowl. . . . [W]hen it is warmer I will get busy with little alligators and chameleons.

Excuse me, Grandmother dear, if I talk snakes and alligators with you, I was forgetting your apprehension of these kinds of animals; I hope that a cardinal or a pope [This is a pun: both are birds, and the grandmother is a devout Catholic.] would please you more. I had wounded in flight a very beautiful parrot, which was supposed to be for you, but he died; I would really like to give you a pretty vulture but you would smell it at two hundred feet. Unfortunately the season for hummingbirds has passed, but during that season, a visit to Louisiana would have certainly been deadly for me as the place is becoming more unhealthy each year.

We are leaving here in early April. They absolutely insist on returning through the north and I believe that we will leave from New York the first of June because it is necessary to go back to

Niagara Falls and take a little side trip of a thousand miles. This devastates me, but is a sacrifice that I owe them. . . .[17]

Despite the fact that Théodore had heard from Victor only once, he wrote him a long, newsy letter on February 4, 1830.

Why do I not see any more letters either from Paris or from Angers? The last one is from Weimar; the last one from Papa is from September fourth. Since then, nothing at all. . . . four months without any word about you. . . . The news from France in the newspapers is quite insignificant. Nonetheless, it is to this that I am reduced.

Dear friend, these are my pleasures and pastimes here: bringing order into some notes on the land and the manners of the savages, collecting curiosities, admiring nature and thinking of you; this is how I spend ordinary days as beautiful as possible under the solemn vaults [skies] of the New World, isolated from my family without receiving any news of them. I often go hunting, that is to say I take a shotgun and wander in the woods killing ducks, squirrels, and buzzards. Sometimes I hunt deer, so numerous in this region. But to all of these I prefer a solitary promenade in certain sites that surpass in solitude and power all the nature that you can imagine. Yesterday I saw a rather curious spectacle. It was the New Year's greeting that the savages were cautiously celebrating, dancing to the sound of the tambourines and the cane flute. They all jump in a circle emitting surprising cries, always accompanied by the pure voice of the women singing an octave higher. They entered the houses and the Manitou shook some little flags around the one who was talking.

Day after tomorrow I'm leaving with several people to take a four-day trek into Mexico, mounted on a big mule with a carbine and two loaded pistols, without forgetting my dagger. I ask you not to tell the parents for fear they would be worried. However this journey offers almost no danger, and the cannibalistic savages

17. Théodore Pavie to Marie Pavie (Bonnemaman), February 2, 1830, in private collection.

hold up more than ten days from here, and we're arming only as a precaution. You will perhaps see on the map the place where I'm going named Nacogdoches, a little to the left of Natchitoches. My goal in making this trip is to see a little of Mexico and to find some curiosities in these places little lived in and not at all cultivated.

I am overwhelmed with care by everyone. We talk every minute about you. Here is what this kind aunt who loves us so much was saying just then: "Tell your brother that I'm anxious to see him, get to know him, and that I will know no consolation far from my family than to have him beside me sometimes." . . . [W]hat have I done to deserve all the care lavished on me here, all the kindness that they heap on me. For the last four years, what harm have I caused those who love me. I often say this maxim of René: "It is better to resemble a common man more closely. . . ."

Yesterday I played the overtures from the *Caliphe de Baghdad* and from *Iphigenia* on a beautiful organ they have here. The savages were passing by, they rushed to the gallery and listened keenly. Their severe faces wrinkled up little by little. They spoke enthusiastically among themselves and danced with abandon: Cherokees, Caddos, Appaloosas, etc., all were in admiration. I yelled out to them to admire the music of Boildieu and Gluck. I gesticulated and they were stupefied. I noticed among them a tattooed _____ [looks like "Tharmoué"] who had a horrid scar on his forehead from an arrow shot by a Choctaw: I bought his bow and lead-tipped arrows from him. I have a rather large quantity of arms and arrows of all kinds, panther skins and other curiosities.

Farewell, dear Victor, dinner is waiting and the mail is going to leave. I won't tell you to write to me; this time it will be too late.[18]

Troubled by the isolation from his family because of lack of mail (probably owing to weather conditions in the Gulf), Théodore laments his aloneness in a letter to his father written the last week of February, 1830. Homesickness seems to have overcome him when he returned from Texas and no mail awaited him.

18. Théodore Pavie to Victor Pavie, February 4, 1830, in private collection.

Mardi Gras (23/28) February 1830

Already ninety suns have risen over the horizon of forests surrounding me, the Savage has counted three moons since I received
the last letter dated the fourth of September and afterward: nothing. I did receive a delicious letter from Victor, but it was from
Weimar and, consequently, dated before yours. My last words
from the one who is everything to me cease, therefore, on the
fourth of September, that is, nearly six months ago. Imagine what
my concern has been . . . Storms have sunk many ships along the
coast, especially in the Gulf of Mexico. Doubtless your letters are
lost, however I know positively that the steamers from New York
have always arrived safely; and, moreover, every day I see happy
people who receive letters with recent postmarks, directly. What
should I think?

Today is Mardi gras. Yesterday there was a ball; another is
being prepared for tonight. Judge what evenings I spend like this
all alone with my concerns, trying in vain to penetrate this thick
impenetrable curtain that has fallen since this fourth of September
and on which are painted a thousand ghosts that I am having
trouble erasing. I will spare you the terrible visions that worry me
and I pray God that they are just dreams! I have taken down all of
my wild trophies that decorated my little room, whose embellishment I enjoyed every day saying to myself, "This is for him; this is
for Victor, etc." It is all over, all joy has ceased for me; my arrows
are in the quiver upside down, my pistols are tilted toward the
ground, my belt no longer festoons the deer's antlers, my flute is
disassembled, my music locked up—there is only my mysterious
little trunk that I open all the time. It contains my treasure: your
letters.

Alas! Two days ago I returned from an eight-day trip on horseback to the province of Texas (Mexico). At every mile I found a
stream where I descended to drink, sat at the foot of gigantic magnolias, so numerous in that country; the parrots came in uncountable flocks, squawking above my head. I suspended my Mexican
whip over the butt of my pistols, I traced names dear to me in the
sand with the tip of my dagger; I was mute in the bosom of this
wilderness that seemed sad to me; however, spring is beginning, it

was very warm; and the prairies that interrupt the sassafras woods at every mile were often crisscrossed by the rapid flight of deer, the barely visible trail of the wild turkey. The breeze murmured in the cedar trees, the wild mulberry trees, the cypress, all that was sad to my ears, to my eyes, and to my heart. I saw the chief of the Cherokees with his lance decorated with enemy scalps, the Delaware exiled from the banks where Philadelphia rises up, the Shawnee descended from Illinois; I smoked with them, they shook my hand and asked me in English where *my home* was and, turning toward the east I told them, "On the other side of the Great Lake." As the fierce traits of the savage relaxed, he gave me his hand with a look of pity for the young voyager—and you, my father? Of course not, you haven't forgotten me I hope.

Here my aunt interrupted me to tell you every kind, good, and tender thing imaginable. I will let her speak for herself, you will judge her heart: "Tell your Papa that it is impossible to leave without you. God sent you to me to give me the courage to leave my family. Perhaps your concern will push you to leave without us, but I cannot leave without you." Really, dear Papa, their tenderness for me exceeds anything imaginable.

Lent is easy to keep here. The Priest gave permission for meat every day except Wednesdays and Fridays. Religious obligations are almost impossible to fill here; but don't worry about me; everything reminds me of this religion which is today, more than ever, my only consolation.

Good-bye, excellent father, I cannot believe that you are deliberately hurting me like this; in reality, I have much pain. I will always love you.[19]

Louis Pavie added this note to the end of his son's letter before sending it to Victor in Paris:

What shall I add to this letter where the feeling for us, especially for you, is so well painted! Nothing. It is quite eloquent. Agitated by diverse thoughts, he does not know what to do. Whatever

19. Théodore Pavie to Louis Pavie, February 28, 1830, in private collection.

his choice, he will be welcome [to join the Charles Pavie family on their journey] just as he was anticipated with joy. If I could advise him, I would tell him to wait for his relatives and share the difficulty of the crossing with them.

I was counting on a letter from you this morning where you would share with me the pleasure you felt at the news from your brother.

Didn't you need to reassure me about the evening at the Théâtre français, if it took place?

I embrace you as a father,

L. Pavie

A copy of the new *Views* by M. Daguerre has been purchased by the library. I forgot to tell him about it. I will do everything to place the others.[20]

In April, Théodore Pavie turned his activities toward his imminent departure. Still believing that he would accompany Charles, Marianne, and their daughter Eliza on their journey through New York, he organized his collection of souvenirs in a trunk that he entrusted, along with a letter, to one of his father's contacts who would be traveling directly to France. This list of the contents of Théodore's trunk is among the most difficult to read of the surviving documents.

Trunk[21]

List and explanation of objects contained in a trunk consigned to Mr. Maës on April 8, 1830.

—8 bows, 3 of them yellow wood, formed into bows; three others pliable in either direction made by the captain of the Caddos, another very hard large one, and an insignificant small one.

---

20. Louis Pavie to Victor Pavie, February 26, 1830, in private collection.

21. Contents of Trunk, April 8, 1830, manuscript in private collection. These objects have been dispersed over the years although a few pieces remain in the family. I have seen a fragment of the bearskin mounted on a board to be used to keep the drafty air from passing under a door, two pipe bowls in poor condition (including the one from the Cherokee medicine man), the rattlers, the trefoil and silver-plated pipe/hatches, spoon, and one red feather from a "pope" that Pavie transported between the blank pages at the end of some of the notes used for *Souvenirs atlantiques*.

—84 varied arrows of the following descriptions: 19 arrows in yellow wood, tipped alike, many of them are stained with blood, 7 others also tipped, but in iron; another bundle of arrows in bois blanc,[22] and others longer stained with blood from deer; wide tips, pointed, square, etc. . . . ; the rest, made of light reed arrows (of which 3 are very long) with wild turkey feathers, some _____, others with wide tips and without feathers. (All these arrows and the 7 bows are in very good shape)—plus a large quiver in "tiger" skin from Santa Fé.

—3 lead pouches, two embroidered in porcupine, another striped and plain, a single new one.

—1 lead pouch made of bearskin, and a powder horn with two measures, one made from a deer antler, the other made from reed.

—2 belts. One Algonquin, of one color, the other Choctaw, striped. One other straight and single-colored, two pairs of garters[?], one of them especially remarkable. One swan skin a little dirty in the shape of a turban.

—An embroidered hat and some _____ [mitasses?] also dyed and embroidered, as well as a pipe shaped like a trefoil from the Quonchtees[23] of Mexico, another pipe plated in silver that I brought back from Texas. One deer head.

—2 pairs of moccasins, one new yellow pair from Texas, the other a bit used, embroidered in porcupine from the Oneidas; plus a small birchwood box, also embroidered, coming from Canada.

—2 purses, one is beaver pelt, from a Seneca chief, the other a long-haired pelt, here called a "stinking beast" [skunk]; a savage's flute.

—A small chest full of Indian pans of all shapes and sizes. One spoon from savages; a mirror encased in the effigy of a alligator; a

22. Bois blanc, literally "white wood," is the swamp privet, *Forestiera acuminata*. According to Reese, country Cajuns still call this wood "bois blanc."

23. Juan Antonio Padilla wrote a report on the barbarous Indians of the Province of Texas in 1819. He mentions five hundred "Conchaté" who live further down the same river (the Trinity) as the Alibamó, who go to Nacogdoches to trade. The Conchaté wear their faces painted in vermilion, trade in furs, hunt, and cultivate the soil. Eugene C. Barker, *A Comprehensive, Readable History of Texas* (Dallas: Southwest Press, 1929), 35.

pipe in the form of a turtle, very dirty coming from Texas; I got it from the Manitou of the Great Chief of the Cherokees. A tuft of feathers from ducks and ivory-billed woodpeckers. Several tails[?] in pearls.

—3 gallons of pecans. Seed from wisteria, magnolias, sweet potatoes, a creeper vine called "crocodile," Papouais or wild tobacco, sassafras roots. All of these little objects are contained in Shawnee baskets that crowd the trunk; one must take care of the dried Spanish moss surrounding all of these objects.

—3 cowhides, 2 panther skins, 1 skin from a black bear. 1 "armed fish" [alligator gar], 2 large rattlesnakes, plus a large rattler of 15 nodes from the chief of the Tahatees [the name he gives a tribe in a chapter called "The Indians"] and three small rattles. (The skin from the stinking-beast contains arrow tips in stone [arrowheads] in use before the arrival of the Europeans; be careful of them, I believe they are poisoned.)

Open the box immediately for fear the objects will spoil; take care of them; keep them a bit hidden from curiosity until the happy day for me; please allow me the pleasure of disposing of these things regardless of the claims of the people to whom I have assigned this or that. I also have some birds, but I am keeping them to bring with me so that I can better take care of them. Since Easter I have killed ten hummingbirds; I easily skin them, then dry them in books like flowers in an herbarium. Good-bye, it is overwhelmingly hot, I am leaving to go take a nap.

On April 15, 1830, Théodore wrote his final letter from Louisiana to his father, to be hand-delivered by the same person who took charge of his trunk. In it, he captures the emotional intensity of the imminent leave-taking, fusing homesickness with future nostalgia. He also speaks of other members of Marianne and Charles's extended family: Marcelite, the widow of the Neutral Strip interpreter Juan Cortés, and Hélène Poissot, the aged daughter of the murdered Étienne Pavie, whose widow married his best friend, Pierre Metoyer.

I must explain to you the thought under whose spell I find myself since yesterday so that you might understand something about this tangled web of sad and melancholy ideas.

Among my aunt's sisters, there is one [Marcelite Cortés] to whom I am especially close from a double attachment. It is she who, under the pretext of having been ordered by my uncle to do so, kept me from joining him at his plantation, and it was she who first received me upon my arrival with surprising solicitude. Add to that that a ghastly double blow has struck twice in one year: she lost her husband and finds herself a widow, mother of 5 children brought up in opulence, and the father's estate is insolvent. Her children show me a priceless kindness and openness. The oldest, married for a year and living far from home, had been expected for a long time. Finally, last night, we were all gathered together— nieces, cousins, everyone . . . I was rather gay and joyful, contrary to my usual; I had even provoked general hilarity by a few jokes when, at ten o'clock, the Negro man arrives, the steamboat having been heard in the distance across from the plantation of cousin Poissot [Aunt Helen] which can be seen among the trees. Everyone rushed in a group to meet the one whom my aunt calls her beloved. We all crowded under the florid dome of catalpas and black lo- custs whose flowers, swaying in the delicious evening breeze, per- fumed the bank of the Red River. A light shines, the cannon re- sounds, no more doubt, there she is. There she is; the sailors sing in cadence, the boat appears under the starry sky like a fiery furnace.

"What's wrong with you," asked all the young girls, turning the torch toward me, "you're so deep in thought." And me, I said nothing, for they must have seen a tear welling up in my eyes. Oh! When will they be able to cry out "There he is," when will you be able to press your son in your arms—you who, all of your life, have sacrificed yourself to the happiness of your family; Oh! dear Papa, perhaps I wound you by telling you all that, but I am so happy here that when I think of you who are all alone over there, all alone working while I enjoy this, it makes me cry like a child. It has been said that I am cold as ice, it could be so, but ask the Night which alone has seen my tears flow; ask this aunt who has already wiped them so often. No, it is not for the child who misses his cradle, his toys, and his rattle, it is the son who feels all that he owes to his father, all that his father has done for him. Once more, I am doing so well here, I take so much pleasure in smelling the perfume of the forests, seeing the feather of the crane poised on the melancholy head of the Choctaw, seeing him swing his bow, his quiver dyed with the blood of bear and bison. They are so pure, these pleasures that Nature bestows when one senses in them the name of the Creator. But you, why are you not here to enjoy it too? I have braved storms, dangers, death, and I will brave them a thousand times more, but when I think of you, it is the chink in my armor, the place where the faintest blows wound me, it is my Achilles heel.

Until midnight, I wandered across the hill, everyone was watching me. "What's wrong with you?" the girls asked, "you no longer laugh." And me, heartbroken, I couldn't answer; until midnight I shed tears and this morning, I was still moaning in my bed when a hand lifted the mosquito netting and clasped mine; the kind hand of my aunt sought to console me. It is less hot today, I am going riding. I shall gallop across the woods, but sadness will climb up behind my saddle to ride double and gallop along with me, and this suffering of a soul that loves you could be offered to you in holocaust, I offer them to you with all my heart.

Join to that that I find out from Mr. Maës that he is embarking in ten days directly for Nantes. He will bring you this letter. My feet burned at this news, but gratitude will keep me here until I can't tell you exactly when; three more weeks at Natchitoches.

Perhaps you have read that several steamboats have sunk, blown up on the river, in New York, on the Ohio. These are rare, besides don't worry about anything. Your benediction follows me everywhere.

My fond greetings to all the relations, friends, acquaintances and the good people of the house, the men of the Press. M. Prunair, of whom we often speak, and you, whom I love as much as I can. Theodore P.

Grandmother, dear, I am doing my Easter duties Friday.

Why have I not received a single letter from all of you since yours of September 4? How you make me worry.[24]

24. Théodore Pavie to Louis Pavie, April 15, 1830, in private collection.

Pavie's papers also contain two poems that he may have written after he returned to France and discovered his emotional loss from being separated from seeing the one whom he called "Élise" daily. Though undated, they seem to belong here, at the end of his letters from Louisiana.

So far from me will she—

And you ask me why, Friends, why I love her
with such a great love; why, without her,
nothing pleases my vexed heart; why, fed-up with myself,
I leave the brilliant ball and my gaiety is silenced.

And what do I care for your beauties, so vaunted
that a cloud of incense surrounds them, and that I see
them carried into the brilliant circle of the quadrille,
spinning like a swarm of bees in the woods.

Casting everywhere her glance, intoxicated by her jewels,
admiring to my satisfaction her quickened waltz steps,
balancing her fragrant head proudly,
and sweetly murmur, "Were you applauding?"

She is not like this, the woman I adore;
Her face is much more humble, and the sparkle in her eyes
Like a sacred ray from a falling star
Knows how to slide across a heart and return to the
heavens.

She is not a queen of this world, intoxicated by her vain
    beauty;
from heaven she has left, in livery borrowed from
    misfortune,
to console a heart
Cast down upon earth.

How I loved to hear her in pious prayer
blending her sweet voice, or joining her two hands
to pray in silence, how these mystical voices
travel from arch to arch in the holy places.

I went and sat down beside her;
near her, I felt so well and my heart was less afflicted,
near her it forgot all the hurt that it holds,
it was as if a burden were lifted.

If she happened to pass by in a group of young girls
giggling together; her glance would soon be directed
        toward me,
under the arbor and then, always walking slowly,
she would arrive too late.

When she saw me across the fields
depressed, wandering far, very far from the happy ones,
"Why," she asked her young friend,
"am I also sad whenever I see that he is unhappy?"

And I, too, loved her so! But far from my homeland,
a voice had long ago recalled me;
across the ocean I hear it calling to me.
what could I expect; that she love me anyway?

Also I said to her: "Do you see at dawn
Under an azure reflection the days recommence;
We will only see one another for a few more suns,
But when the rose dies, farewell. It is forever.

And the rose was soon withered . . . with it
the sweet illusion vanished forever;
but to the memory of it I shall always be faithful;
Alas! . . . So far from me, will she forget me? Oh! No!

The other is a prose poem:

For me, my friend, life is finished!
There was a time when I was in love without knowing it . . .
    when her eyes met mine, then lowered, a time when I trembled
at the sound of a voice, the rustle of a skirt along the bushes, then,

half opening my curtains, I saw her pass by and turn back toward me, with each step smiling;

when in the evening seated under a blooming wisteria, we would chat while the thunder roared, and the lightening illuminating her face revealed eyes fastened on mine;

when at night, I was sleeping happily, I awoke to marvel at my memories and, opening my window I could see on the horizon only the oceans of forests, turned silver by the moonlight, and everything in the distance was repose and silence. I stayed awake, leaning on the windowsill, dreaming of the day just passed, and of the morrow.

In mid-April 1830, Théodore Pavie and Charles and Marianne Pavie and their adopted daughter, Eliza, left their plantation on a steamboat bound for New Orleans. In *Souvenirs atlantiques,* Pavie recounts the strong emotions they all felt, and describes the port city. To the second edition, he appended a description of the Battle of New Orleans, apparently dictated by Charles during their visit to the battlefield at the Plains of Chalmette. Contrary to everyone's expectations, Théodore Pavie made a precipitous decision to sail directly from New Orleans to France rather than accompanying his hosts to New York and returning to France in their company.

From Bordeaux, Pavie wrote his father on July 2, 1830, to announce his arrival in France. "Home Sweet Home," he proclaimed in English, "I have finally arrived! Oh! Thank God, who protected me in the middle of . . . ," listing trials and tribulations, including a ten-day tropical stall and a storm so violent that the mast was sheared from his ship, the Henry Astor. All of the boats coming from New Orleans were also held in quarantine. He could not explain to his father his decision to leave alone: "Why I left my relatives in New Orleans, I don't even know myself, I owed them everything, and what happened was that a finely outfitted, deliciously masted ship turned my head. Then, how it tortured me! . . . I have to stop at La Rochelle, at Nantes. . . . I'm so anxious to see you and Bonnemaman and Victor and all the relations and friends—I'm so happy I can't write. Good-bye."[25]

25. Théodore Pavie to Louis Pavie, July 2, 1830, in private collection.

4

THE HISTORICAL MOMENT

La Rochelle 8 July 1830
Dearest Bonnemaman,
   I have been here since yesterday. . . .
   My hand is trembling from joy so badly that I can't write. . . .
In the place I left were found some people whose souls understood
mine, but silence, it is to you and nothing but you that I aspire.[1]

Chateaubriand's writing so strongly inspired Théodore Pavie that he carried a copy of the author-diplomat's work in his knapsack through most
of his American journey. Through imitation and tribute, the young writer
used his hero's creations as a tool for processing his own experience and
as an aid to his personal development. After a period of immersing himself in and imitating the older man's work, Pavie eventually transcended
it and developed his own style. Though he outgrew the youthful ardor
the two writers had shared, Pavie never mocked or put down Chateaubri-
and when the visionary went out of favor.

1. Théodore Pavie to Marie Pavie, July 8, 1830, in private collection.

Chateaubriand had been subjected to intense public criticism starting in 1826 following the publication of his complete works because he had not visited in person all the locales he described in *Atala* or *Voyage en Amérique*. Some places he had visited only in his imagination while sitting in Parisian libraries reading the works of travelers whose observations he folded seamlessly into his narratives, without citations. He claimed to have written *Atala* "in the wilderness under the hut of Savages," which he did not. A more significant breach of the reader-writer contract occurred in *Voyage en Amérique*, wherein he reports that he interviewed George Washington at Mount Vernon. This did not happen. Whereas the "hut of Savages" could be labeled fiction or literary convention, the standards of accuracy for mentioning a famous leader in a travel account were stricter and, at a time when readers brought more innocent expectations to accounts of voyages, Chateaubriand's indiscriminate combination of travel writing and fiction violated unspoken, emerging conventions. Although his methodology extended back to Homer, it was not condoned by many commentators in 1826. The virulent disapproval was symptomatic of the upsurge of positivism amid a changing conception of history. Positivism's quasi-religious devotion to the scientific method resulted in a need for authors to write disclaimers about their "inventions," such as Pavie's notice in the preface to *Souvenirs atlantiques:* "Above all, I told the truth, except a few stories—not strictly true, at least probable, and in the character of the places and the inhabitants: I restrained myself from introducing anything not based on facts."[2]

In addition to countless references to Chateaubriand in his private correspondence, Pavie explicitly recalls him eight times in *Souvenirs atlantiques*. During the early part of Pavie's journey, the great author seems

2. Théodore Pavie, *Souvenirs atlantiques* (Angers: L. Pavie, 1832). Joseph Bédier concluded in 1903 that "Chateaubriand never set foot in the land of Atala" (Armand Weil, introduction to *Atala* [Paris: Cortir, 1950], lxix). No one has seriously questioned his conclusion. Gilbert Chinard and others have, instead, sought out Chateaubriand's literary sources; see especially Chinard's *L'Exotisme américain dans l'oeuvre de Chateaubriand* (Paris: Hachette, 1918). Sources discovered include texts by Le Père Charlevoix, Rousseau, Marmontel, Bernardin de Saint-Pierre and several naturalists, such as Carver, Imlay, and Bartram. In *Défense de la Génie*, Chateaubriand invoked William Bartram's *Voyage dans les Carolines et dans les Florides* in his own defense, citing Bartram as the source of his much-ridiculed dancing bears, intoxicated from eating fermented raisins. Weil summarizes these texts in his introduction.

to have dominated Pavie's perspective. He appears not to have found Chateaubriand's embellishment of the truth unsettling because he found the imaginative aspects of the narrative so accurate and so impressive, even when he compared the reality of America to the literary illusion. On a steamboat on the Ohio River, Pavie recognized the spot where Chactas tells René the story of his life.

Was it not in these same places, under these same trees, under the rays of the same melancholic star, that Chactas recounted to René the misfortunes and joys of his youth, and spread like a tardy balm consoling advice onto the soul of the exiled man! Undoubtedly America never nurtured at its breast a man like the blind Sachem, patriarch of days of old; the heavens never gathered together in a single heart as many pains as René devoured; but let what should be the magnificence of a solitude that inspired such thoughts in the author of *Atala* be judged and see how noble must be the impressionable and melancholic mind to cause to spring forth such pure and generous creatures in the middle of the wilderness.[3]

Pavie struggled to reconcile Chateaubriand's elaborations with the resonance he himself experienced. It is the "magnificence of a solitude that inspired such thoughts" that is real to Théodore, whose own persona alternates between a self-absorbed, moody youth deep in solitary contemplation and an intellectually bold adult. "For me, the picturesque infinite harmony of nature is everything." At the sight of the Mississippi River, he rescued himself from inarticulate bewilderment by calling up Chateaubriand's prose to mediate between the sight he beheld and the sensations he felt: "Having arrived at the loveliest part of my voyage, surrounded by these places of which I have dreamed so many times, of these images of fantasy and reality at the same time, I pause and words escape me. Chateaubriand passed here with his genius and his words of fire: each day travelers see these same places without understanding them and find nothing here to ponder, but you must go there anyway. I will try to gather up all the scattered memories whose waves float so deliciously for the one

3. Part II, p. 118 herein.

who loves to remember his sensations, and I will tell you about the Mississippi as it presented itself to my delighted eyes."[4]

The description that follows recalls Pavie's idol to the reader. Though transported at the sight of the Mississippi River, which amply fulfilled his oversized expectations, Pavie warns his readers that the village of Natchez would fall short of one's hopes if those were based on Chateaubriand. Disillusioned, he warns that " 'Natchez' is a beautiful name full of memories celebrated by Chateaubriand, known in Europe as the ideal Indian village. You who have read *The Natchez* must never go near this village if you want to keep your illusions. All that remains is very tall hill piled high with shabby houses, crudely built, with weeds sprouting from their walls."[5]

Apparently his disappointment with Natchez did not extend to the author who had described it, for Pavie quickly resumed his reading of the master. On an early November evening when the boat was anchored, "I sat down at the table and opened a volume of Chateaubriand whose writing, always full of enchantment, never had more of it than in this place. A thousand thoughts rapidly followed each other in my mind: my memories, combined with the ideas given birth within me by *The Natchez,* oppressed me so much that I went back up on deck. Oh! delicious solitude!"[6]

After Pavie had settled into his aunt and uncle's plantation, his appreciation for Chateaubriand continued to grow. Recounting a visit to the Lake of the Natchez, a small lake south of Natchitoches, he wrote, "The author of *Atala* was my faithful companion, whether I directed my course to the banks of the Lake of the Natchez where I picked my way through the tombs over which brambles were growing or, seated on a vine swinging from the summit of a liquidamber tree or climbing back to the crest of a plane tree, I remained a few hours to read and reread these sublime pages—balancing myself pleasurably like a bird."[7]

Pavie even takes the opportunity to confirm the games played by the natives and described by the discredited Chateaubriand before updating

4. Ibid.; Part II, p. 130 herein.
5. Part II, p. 151 herein.
6. Part II, p. 155 herein.
7. Part II, pp. 167–8 herein.

the earlier description with a recent report and a personal account. The passage serves as a testimonial account by an eyewitness. "The solemn games of which the author of *Atala* gives such an exact and poetic description in *The Natchez,* are still celebrated sometimes in the great plain of Natchitoches, the racquet game being the one that attracts the largest number of Indians. . . . In the contest that took place in October, the Pascagoulas, a weak tribe of the Red River, were victorious over the combined Choctaws and the Caddos. . . . Later, when hunting, I came across an Indian camp where one of them limped with the help of a stick. I recognized in him the winner of the racquet game. He had me sit on his mat and smoked with me."[8]

Recalling the warm day at the end of January 1830 when he left Natchitoches for Nacogdoches with his uncle Charles, Pavie lyrically evokes Chateaubriand for the last time. This time, while clinging to local tradition, Pavie nevertheless says he found no evidence that Chateaubriand had been there. Perhaps because Victor Hugo spoke frequently in private about Spain, Pavie's thoughts turned from Chateaubriand to Hugo when he passed the magnolia tree—symbol of exotic Louisiana—and approached New Spain, that is, Texas.

I pushed myself cheerfully toward the route to Texas. . . . After several miles we let our mounts drink at the Hondo River, a delicious stream that for a long time served as the boundary of the two powers. We noticed near the path two admirable magnolias, the most beautiful in all the land, on the bark of which each traveler customarily wrote his name. I looked there in vain for the name of Chateaubriand, which nonetheless should have been there according to the local learned ones. When I dismounted on the bridge to carve into this consecrated tree the five letters of my unknown name, I found a young alligator on the route. He did not dispute my way very long and plunged into the bayou, playing in its silvery waves.[9]

With this gesture of etching his name on the face of the land, Théodore Pavie symbolically claimed—based on his intimate knowledge of the

8. Part II, pp. 173–5 herein.
9. Part II, p. 185 herein.

foreign land—the geographic and intellectual territory where Chateaubriand had not preceded him either in person or on the intellectual map
of French readers. Only once after his January trip to Texas does Pavie
mention Chateaubriand, his companion in his "passage to Romanticism,
to adulthood and to writing itself." In the final reference to his former
idol, instead of waxing poetic, the young man realistically admits that
"Nothing is more terrible, more distressing, or more sublimely horrible
than the mouth of the Mississippi. I know more than one Frenchman, attracted to the banks of the 'Father of Rivers,' by the descriptions of Chateaubriand, who cried from disappointment at the site of La Balise."[10]

True to Pavie's claim to be an authority regarding the territory, this
passage introduces several pages describing La Balise. He has now shed
the skin of his hero and entered into the ranks of literary discoverers creating a new world on the French public's epistemological mappemonde,
the map in the mind's eye.

When he arrived back in France on the first of July 1830, Pavie recognized not only how rapidly France had changed in his absence, but also
how radically it was changing every day. In the conclusion he appended
to his journal, he denied the existence of significant change in America at
the same time he equated the artistic revolution in France with the coinci-
dent political revolution. "During the year of travel in America, no event
took place that was worth the trouble of being mentioned. But I had
barely disembarked before I was applauding *Hernani* at the *Grand Théâtre;* the stage had had its revolution. A week later, Algiers fell like the
walls of Jericho in front of the French army! Another week later, an ancient dynasty collapsed, and all of the kings of Europe trembled on their
thrones! Who would not have been awakened at the noise of a whole
world shaken loose at its foundations!"[11]

It is true that no American event took place that year that could compare to the three revolutions Pavie refers to: the fall of the classical French
theater, the fall of Algiers, and the fall of the Bourbon dynasty. The military conquest of Algeria, begun that week in Algiers, established a French
colony in Africa that endured for 133 years. The three-day July Revolution dethroned King Charles X, the last hereditary Bourbon monarch and

10. Part II, pp. 234–5 herein.
11. Part II, p. 239 herein.

king of France, whose power supposedly came exclusively from God. He was replaced by his cousin Louis-Philippe, the former duc d'Orléans, who presided over the social and industrial revolution in France from 1830 to 1848. As King of the French, he ruled under a charter, with the consent of at least some of his countrymen. A constitutional monarchy had thus replaced the traditional monarchy, and never again would birth be the sole criterion for ruling France. Much to his credit considering his age and time, Théodore Pavie realized that it was "a" whole world, not "the" whole world, that had been "shaken loose at its foundations"—the world of those European and South American countries still ruled by absolute monarchs.

And what about the revolution of the stage? More or less continuously since the days of Louis XIV and Molière, whose troupe became the national theater when he died, the government had controlled both the form and the content of French drama. On the stage, stories of noble characters unfolded in five acts observing the three unities of time, place, and action. Every line contained twelve syllables, known as alexandrines. Victor Hugo, who challenged these classical conventions in print in the *Préface de Cromwell,* organized a revolt held at the Théâtre français, an event known as the "Battle of *Hernani,*" after the title of his play, the opening of which formed the backdrop for the clash. The "revolution" in the theater was an orchestrated shouting match pitting Hugo's friends—several hundred enthusiastic young men, primarily long-haired students—against an even larger number of older men, bald or wearing wigs, who wanted the stage to remain as it had been before the 1789 Revolution. They fought symbolically over a three-syllable word that did not fit within a line according to the conventions of syllabification, thus causing the deliverer to inhale after the "wrong" number of syllables. This event took place during the premiere of Hugo's play *Hernani* in Paris on February 25, 1830. Victor Pavie attended and participated, and even brought a cohort—but our traveler was able to see only a repeat performance in Bordeaux in July of the rather unremarkable play, whose opening he had missed because he had been either in Natchitoches, Louisiana, listening to Creole girls sing French songs, or in Nacogdoches, Texas, witnessing the Cherokee Indians' victory march and listening to the Mexican soldiers sing their new national anthem, "Viva la Libertad."

But America was changing just as rapidly as France, even though the young republic of twenty-six states had few watershed events to mark its course through intellectual or geographic cultural borderlands. Unlike France, the United States had no classical theater, no absolute monarch, and certainly no desire to load thousands of soldiers in boats and sail off to conquer and colonize a distant country. In 1830 the young nation concentrated its efforts on exploring, conquering, exploiting, and settling the territory west of the Mississippi River. The government chose to ignore the activities of its people who crowded into Louisiana for the express purpose of separating Texas from Mexico, being more concerned with expanding across the continent. North America would be conquered and tamed by individuals on foot or horseback, and finally by train, using a "westering" process—slashing, burning, planting, chopping, and squatting, pushing ever westward across Mexican Texas (in existence from 1821–1836) and onward toward the Pacific Ocean, the only border Americans were willing to recognize. The people of the new republic overwhelmed the people who were on their way, or in their way, with force, disease, unkept promises, or simply by assimilation through intermarriage and forgetting of the languages of their grandparents or parents. The naïve witness from France mourned the giant trees, felled merely to feed the hungry steamboats on the Mississippi, and the soon-to-be-extinct virgin forests, feverishly cleared by land-hungry pioneers. He also mourned the passing of Indian tribes. Théodore Pavie comprehended extinction, but not assimilation. *"Ceci tuera cela,"* Victor Hugo would write in *Notre-Dame de Paris* during the summer of Pavie's return, meaning not simply the literal "This will kill that," but also "This will replace that," irreversibly and forever. Pavie did not travel to Florida and seems not to have understood the full purpose of the troops gathering in New Orleans in May 1830—the initiation of the Trail of Tears, which would be the consequence of the Indian Removal Act. It would be the fate of Sam Houston, Alexis de Tocqueville, and Gustave de Beaumont to happen upon the tragic removal of the Choctaw tribe west of the Mississippi two years later.

With a century and a half of hindsight, we can now see that *Souvenirs atlantiques* rescued from extinction some of the ephemeral sights, sounds, motions, and feelings of the vivid borderland cultures: Indian, Spanish or Mexican, and French. Although his visit was brief, the event-hungry young writer captured for us a grand finale. He seems to have sensed that the years 1829 and 1830 would be one of the last times that these vulnerable groups could live out their distinctive cultures in all of their finery before being overwhelmed, swallowed up, assimilated into the Anglo tide as Louisianans or Texans, and eventually as Americans. When the youthful adventurer crossed the Sabine, he situated himself culturally—in time and in space—in an "England, imitated by all Americans, . . . giving way to Spain, now the Republic of Mexico." Things "gave way" in that part of the world. Ripples, then waves, of colonists flooded over the previous inhabitants. Even the great logjam of the Red River gave way in the next decade to the skilled engineer Henry Miller Shreve, robbing Natchitoches of its strategic geographic location as the most westerly port accessible from the Mississippi River. Moreover, the French planters, the Mexican soldiers, and the Indian traders were the borderlands' wall of Jericho, which gave way in the 1830s. It all came tumbling down.[12]

The Old World seemed to change more illustriously, that is, with more preemptive drama. With so much concentrated intellectual and political power, Paris was the epicenter of the adjustments that Europe made in the face of the industrialization and democratization taking place in the nineteenth century: it did produce "events," which France needed and was ready for. Visiting Louisiana and Texas in 1829 and 1830, Théodore Pavie missed the two main events, being too late for the Battle of New Orleans in 1814 and too early for the Battle of the Alamo in 1836. Yearning like a true Romantic for events to relate, events against which he could test his mettle, he was forced to settle for observations, descriptions, and episodes. He witnessed no important events—or so it seemed—yet in recording facts and stories of exotic local color, Pavie rescued from oblivion the disappearing patriarchal culture of the rapidly changing Sabine Borderlands.

Victor Pavie first mentions his brother's book in a letter to Victor Hugo dated August 12, 1830, wherein he asks for the noted author's help. "My brother is writing a book about his memories of America that is truly remarkable, at least for us. He is publishing it within the family and that is a shame because, by reaching out, and with the protection of some stronger friends, this book could circulate generally. Take him in

12. Part II, p. 197 herein.

hand and encourage the poor author who loves you, and not just a little, even though he does not tell you."[13]

In his reply to Victor Pavie, Hugo complimented Théodore on those writings of his that Louis Pavie had published while he was still abroad: "Tell our friend Théodore that he has his share of your lively and beautiful imagination. What I read by him in the *Feuilleton* enchanted me." He then updated his friends on the Hugo family, relative to the three-day July Revolution and the birth of their second daughter. "My wife delivered nicely, a little after the machine gun fire and cannon shots, a little girl with a little mouth, for whom Sainte-Beuve is the godfather, whom we are naming Adèle and are baptizing Sunday. We will drink to your health." Hugo, however, reported maintaining his focus on his new novel, claiming to be buried up to his neck in *Notre Dame*. "I am stacking page on top of page, and the contents expand and stretch out in front of me so much so that, as I progress, I do not know if what I am writing will end up as high as the towers."[14]

Amid the following winter's excitement surrounding the publication of *Notre Dame de Paris,* Théodore Pavie experienced the second great sorrow of his life: Marianne Pavie, who had been so fearful of leaving her family in Louisiana, died in Bordeaux in March 1831, at forty-three. "Our dear aunt has died," he informed his brother Victor on March 22. Théodore lamented, "She who was a sweet mother for me and who loved both of us like sons. Did I have to attach myself so closely to her to feel this horrible blow so deeply? Sometimes when the sun cast its rays on my pale forehead, she would say to me with that Creole tenderness: 'What

13. This letter is housed in the Artine Artinian collection at the Harry Hunt Ransom Humanities Research Center at the University of Texas at Austin. It is quoted here with permission.

14. Hugo's letter to Victor Pavie of September 17, 1830, concerning the July Revolution, the birth of daughter Adèle, whose godfather would be Sainte-Beuve, and his writing of *Notre Dame de Paris,* is frequently cited in books and articles about Romanticism not only because of the intimate nature of Sainte-Beuve's relationship with Madame Hugo (and Hugo's with Juliette Drouet), but also because the book Hugo was then writing became one of the three best-selling French novels of the nineteenth century. The historic missive has been published in various collections of correspondence (Hugo's, 478; Sainte-Beuve's, 205, n.5; and Théodore Pavie's biography of Victor, 82); it was among the letters that the Pavie family exchanged with the Hugos after the deaths of the correspondents, according to the practice of the times.

good does it do for us to become so strongly attached to each other? Soon we will have to separate from each other.' Yes, my dear friend, we had to separate and forever. It is the deepest wound that has ever caused my soul to bleed. And our uncle and this poor Eliza, alone, twice without the one who was her mother. There you have the deplorable situation of this family that was so brilliant and happy . . . I am cruelly devastated."[15]

From Bordeaux, where he went to console Charles and Eliza, Théodore Pavie reported to his father that Eliza was better than usual and "as lovable as in Natchitoches. We have renewed that sympathetic fraternity from the Golden Age and I cannot forget the one who no longer lives that I have lost." Charles and Eliza soon returned to Natchitoches where she married Edward Orlando Blanchard in 1835.[16] Théodore Pavie returned to Angers from his aunt's funeral in Bordeaux, but remained in France only a few months. He would travel nearly around the world—sailing once to the West and once to the East—before he would get married and stop traveling.[17]

Just as Pavie set sail for South America, Victor Pavie wrote to Hugo October 17, 1831, to express his gratitude: "My father, my brother, how you treated them. Who could repay that[?]" Hugo had apparently interceded with one of his publishers, Roret, on behalf of Théodore's book. Roret published the two-volume edition in 1833. David d'Angers, an-

15. Théodore Pavie to Victor Pavie, March 7, 1831, in private collection.

16. Marie Eliza Bludworth Blanchard, who lived at the "Ile aux Vâches" Plantation which she inherited from Charles Pavie, named her son Charles Pavie Blanchard. Her daughter, born July 8, 1846, was given her name, Marie Eliza. The thirty-four-year-old mother, Théodore Pavie's first love, died one week after her daughter's birth, from complications arising from delivering twins. Her widower married Celeste Cornelia Dranguet. Marie Eliza Blanchard married a certain William Payne from Ireland and divided the Pavie plantation with her brother. According to her great-grandson, Judge Richard B. Williams, Mary Eliza took the south portion, Charles Pavie the north, and the land remained in the family until 1975. Louisiana journalist and genealogist Marie Wise, Eliza's direct descendant, has graciously provided the portrait of Marianne Rouquier Pavie. Wise, *Norris-Jones-Crockett.*

17. In 1841, at thirty, Théodore married eighteen-year-old Cornélie Gennevraye in the cathedral at Angers. Apparently having more confidence in his father's judgment in family matters, he asked his father to help him select a partner. The marriage apparently was quite happy except for the fact that they had no children. They went to Portugal on his mission to translate documents discovered by Geoffroy St. Hilaire, then lived in Paris for a decade before returning to Angers where they spent the rest of their long lives.

other important figure who earnestly admired Pavie's work, may also have influenced the publisher in favor of the book, which met a market demand generated by the political changes of the summer of 1830.[18] The primary competition for *Souvenirs atlantiques* was a French translation of Mrs. Trollope's *Domestic Manners in America*, which also appeared in 1833. And Chateaubriand's young cousin, Alexis de Tocqueville, published *Démocratie en Amérique* in 1835. Tocqueville was six years older than Théodore Pavie. The itinerary of his journey, made two years later and in the company of his friend Gustave de Beaumont, was entirely east of the Mississippi River. *Démocratie* eclipsed *Souvenirs atlantiques* in 1835.

Théodore Pavie left his manuscript in Paris in the hands of publisher Roret in 1832. At that time, he hoped to receive a government appointment whereby he would accompany a diplomatic mission to North Africa and serve as artist-secretary recording the local sights and customs. Despite the intervention of David d'Angers, however, the government assigned the older, better-connected, more experienced Eugène Delacroix to be the artistic secretary of the mission. Pavie then decided to follow the route of the scholarly adventurer Alexander von Humboldt to the Cordillera of the Andes and across the revolution-ravaged South American continent.[19] He returned to Paris in 1834 and recounted his story in the *Revue des deux mondes,* France's most prestigious literary periodical in the nineteenth century, for which he wrote over seventy articles between 1835 and 1865. Next turning his sights from the New World to the Orient, he remained in Paris eight years studying Chinese, Sanskrit, and other languages to prepare for his journey east. In 1838, Charles Pavie died in Paris after a lengthy illness during which Louis and Théodore were frequently at his bedside. In his will, he left Théodore and Victor each a small fortune ($5,000). Théodore finally headed east, spending

18. Victor Pavie to Victor Hugo, October 17, 1831, Artine Artinian collection, Humanities Research Center, University of Texas at Austin. It is certain that Sainte-Beuve had no part in helping Pavie with his publication, which, despite a request from Victor Pavie, he did not even review. His first contribution to Pavie's career came after the traveler returned from South America. Sainte-Beuve then presented him to Buloz, editor of the *Revue des deux mondes.*

19. Ironically, Humboldt had wished to go to Egypt, but Napoleon's war maneuvers there disrupted his projected journey; South America was a consolation prize to him, also.

two years in Egypt and India studying in a monastery and collecting inscriptions from monuments and stories from the people he encountered. On his return he published French translations of the Indian epic *Mahabharata*, a life of Krishna, and other scholarly translations as well as ethnographic fictions—stories of ordinary people told in richly developed cultural contexts. These stories differed from historical fiction by the social classes of the characters, and from the local color of his Romantic colleagues by their derivation from on-site observations and personal transactions with "native informants" in their languages. After teaching in the position of his renowned mentor Eugène Bournouf as professor of Sanskrit at the Collège de France for five years without receiving a permanent appointment, he resigned and returned to Angers with his wife. There he lived for forty years in his small chateau, La Chaufournaie, continuing to write and correspond with linguists throughout Europe.

How can we categorize this prolific itinerant scholar whose writing is so dispersed into a variety of seemingly unrelated fields, so that his work might be appreciated today? Perhaps we should view him as a particular type of French explorer and conqueror. Historians usually refer to the first great stage of Renaissance exploration as maritime, the second inland. During the age of maritime exploration initiated by Columbus, "Overseas France" grew into an enormous global patchwork. Then it contracted in the eighteenth century, especially in 1762–1763 when India, Canada, and Louisiana were lost with the stroke of a pen. After thus losing most of her colonial empire, France's nineteenth-century endeavors came to be characterized by two other forms of conquest: military and intellectual. As certainly as Louis-Philippe and Napoléon III dispatched troops to conquer Algeria and Mexico militarily, travelers like Humboldt, Chateaubriand, and Théodore Pavie set out to conquer the world intellectually through writing about the lands and peoples they observed and imposing their visions on the minds of their readers. The collective published knowledge, the erudition of places, forms the previously mentioned epistemological mappemonde. Through his publications, then, Théodore Pavie intellectually reclaimed for France portions of India, Canada, and Louisiana.

Certainly no one in Paris realized in 1833 that young Pavie was one of the last observers to carry a pencil and pen into a world on the verge of vanishing. Nor could the significance of events of the next few years be comprehended immediately in France. The Battle of Nacogdoches pitted a handful of English-speaking Texans against a few ragtag Mexican soldiers—many of them cavalrymen without uniforms or horses—in a standoff that lasted for a few hours on August 2, 1832, until it was settled in a white-flag conference between former friends John Durst and José de las Piedras, who withdrew rather than support Mexican general Santa Anna. Mexican soldiers then left east Texas, and Anglo militiamen replaced them. Four years later a Frenchman who survived the drownings and beheadings of the Reign of Terror would have been reluctant to call a handful of skirmishes lasting from March 2 to April 20, 1836, a "revolution." A Texas revolution? When was there a revolution? Where? When fewer than two hundred men fighting on the side of Texas independence died at the Alamo, how could any epic significance be seen by the French who lost twelve thousand soldiers at the Battle of Austerlitz in 1805, *which they won*? After three hundred years of Spanish dominion, Texans finally gained their independence in one eighteen-minute battle with a Mexican army at San Jacinto, where only two Texas soldiers were killed. It took weeks for word of Texas independence to reach France, but months more to be taken seriously because the news emanated from New Orleans—a notorious rumor mill. The report of Théodore Pavie's visit was buried in a two-volume travel account superseded by Tocqueville's analysis of American democracy and further obscured by the 1838–1839 French intervention in Mexico.

Mexican Texas was gone forever in 1836. Extinct. The future of the Native Americans the Mexican government had encouraged to come to Texas was threatened. Chief Bowles, with whom Théodore Pavie had smoked a pipe, was shamefully murdered in 1839. Even the friendly Cherokees whom Pavie had met in Nacogdoches were "removed" in 1839, the same year Santa Anna had his prisoner Piedras executed. East of the Sabine, the Caddos were ordered out of Natchitoches. In the decade following Pavie's visit, Shreve and his log picker broke up the Red River Raft, causing the water to jump its bed and leave Natchitoches stranded high and dry. The grateful citizens of the village that captured Natchitoches' economic role renamed itself in the engineer's honor: Shreveport. Natchitoches was transformed from the "sentinel of civilization," the most westerly port accessible by water from both Canada and the Gulf of Mexico, into a stopover on the overland trail for settlers bound first for Texas, which was annexed in 1845, then to Mexico to fight in the war caused by the annexation, and last, to seek gold in the newly acquired territory of California. A modern dam created the beautiful Cane River Lake where rowers now come from universities all over the United States to compete in the warm spring weather.

Thus Natchitoches and Nacogdoches turned into sleepy college towns, today bustling with weekend tourists. In Nacogdoches, the Old Stone House built by Antonio Gil y Barbo, where Théodore and Charles Pavie stayed with John Durst in 1830, has been rebuilt. Relocated to the campus of Stephen F. Austin University, it is called the Stone Fort Museum. East of the Sabine, in Natchitoches, Louisiana, the campus of Northwestern State University occupies the Rouquier land, some of which passed through the estate of Eliza Bludworth, Théodore's bittersweet first love. A local historian told me that the Red River probably carried off Charles and Marianne Pavie's plantation house with its galleries, Théodore's cottage, and the slave shacks.[20] What remains is *Souvenirs atlantiques,* which he introduces as *"incoherent pages, the disorder of a melancholy and suffering mind which I deliver to you regretfully for I sense what is incomplete in this work, first for its absence of interest, by the insufficiency of things, the palpable inexperience of this fragmented style, and especially because I find nothing in reading it of what I felt so strongly in the forests; and then I had to silence what is directed at no one and has charms for me alone . . . I did my best."* The journeys of the writers of Théodore Pavie's generation were considered to be works of art in themselves, as sincerely conceived and as deftly composed as their journals. Undoubtedly Pavie's greatest creation was his emotional discovery of the Mississippi River and his youthful trek west alongside the Red River alone and down the Camino Real with his uncle to the distant Mexican outpost of Nacogdoches with a pencil and pen in his saddlebag.

20. Bobby DeBlieux, who is a descendant of Charles Pavie's close friend Alexander de Blieux.

1. Théodore Pavie. Oil portrait on canvas from about 1830, by his friend
Alfred Ménard.

2–3. Joseph Pavie, founder of the Pavie printing dynasty, and his wife, Marie-Jeanne. He was a licensed publisher and *cartier* of La Rochelle before the French Revolution.

4–5. Louis-Victor Pavie, fifteenth child of Joseph and Marie-Jeanne, and his
wife, Marie-Marguerite Fabre Pavie ("Bonnemaman"), who was licensed to
publish in Angers as Veuve (Widow) Pavie. She originally worked as his assis-
tant and was imprisoned during the Revolution when the press was destroyed.
He died soon after the Revolution, but she carried on to rebuild the press.
*Left portrait courtesy private collection of the descendants of Françoise de
Sainte-Lorette; right portrait courtesy Chasle Pavie Collection. Photographs by
Betje Klier and Yves Pavie.*

6–7. Louis Pavie joined his widowed mother at the Pavie Press during the Restoration. His wife, Monique Fabre Pavie (right), died at age twenty-one, when Théodore was two and his brother Victor was five. Théodore worked at the family press from the ages of fifteen to seventeen.

8. Manette Dubois ("La Chouanne"), in Vendean peasant costume, which connoted fidelity to the Catholic church during the Revolution. She assisted the widow Marie-Marguerite Fabre Pavie in rebuilding the press and in raising her son and grandsons. Manette's stories strongly influenced Theodore's imagination and storytelling style.

9. Dufour's panorama *Sauvages de la mer Pacifique*, popularly known as the "Captain Cook wallpaper," depicts the voyages of both Cook and his French counterpart, La Pérouse. "Feasting his eyes upon" these scenes stimulated Pavie's imagination as a child and fed his desire for adventure at sea.

Photograph by the author

Seven Drawings from the Sketchbook Théodore Pavie Took on
His Journey to the Sabine Borderlands

10. Descending the Mississippi River in the wake of Chateaubriand, Pavie
observed nature with an almost religious fervor.

11. When Pavie was sent ashore to get supplies, he discovered several destitute orphans whose plight made him appreciate his own good fortune.

12. Charles Pavie and his brother-in-law took Théodore camping in the former Neutral Strip. He appreciated the abundant game, savored the squirrel gumbo, and was thrilled by the hurricane that struck the camp in the middle of the night.

13. Lac de la Terre Noire, one of Pavie's favorite sites for communing with nature, is called Sibley Lake today. Note the nearly invisible alligator in the foreground.

14. A lake in Texas. When he crossed the Sabine River, Pavie exclaimed, "Texas is a whole other country!"

15. Pavie titled this exquisite sketch "Choctaws on the Washita," and it is probably his most historically significant drawing. Most of the Native Americans whose paths he crossed were forced to join the Trail of Tears migration to the Indian Territory within a decade.

16. "Lower Louisiana," Pavie titled this scene of roseate spoonbills in a southern Louisiana cypress grove. Unlike John James Audubon, who spent his youth in the same region of western France as did Pavie and minimized the flora to focus on the fauna, Pavie considered the landscape sublime—the touch of God's finger on earth.

17. Poet Victor Pavie, Théodore's brother

18. The closing scene from Victor Hugo's play *Hernani*, the famous "battle" which signaled a cultural watershed—the triumph of Romanticism over classicism in the French theater. Victor Pavie attended, led a claque supporting his friend Hugo, and described the event in a letter to his father.

From the author's collection

PART II

EXCERPTS FROM *SOUVENIRS ATLANTIQUES*

SOLITUDE

Louisville was disappearing. With it the noise of civilization faded, the falls of the Ohio tucked themselves away behind the island willows, and the sound of axes chopping the flanks of the trees dully beat out its monotonous measure amidst the cries of the sailors. Little by little, all of this blended into a distant murmur carried in waves on the evening breeze. Another lost sound echoed back—the chance shooting of a carbine, a wheel of a passing boat, one more sigh from this huge body—then silence, darkness, solitude.

It was completely dark. We were no longer moving: two cables tied to some roots held us to land, and the rope of the anchor cast into the deepest part of the river vibrated in the current. On board, everything was at rest. Passengers who had not arrived in time to choose their berths slept on mattresses on a long table, stretching the length of the lamplit sleeping room. Behind the curtains of the cabins other travelers were snoring, sleeping draped over their trunks. At the least movement in the draperies, the darkness deepened in the undulations of the silk, then a pale glimmer wandered across all these furrowed brows, wrinkled variously from age or sorrow, modified by a smile of memory or hope. In the rear of the boat was the women's cabin, a solitary retreat [where] a Negress swung her baby in a hammock suspended from the ceiling, and hummed an African song in a hushed voice. On the lower deck, slaves slept among the horses' hooves, sharing their litter of straw and moss, while the coal stokers, their skin darkened by smoke, recuperated from their heavy work in the coal bin, the oat sacks, or the planks of the bridge. The boat, anchored to an old tree and shaded by its boughs, was bathed in darkness, like a black spot amid the silvery waves of the moon's first rays.

I was alone on the ground, alone in a new country, at least in harmony with all that surrounded me. I could pick the flowers that hung down on my brow, write a name on the bark of this plane tree, dive into these transparent waters, let my feet and my thoughts wander from bush to bush, without encountering a person with a patch on his arm who could seize me like a criminal, crying out, "Stop in the name of the law!" I was alone with my memories, admiring the earth and the heavens, gathering inside myself those sounds exhaled in gentle harmony by the night, without an armed guard who could ask me by what right, vagabond and wandering, I contemplated the stars. I was alone in the middle of my domains; these woods, this river, these hills and their innumerable inhabitants, these evening voices that moved and breathed like everything in the world, it all belonged to me. That which does not belong to anyone in particular, belongs to everyone.

Then I began to dream of Europe. It is strange for someone who was born in the cities, has spent his life in the cities, and should someday die in the cities, to feel once, at least in passing, that he is master in the middle of the world, independent, owing no accounting of his actions to anyone besides the One who also sees our thoughts. For these men have called this country Indiana, and the other land washed by the same river, Tennessee. They have applied names to the wilderness, they have said "This belongs to us, North Americans," but their footprints have not been imprinted there yet; when I staked a claim on their shade, the forests did not ask me "Are you a citizen of the twenty-six republics?" The birds sang for me, the waves bathed my feet, quenched my thirst; the moon shone on my forehead: nonetheless I was a foreigner, a European come from far away across the seas, from a country where each thing has a master who exploits it and keeps for himself everything he has paid for with gold! Here, at least, I breathed freely without owing to anyone for the moss that I trampled nor for the root on which I rested my weary head.

Of course, I also have a fatherland of which I am proud when I sit face to face with those who extol the country where they were born. I have shed some tears, and I have even more to shed for those who shared the care of my childhood and who were frightened by my adventurous excursion. But when one is in a wilderness, it is as if one were on the Ocean: all of that is erased. The world in which one lives is just one family, the earth, the public sphere in which every man has his share. Then distinctions disappear, the universe is an idea, and how could the soul not embrace the idea in a single flash—it is so infinite!

Thus it was that thinking of Europe, and in the wave of my ideas, I wandered like the smoke of a fire that dies down near a bivouac. I thought I saw in the distance a luminous point obscured by thousands of insects swarming in perpetual oscillation, searching for happiness, they said, but off track, haphazardly following false or deceitful systems, hurtling against one another, swarming and vying with one another, emitting here and there boisterous exclamations in bitter and lugubrious voices that almost immediately blended into the cries of the populace. Glimmers of an angelic brightness crossed this space, but they were more swift than lightning, and the howling of this eternal tempest began again more frighteningly. From incessantly shifting waves rose up glittering glories cast by the storm, like a vessel that fights and triumphs. Then came the fatal, rapid shipwreck and the debris floating on the surface for a long time, from generation to generation, from centuries to centuries, sad recompense for the noble ship which had already sounded the depths of eternity. [See note 5 on page 133 below.]

So many people were looking for the truth, but were not really searching for it; they fabricated it at their will, decked it out as they would, silenced it, or whitewashed it according to their fantasy, whereas a wise and prophetic voice said, "Let it speak in the bottom of your souls; listen, philosophers, and be silent." The angels trembled and the gaping earth swallowed them up, vomiting their debris, which was then hastily reconstructed by a foolhardy or guilty hand that failed to notice that this ephemeral temple, with its foundation of moving sand and its people with their thousand heads, was still trembling and cracking on all sides.

Then I realized that I was taking my turn philosophizing in the clouds! And, I too, was an ambitious child driven there by the rage to see, in search of new things, disdainful of my part in the world. I could no longer naïvely enjoy the great spectacles of creation like an Indian who has an instinct for it. True, I saw them from a higher plane, but no, civilized man carries his pride inside himself, and cursed be the one who wishes to stand up in the middle of the forest and lay blame for the eternal agitations of the great societies. Let us therefore leave everything in its place; everything that is done with the permission of God is good.

What good does it actually do to allow oneself to experience such sudden recriminations or these hatreds for what one has loved and what still loves us, to become infatuated at every moment with some novelty of which one tires very soon? Listen, you who travel young—a thousand things will strike you that you will embrace ardently. Good-bye, Fatherland and friends! All that is nothing, everything is forgotten. Alas! One day later and you will cry for this fatherland, you will grow thirsty for this friendship, you will not change your nature, children! You are born in our cities, you have tasted the joys, too rare but profoundly felt, of social life. These things you have disdained will come to you in a dream and murmur in you a bitter complaint. Entire races marching to glory feel this *homesickness* so terrible, even in the words of the impetuous Byron. This remorse will eat at you. Then let us admire at leisure, let us love with appreciation these good and hospitable far-off lands that have welcomed us, these waves that have rocked us, these streams that have murmured their mystical sounds in our ears; let us nurture our memories, perhaps attach something even sweeter to them! But let us keep inside ourselves these thoughts that would undoubtedly wound other hearts; let us live on unknown remembrances, unknown to everyone, that we will cherish and search out in our reveries like an intimate friend. May an infinite charity admit all that presents itself at our feet wandering from one pole to the other, and if we compare ourselves to those who do not feel these things, may this just be to pity them and to wish them happier days.

One more idea: was it not in these same places, under these same trees, under the rays of the same melancholic star, that Chactas recounted to René the misfortunes and joys of his youth, and spread like a tardy balm consoling advice onto the soul of the exiled man? Undoubtedly America never nurtured at its breast a man like the blind Sachem, patriarch of days of old, and the heavens never gathered together in a single heart as many pains as René devoured. But let what should be the magnificence of a solitude that inspired such thoughts in the author of *Atala* be judged and see how noble the impressionable and melancholic mind must be to cause to spring forth such pure and generous creatures in the middle of the wilderness.

The Shawnees

Let's leave the Ohio River, flowing swiftly through the middle of its verdant islands, so powerful in picturesque effects, and penetrate into Indiana for an instant. There we will find an opaque shadow in the evening at sunset and limpid streams with yellow and white water lilies and bro- ken rushes, the natural landscape more guessed at than understood by Newton Fielding and poeticized in France by Paul Huet.[1]

We were coming back from Vincennes, descending the Wabash—a strange juxtaposition of two names that one would believe to be very for- eign to each other. The French who founded this village in the middle of the wilderness of Indiana brought along with them memories of France, of Paris; and the Shawnee savage never suspected in the least, while pointing out to us the smoke from the roofs of Vincennes, just how much this word pronounced with the guttural accent of an Indian would cause us to recall.

Two canoes formed the entire fleet. This is another delicious way to travel that is unknown in Europe: to row this way for eight hours, a month, to camp in the evenings, light a fire which shines in the thick darkness like a torch and around which gather hungry vultures that fight over the scraps from our hunt, to sleep without fear, care, or worries on a bearskin, head on the trunk of a tree that stretches across the camp and serves as a common pillow and, when it rains, to gather under the tent, plunge into the ground a burning pine branch which furnishes light, and there, well hidden, smoke cigars with our arms crossed, waiting for the return of the sunshine while the rain runs in torrents around the stakes and floods the countryside. Could there be a sweeter life, more pictur- esque, more adventurous, more exempt from political troubles, in a word, freer? Many times in the most brilliant capitals, under the golden domes of palaces, in the middle of noisy joys of an entire people, I have missed my bearskin, the hard earth where I slept in peace, the tent that sheltered me from the storm, and my rifle. Moreover, were there not mag- nificent scenes that had only us as spectators? Falling stars in an autumn

---

1. Newton Fielding (1797–1856) was a British landscape artist who lived and worked in Paris; Pavie probably met him during Pavie's visit to the capital in 1828. According to Patrick Noon in *Richard Parkes Bonington—On the Pleasure of Painting* (New Haven: Yale University Press, 1991), Delacroix painted Fielding's portrait in 1823 (p. 280). Through Victor Hugo, Victor Pavie befriended both Delacroix and Paul Huet (1803– 1869), another leading avant-garde Romantic artist. The influence of Huet's early litho- graphic style is clearly visible in Théodore Pavie's sketches of Louisiana and Texas. This generation commonly paid tribute to one another by cross-referencing their friends' accom- plishments in their writings just as the artists "quoted" each others' representations.

evening, heavenly bodies rotating silently in their celestial sphere, the moon, itself a world, dominates its own vast empire in its turn. What more could one want than this immense harmony of a world fulfilling its destiny?

It was night when we stopped to hunt a flock of turkeys that were walking in a close file on the banks of the Wabash. When we were all gathered in the camp, we cleaned the game. Then each one gave in to his sleepiness, except some Indians who accompanied us as rowers,[2] who gathered together around the fire according to their custom, turned their wraps down over their shoulders, and all arranged in a circle, smoked their hatchet of peace,[3] passing it to each other one by one. When the last puff was gone from the common pipe, they spoke in low voices with expressive and animated gestures. The oldest soon imposed silence on the others, and here is what he said:

"When the chief lets out a war cry each warrior should march, his bow should not stop until every one of his arrows is red with the blood of the enemy or upon returning to his tribe or it will be said on pointing him out to the children: 'Look at the woman.' We would snatch his arms away from him, his hair would be shaved, and the coward would be chased from his village. But when the two nations have sworn peace and friendship, when the two chiefs have drunk from the same gourd and smoked the same peace hatchet, let them be united like the dangling vine and the oak. May misfortune then come to him who forgets his oath! The Great Spirit will turn his arrow against him on the day of combat even if he burns in his honor the tuft that grows between the horns of a buffalo, the tongue of the squirrel, or the first cob of corn grown by his wife at the door to his hut. It would be better for him had he never been born, or that he had died when he slept among the leaves of the lantana tree, suspended from the *téchis* in bloom, or that his mother had sent him to

2. This section of the journal echoes a letter home up to this point when Charles Pavie's slaves are transformed into Indians for the purpose of telling this story, which is corroborated in the letters of John Sibley.

3. Théodore Pavie purchased at least two hatchets during his journey to America. One is a peace pipe, a metal trefoil or club-shaped tomahawk tip hatchet attached to a wood handle approximately twenty inches long. Opposite the chopping edge is a circular pipe bowl for smoking.

the regions above by unleashing toward the heavens the branch where his cradle was suspended."

The Indians inclined their heads in a sign of approval. They gathered their half-consumed logs together and the flame, leaping up in the middle of the circle of men with red skin, lighted their severe features, etched with all the impassivity of an Indian.

"You know," the one who had been talking started over, "that a truce has been concluded between the Miamis who live on the banks of the Ohio and extend toward the source of the Father of Rivers, and the Shawnees, descended from the high hills where the Wabash has its source, meandering from the Rocky Mountains to the Red River, and to the prairies where our common enemy—the Comanches—roam. A solemn peace was made, the smoke of two villages and the evening chant around the cabins mixed like the flame of two fires, like the water of the Wabash and the Ohio, before getting lost together in the Meschacébé [Mississippi], then in the great lake of salty water. It was strange to see the warriors of two nations mingling together in the forest, hunting the same buffalo, sharing the remains of the enemy. But that truce could not endure longer than the overflowing of a river; all that was finished in a single moon. From the frozen lakes of the west to the lakes of the alligators, who could ever find the tiger and the wolf together pursuing the same doe, the eagle and the vulture united together against a turtle? So one day when they were reunited among the habitations of the Whites they drank firewater, their reason went up in smoke, they tottered like children, and then they happened to remember their old hatred. 'Oh!' cried a Shawnee raising his arm up over the other warriors; 'There was a time when the proud Miamis fled in front of my tribe faster than the buck in front of the jackal. Never did we see the *totem* that covers their chests and never did our arrows reach the backs of the cowards. Never was there a truce then, and their villages disappeared under our feet like the grass of the prairie under the passing fire. Today we must share everything with them: hunting, furs, herds of buffalo, even the scalps of the enemy. We see them raise their shaved foreheads to the height of the Shawnee who puts on his two ears the plume of the eagle and in his nose the tooth of the alligator, emblems of his tribe. Go now, dog, go away! The Great Spirit crushes you underfoot!' Shaking his tomahawk, he struck the forehead of the young

Miami warrior. Mortally wounded, the warrior let out a cry and reached for his knife, but soon, bathed in his own blood, he expired.

"It happened on a holiday for the Whites. The wife of the dead warrior, beating herself in the face, untied the strings that bound her hair, snatched out the ornaments dangling from her ears, turned, and howling like a wildcat at the tip of a cypress, disappeared. Those of her tribe retired, murmuring. They polished their arms, but a captain of the Whites came and said, 'Prison!' and they dispersed, for you know that the Whites want to punish the actions of the free Indians like those of the people of their own color.

"The wife of the dead man walked and walked and kept on walking. Those who encountered her watched her pass in the same manner as the shadow of a warrior killed in combat, without turning her head: her gaze fixed, her breath seeming to dry the grasses of the forest and the flowers of the dangling vines. It was death, crossing the earth from the east to the west.

"Thus she went as far as the habitation of a White whom she had known. They were all gathered together in prayer when she threw herself, disheveled, into the midst of these men on their knees with their frightened wives, and everyone remained stupefied, the color of the snow of the highlands. The widow of the warrior raised her bleeding arms and cried out: 'Vengeance!' Then, wresting the cover from her shoulder, she presented them her newborn son, who could not yet hold himself up on his own feet, and the women wept.

"The planters had understood. They ran to the village and arrested the murderer and the Indian woman seemed satisfied. She looked the Shawnee in the face with the eyes that hungered for his skin, shook the hand of the chief of the Whites, and disappeared. Those who travel in the summer near the mountains of Missouri swear they have seen her with her child and that in the night a voice can be heard moaning in the rocks—

"Well, Warriors, what do you believe was done to the guilty man?" The savages raised up their coats of fur, pushed aside the hair that fell over their ears, and returning to immobility, seemed to double their attention. Everything was silent around them. Far away in the forest the cry of a jaguar seemed to mark the minutes of the night. From the place I occupied unobserved in an obscure corner of the tent, I could distinguish the gravest gestures of the Indian and his tattooed companions, as stiff as the mummies of Egypt.

"For a whole moon, they left him in a narrow cabin with iron bars through which he poked his head, looking from there at the forests and the smoke of our huts scattered across the plain in the distance. He roared, striking his forehead against the stones of the wall and crying out for a carbine to pierce his skull, a knife to open up a path for his spirit toward the land above; to hear him wail, one would have taken him for a bear caught in a trap. The warrior had become skinny and frail like a reed, his legs folded under him. Finally the chiefs of the Whites assembled, the chiefs of the Shawnees came also, and they judged him.

"I told you that he had been there between iron bars for a month without arms with which to take his own life. This had been his punishment, more horrible than the iron box, the arrows with iron tips, or even burned wounds, reopened and burned more. After a long powwow of eight suns, the captain of the Whites made a sign to him that it was all over, and the guilty one saw the doors open suddenly. He awaited the death blow, intoned his war cry, but everyone had retired. They said there was no need for punishment because he had lost his spirit, and so the prisoner found himself alone, free in the middle of the village where the children pointed their fingers at him, saying 'Warrior, go back to your tribe!'

"Go back to his tribe," all the other Indians who had listened in the most profound silence said together, and "Who among us would have received him in our hut? One says to the stranger 'you are welcome,' to the enemy 'our hatchets are ready and demand blood,' but to a murderer 'go, I do not know you at all,' and the chief has him tied to a post like a captive."

"He did not return there, my Brothers," continued the Indian in a solemn tone. "Two days he wandered among the habitations without seeing a red face, for they were ashamed of him. The Blacks worked around the sugarcane, whistled, sang, and laughed, staring at him; the masters of the slaves said, 'There's the Shawnee,' and he did not reply. His wife had closed the door of her hut on herself, the weapons of the warrior were suspended from the branches of the pecan tree beneath which he was accustomed to sleeping, and at night his dog barked, muzzle pressed on the earth or raised toward the sky, but nothing responded to his lamentations, and he was killed by a wolf. 'Go back to your wigwam,' the children always taunted while playing around him, and the Indian, leaning on a stick like a little girl who is following the steed of her brother on foot, looked at them without seeing them. Poor son of the tribe of the Shawnees, he begged for a bullet, and everywhere he passed the doors of the huts closed, the women hid their faces in their hands.

"Although he was a warrior, prison had made him like a child; he laughed and cried, and tottered down the paths; one would have said that his body stayed on the earth while his soul was in the clouds. One night, without thinking about it, he walked toward his old dwelling. The moon shone on his pointed roof, and a bit of smoke chanced to escape from it. His weapons swinging from the branch of the pecan tree cast their shadow across the brambles, the thorns, the papaya flowers. Then he woke up from this painful dream, and seizing his bow and the longest arrow from his quiver, he examined them lovingly. The rays of the moon reflected on his weapons and he smiled; his bow stretched, he tried it out, the cord resonated as on a day of battle. Oh! how he jumped, roaring with joy! He knocked with his foot at the door of his hut, and threw himself armed in front of his companion. She wanted to recoil in horror, but he shook his bow with one hand and his arrows with the other, he opened his arms, and the wife of the prisoner fell into his arms, crying. Soon she stood back proudly and awaited his orders.

"The eyes of the Shawnee sparkled as in the moment of victory. He returned his shiny weapons to his wife and walked out. Immobile in the middle of her hut, she rested her head in her hands, and her children came to play, to jump on her shoulders as they were accustomed to doing. Already the youngest had managed to lodge himself in the corner of the pouch that was intended for him when his mother carried him on a trip, and had gone to sleep, while the other was testing the bow, which he could hardly lift, and the heavy arrow which was higher than his head.

"Suddenly his mother cast him down and rushed out of the cabin. The Indian made a gesture, standing on the edge of a pit that he had dug in the sand, and pointed to his heart. An arrow from the hand of his wife vibrated in the chest of the warrior—a sigh terminated his death chant, and he rolled gloriously into the tomb.

"The hunters report having seen his widow throw a little earth over the body of her spouse, and as was the custom, bury his weapons with him. Then, loading her young baby on her shoulders, she took the other by the hand and walked straight north."

The Indians added a few words to this narrative and fell asleep around the flames.

At the first ray of the sun, they were ready to leave. With the tents folded and the baggage loaded in the canoes, the flotilla set off. Some hours later the one who had told the story of the death of the Shawnee pointed out to his companions a clearing on the left bank of the Wabash. We allowed them to go ashore according to their desires and I saw them disembark in silence on a bare plot, cleared of these dangling vines which are so prompt to usurp the land abandoned by the hand of man. In the clearing there stood a pyramidal hut, strung with enormous gourds, still green, and covered with jasmine, with a swarm of hummingbirds buzzing in its flowers. On the end of a branch of a pecan tree was suspended an embroidered belt. In the back of the enclosure, the Indian stopped at a plot of freshly worked dirt and said, "It is here, my Brothers."

Then they came away in the same silence.

Much later I met the son of the Shawnee warrior in the village. The story of his father aroused my interest in him, and I exchanged a filled powder horn for some arrows of reed, decorated with feathers of ducks and parrots, that still remind me of the tragic story of the Shawnee.

The Illinois River

Undoubtedly, it may seem monotonous to navigate a long time on a river, especially when the forests, sometimes tall and majestic, sometimes painfully entangled in the cracks in the rocks, restrict your view in every direction. But a traveler is no longer the same man once his steps are engaged in the great career opened in front of him. The powerful cities, magnificent in their monuments and memories, are of little importance to him; he stores all of that in the depths of his soul. When he finds himself, as we do at this moment, carried along by the rivers' currents through a succession of new, little-known regions distinguished only by names as strange as this nature, then he abandons himself to his thoughts, plunges with love into an imposing wilderness, and like the eagle above the clouds, sees provinces and empires pass around him. He dreams, remembers, hopes, contemplates; he is happy, for isn't happiness that exemption from all care: repose?

The water was very low, and at the juncture of the Tennessee River, we encountered the *Caledonian*, an enormous boat from Cincinnati, run aground on a sandbank for several weeks. At least a hundred passengers and sailors had to be fed, and with the Ohio River growing shallower by the day, the hope remained for winter floods; still they could not arrive until many months later. As for me, I would have lost my patience in a similar predicament, but Americans know how to resign themselves, and there they were, spread out on the galleries, smoking and reading. Perhaps some among them were grumbling deep down inside themselves, but once again, what good does it do to spit fire and flames when you feel the keel of a boat sink three feet into the strand? We too had been threatened by a similar misfortune. All those who have descended the Ohio River know, among the hundred islands washed by this delightful river, the one that carries the name of Flint Island. The strand that divides the flow of the river makes the passage very narrow, and it is there that the most arrogant pilot is obliged to have recourse to sounding and bringing all of his talents to bear. The day was slipping away, and already the moon had raised its silvery crest above the hills of the Illinois. A deer swam peacefully across the limpid and solitary waves. We saw him get out onto land on the opposite bank, rest an instant, shake off his antlers glistening with drops of water, and disappear, frolicking through the grasses. However, the moment of crisis was coming for us; the two pilots were out on the sand bar and from each side, a sailor threw in the sounding plumb, repeating in a clear and sonorous voice: "six feet, six feet, five feet and a half." On board everything was silent, only the boat raised its voice, frothing up foam with its wheels. "Five feet," the sailor in the front suddenly cried out and he suspended his plumb feeling the keel touch. Five feet of water did not leave us anything below the hull, and we smashed with so much force that the strand opened up, and the *Trenton* navigated gloriously into the open river. A collective cry came from every mouth, and we rejoiced through the night by the light of the full moon. The ration of *grog* was doubled for the crew and the Blacks resounded their joy with African roars that resembled delirium.

Then we fell asleep; the captain and the sailors forgot their duty, the drowsy pilot allowed the wheel to turn as it would. At least, that is the way the security of our people must have gone for the rest of the night because at daybreak every one awoke surprised not to hear the hum of our wheels. Alas! We were in the greatest calm possible, taking our turn to be grounded, twisted by the current so we could see no possible way to set ourselves free. Toward the east the breadth of the river sparkled with morning colors, and in the distance, across the shoals, rafts resounded from time to time with the noise of an oar in the deep water. Everywhere there were forests, and in them, the same silence. Still, sleeping vultures mottled the maples, their bodies resembling those shreds of cloth that we hang from the trees of a vegetable garden to frighten away the birds. Eagles began hunting, pigeons left for faraway emigrations, but

> . . . on the horizon
> Nary a house,
> None.

The surprised passengers rubbed their eyes. The oldest said that we were being punished by the heavens for having kept on going day and night on Sunday. Others lamented, blaming the captain or the pilot, but no one thought of coming up with a way to get back afloat. Thirty of the most impatient jumped into the dinghy, dragging two sailors along with them to pull them ashore. In spite of all our reprimands, they abandoned us and fanned out joyfully into the forest, resolved to go hunting without a guide to show them the way. Nonetheless, it was necessary to worry about getting ourselves out of such a bad spot! Two anchors were cast in back, *espars* fixed to the front. They started the machine running at the risk of lurching, and everyone helped pull the mooring ropes over the capstan. All efforts were useless because the sand swirled up with the eddies, stopped the oars, and continued to resist. As for our hunters, half of them were sitting on the bank watching what we did, the others were firing their guns intermittently. Finally, a mere twelve hours later, we felt the movement of the keel plowing through the strand, then floating. The boat lunged with unbelievable force, gliding like a skate across ice, passing a cable's length from the bank. You should have seen the deserters yelling to us then, running to follow us, waving their handkerchiefs and begging us with the voice of the cruelest desperation. Incensed, the captain would have gladly abandoned them, but someone threw out an anchor. We enjoyed the satisfaction of their distress for a long time, hearing them shoot their carbines to make signals, hailing us with frightened voices hoarse from fatigue. When they were on board, we asked to share their bounty. They had killed one pigeon!

Illinois extended to our right; it is a very long, narrow state, wedged between Indiana and Missouri, extending up to Lake Michigan. The villages are insignificant: Vandalia, Kaskaskia, and other strange names that perhaps have not yet reached our European ears. Its southern extremity must be very cold owing to the effects of the icy waters of the lakes further north. The Illinois River, which gives its name to the state, has its source near the country of the Pottawatomies, crosses the villages of the Kickapoos, and flows into the Missouri above St. Charles.

On the left bank we still had Kentucky, developed on the side of the river like a leaf of a palm, cut in two. The Ohio River continued to widen; the hills of the riverbank were high and forested, ruffled with wild valleys from which springs bubbled up here and there. Eaten back continuously by the current, the islands are smaller, rising out of the waves ever more gently, ever more rounded to the eye, and allow one to see further ahead over this vast sheet of golden water. Huge boats that cannot navigate the Ohio in the summer stop at the Trinity, a sizable hotel on the Missouri side. It was there we first saw the pecan trees, palmettos, and monstrous dangling vines peculiar to the American South, and the parrots and the flocks of sparkling birds which deserve special mention. Let us stop, between two cane hedges, under the shady domes of the plane trees, and cast a glance across the *Meschacebé* [Mississippi].

THE MISSISSIPPI

Unfortunate the European who, deserting the populous cities of our old countries, should come looking for a retreat deep in the wilderness that he had never known. Cast far away from society into the middle of the wilderness, seeing nothing but impenetrable forests, wandering from river to river among ferocious beasts whose howling troubles his sleep, he would turn his yearning glance toward the east and throw himself with ardor into the company of men, a sight necessary to him. Solitude is bad for one who finds himself alone with his misanthropy. But when filled with dreams, his soul free from all distressing thoughts, the young traveler finds deserted places where the savage harmony fills him with thoughts gently imprinted with the blue tint of melancholy, hope, or memories of youth and homeland; when held back for a long time as if suffering from a capricious folly he is finally cast where his passion has carried him, across seas, peoples, new regions, to find at last things according to his heart—Ah! It is then that he should declare himself happy, that he should abandon himself to the pure and generous pleasures that flood him. This happiness I experienced at the sight of the Father of Rivers.

At this old name of the Mississippi, I felt arise inside me all those fantastic expectations that childhood loves to nurture and that reality makes disappear like a dream. When I perceived on the horizon this yellowish line of gigantic trees, I saw these last illusions flee together in a crowd, chased by the tangible objects that struck my sight: as the prow of the boat threw a vigorous wake, a cry came forth from the midst of the crew—the sailors celebrating the entrance into the Mississippi River in their own way. As for me, I was strangely moved, I wanted to gather my thoughts and give them form, but it was impossible for me to seize them as they rushed by, they fluttered around inside my head and intoxicated me like the fumes of a punch. I felt so much joy inside me for all of you, companions of my childhood who shared my pleasures and, not less often, my sadness. All of you who loved me, whose concerned eyes followed me across my far-flung voyages, and who already bemoaned a second departure, I thought of you. You were there at my side and the great voice of the Mississippi spoke to you from a forest abyss.

Then I turned to say a last farewell to the Beautiful River that I reproached myself for forgetting so quickly. It flowed slowly, lined with its constant maples and poplars, its banks crowned with a hedge of slender canes, its plaintive murmur carried to my feet. Suddenly the Mississippi's somber and powerful waters rolled majestically forward, spiked with tree trunks snatched from its banks. At the very spot where a last trace of froth marks the separation of the two rivers, three pelicans, necks extended, standing on the cadaver of a floating catalpa, marked the last sigh of the Ohio. Good-bye then, gentle river of pleasant views, with islands of tender growth, transparent and golden waters which remind me of the Loire and its banks so dear to my childhood, lovely, limpid waves where the deer admires its elegant antlers, its fine bright head, and its sleek legs. Farewell, majestic river, only the *Meschacebé* is worthy of receiving your waters in tribute.

On our right we had Missouri, which already had two cities, St. Louis and Ste. Geneviève, and which extends to the west and joins the territory of the same name, a true prairie shared by the Sioux, the Osages, and herds of buffalo. Further down the river, on the left bank, begins Tennessee—a fertile province in its southern part, neighbor to the two Carolinas, Georgia, and the state of Mississippi. Nashville, the capital, is already powerful; the cotton and tobacco crops make it attractive for commerce, and the Alleghenies, rising in the eastern Floridas and terminating on the banks of the Hudson, cross Tennessee, where their picturesque summits lend variety to the otherwise uniform landscape. Here on the edge of the river there is nothing but forests and swamps; from here to the cultivated lands of Louisiana, we have only insignificant villages: *New Madrid*, Missouri; *Memphis*, on the right bank, *Little Gulf* (Petit Gulph) and further down, on the only hills that dare rise above the floods of the Mississippi, *Natchez*.

Having arrived at the loveliest half of my voyage, surrounded by these places of which I have dreamed so many times, of these images of fantasy and reality at the same time, I pause and words escape me. Chateaubriand passed here with his genius and his words of fire. Each day travelers see these same places without understanding them and find nothing here to ponder, but you must go there anyway. I will try to gather up all the scattered memories whose waves float so deliciously for the one who loves to remember his sensations, and I will tell you about the Mississippi as it presented itself to my delighted eyes: immense, infinite like a sea where the eye sees only waves, like a mountain that limits the horizon and seeks the clouds, like the vault of the heavens everywhere presented to the sight of onlookers, like an atmosphere spilled over this world that it modifies in its own way, like a great idea that governs the universe, finally great like a great God who is great simply because He is. After nine hundred leagues of an impetuous course, impeded at each ebb by enormous trees that it drags along its banks, the Mississippi receives the abundant waters of the Ohio, itself enlarged by a hundred impetuous rivers and streams, and when its turn comes pays the tributes of its waves to the Gulf of Mexico, three hundred and fifty miles downstream. Thus its source is in the frozen mountains at the North Pole, far away in the wilderness. It flows through the uncultivated and unexplored land of the west—the prairies of Missouri, the savannas of Arkansas—waters the sugarcane and cotton plants, orange groves and lilas [chinaberry trees][4] of fertile and sparkling Louisiana, then, impetuous and irresistible in the strength of its flow, it empties itself into the boiling waves that burn the tropics, still keeping its current for twelve more miles even into the middle of the sea, the image of those profound genies that traverse the world and whose glory floats for a long time on the ocean of the ages. Each springtime it extends beyond its limits, breaks its dikes of forests, floods the plains that surround it, and uproots with its powerful hand the giant trees which its beneficial influence has caused to spring up from the earth. The displaced trees crash against each other on their course, assemble and lash themselves together with vines and flowers to form those floating islands on which peaceful voyagers travel: green, gray, and blue herons of all shades and all sizes from the smallest, dark like a cormorant, up to the one whose tufted head reaches higher than the grasses along the shore. One sees them marching along with great strides on those natural rafts or sleeping on one foot with their heads under their wings only to waken with a start when two such *rafts* collide, then they stop parading, surprised to see the islands, forests, and shoals passing by and turning in front of them.

Trees snatched up with their roots often anchor themselves in the mud and continue to protrude threateningly above the waters. The current fights in vain to free them; they jiggle their hoary heads endlessly to counter its efforts, etching their frothy furrow on the tranquil waves. Anyone who saw them from a distance would take these columns from a ruined temple for bears looking for pasture in another region. So true it is that the sickle of time requires a victim, that when places are found where man has not yet raised up those palaces of a day with which he litters the dust, he changes the face of the land and renews the forests like human generations.

---

4. *Melia azedarach* is the modern scientific name for what we call the chinaberry tree or lilas, not to be confused with lilacs, which do not grow in Louisiana.

One notices two very distinct characters on the Mississippi: the islands and the principal shore that one may call the mainland. The islands
are just shoals of a fine compact sand cemented together by the silt left
from the overflow, on which trees have rooted. They have generally taken
on a diamond shape; the interior only is covered with grass, while all
around it the yellow and sparkling shoal extends like a dried river bed.
This thick border of forests along the sands stands out admirably in the
sun; it is a diamond set in a ring of gold. The trees become taller and taller
as you reach the depths of the forest. First come some grasses, green and
close together, that snake around the thickets like a long hedge, then the
trembling willows that bend over into a cradle that protects the young
saplings; behind the willows, the oldest trees lift radiant, bushy heads behind which rise the dark masses of the tallest plane trees, among which
the eye can discern only thick darkness, an image of solitude and repose.
In the heat of the summer, deer like to sleep in the bosom of these peaceful islands of evergreen thickets. Bears rest there in their turn, but emigrate in the springtime to the mountains where they find acorns and corn.
Bands of bear, so numerous that they stop the current, extend from the
edge of the shoals like a moving bridge, then one by one each leaves the
water and plunges, roaring, under the cool shelter of the forests until
hunger chases them out again, leading them this time into the hollow of
a cypress to spend the winter in a lethargic sleep. Under a sky as blue as
the tropical sea, the eagles and the vultures swoop down at their pleasure,
nonchalantly descending from elevated regions where a breeze unknown
to the earth inundates them with cool air. Opaque shadows repeat their
aerial maneuvers on the shoals, and in the evenings the image of their
heavy wings grows proportionately larger as they descend, the noise of
their flight rising up like the buzzing of a beehive, but a hundred times
stronger and more lugubrious. Then you would say they were the vam-
pires, gnomes, and griffins that guard the entrance to Hell!

Except for those shipwrecked at night, their rafts rammed against
treetops, mortals never trouble the silence of these islands. In the most
solitary places, the view rarely encompasses more than an ocean of yellow sand without banks and without grass, sliced up by sleeping waves
which sparkle and shimmer under the burning vapors of the sun that
plays with the lives of us Europeans. Big-throated pelicans gather together in the marshes, parading seriously about, unconcerned by the bul-

lets shot at them by Kentuckians from passing rafts. Cranes, more fearful, come back here during the last rays of the setting sun also, and spoonbills seek shelter here from ocean tempests, bathing their pink feet in the bays of the river. Water hens, bustards, and geese sometimes completely cover the shoals in countless cohorts. But it is in the solitary bays where a carbine has never resounded, in these silent, shady arms of the Mississippi, that the timid egret, whiter than snow, appears, attentive and immobile, standing on one foot, with its *aigrette* [feathered tuft] which adorns the foreheads of sultans.

Alas! What good does it do to sketch so imperfectly the most beautiful works of creation? It would be just as worthwhile to sound the depths of the Ocean. We who have been happy enough to feel the beating of our hearts in front of the Mississippi, let us concentrate our ideas in meditation and let us remember. For you who thirst after this virgin nature, contemplate the inimitable engravings of John Martin for *Paradise Lost*.[5] Admire them at length, penetrate his sublime, inspired pages, and you will have an idea of the solitude of the New World. If such images fall into the hands of people who say that they have noticed nothing and felt nothing because they have seen no men on the banks of the Mississippi, let them exchange the staff of the pilgrim for the cane of the *fashionable*, and let them never again mention what they have the misfortune of not understanding.

RAFTS

From the mouth of the Ohio to Louisiana, there is no more lonely coast than the space between the St. Francis River and the Arkansas River. The

5. British Romantic artist John Martin (1789–1854) illustrated an edition of John Milton's *Paradise Lost,* published in London in 1827. Known in his day as "Mad John," Martin received David d'Angers along with Victor and Théodore Pavie during their stay in London in 1828, which may have inspired Théodore's "philosophizing" passage on page 117 above. Martin had a scheme for reengineering London's sewers. The three Frenchmen spread their enthusiasm for Martin to Sainte-Beuve and Hugo when they returned to France. In *Romanticism* (New York: Harper & Row, 1979), Hugh Honour says that Martin "did his damnedest to rival Turner in scenes of sublime terror by making use of similar compositions, and then overcrowding them with little figures" (102).

shoals are immensely wide, deserted, and barren like the sands of Arabia, without a single habitation on the banks except an occasional *block house* [log cabin], the ephemeral dwelling of some poor and indolent inhabitant who chops down the forest to furnish the steamboats with wood from cypress and sweet gum trees, clears an acre around his garden, then abandons his cabin to begin the same kind of life over again farther away. The river is silent and flows majestically around those islands whose gracious contours it bathes, at one point doubling back on its path to murmur again among the roots of the catalpas, at another, impetuously taking off in its course like a Mexican horseman, reflecting on its golden shield the rays of the setting sun. He who spends his whole day in the pecan groves, so numerous on the open land, would hear around him only the crackle of nuts in the beaks of green parakeets or under the tooth of a squirrel, the whistle of young deer bounding through the grasses, or the long song of the mockingbird who, during the fragrant evenings of springtime, takes pleasure in repeating all that is melancholic in the warbling of popes, cardinals, and jays.[6]

It was in the middle of this imposing solitude, however, that one lovely evening in February a raft appeared, long and heavy like a coffin, maneuvered by twelve oars. It descended the river with no other noise than the monotonous strokes, repeated over and over again, and long afterwards echoed at longer and longer intervals. Sometimes the colossal raft, carried along by the current, was silent, just a black and funereal form on the transparent waters of the Mississippi; then an immense sigh would rise up and twelve oars again beat the wave in cadence. The darker the night became, the sharper appeared the outline of the rowers' white coats against the darkness, but their hooded heads seemed downcast to their chests as they lifted vigorous arms in a single thrust, then let them fall with a plaintive moan. This great animated machine carried in its mysterious silence something frightful that touched the soul. Through the air vents, a multitude of other heads were heaped together that one could decipher only from the glow of pairs of sparkling eyes. It was not cattle,

6. Creoles in lower Louisiana caught the bright red summer bunting for export to the east coast and Europe. They called them *popes,* but in New York they were called *nonpareils.* Alexander Wilson, *American Ornithology,* vol. 3 (Philadelphia: Bradford and Inskeep, 1811), 64, plate 24.

because more air would have been left between them than could have circulated in all of the breadth of this raft, also one heard none of the bellowings that set off the entire plain and are sometimes picked up by stray buffaloes, nor could it be those frisky wild horses whose alert feet never stop stamping the bottom of the boats, which neigh impatiently, throw themselves into the water of the river, and disappear into the midst of the herds of wild horses that lace the prairies. No, it was none of those. A whistle blew in the front. The twelve rowers lifted their oars, sank into the hull, and twelve others replaced them, also dressed in white coats. No, these were not any of those animals that man knows how to domesticate, a noble conquest of which he is proud, it was less than that: Negroes, slaves to sell by the hundreds.

Five hundred Negroes were piled up there, fit and properly delivered, like barrels of sugar or packages of furs in this warehouse of a boat, in the middle of foul and infected air, but nonetheless, in appearance healthy, robust, in good condition, for someone knew well enough to choose the beginning of springtime to unload them. At this time the atmosphere is still cool and invigorating on the river, and the deck was pierced by a million little holes through which *the merchandise* could reasonably breathe. Everything was well calculated, so that no more than ten had to be thrown on the shoals for the vultures to dispose of: little children whose mothers did not want to nurse, young Negroes suffocated under the feet of others, or old Congos who had not lost in Virginia the bad habit from their country of swallowing their tongues in order to be delivered from slavery forever.

Therefore about five hundred remained, at least that was the result of the addition done many a time by the master—the proprietor, the man with a whip—squatting in the front beside a dark lantern. He had a small room with silk curtains, a large bed with mosquito netting, a trunk, accounting books, a carbine, some pistols, a dagger—all things over which he kept very close watch. A short dried-up man in good health, nervous, dark, English in origin but turned cosmopolitan, he was very deeply invested, self-concerned, astute in business, and especially knowledgeable in how to treat slaves. He had done his apprenticeship with a planter in Guyana and knew admirably well that he must cut off a black head and place it on a spike in the middle of the huts to make the other blacks understand that, once dead, they would not be able to return to their homelands, for it is one of their superstitions to believe that if they kill themselves, they go directly to Africa, provided they still have their heads on their shoulders.

This time he had gone to Virginia to buy this beautiful herd to resell at enormous profit in Louisiana. He was busily giving them names, so that you could see on his catalogue all of the days of the week, the gods of fable, and the months of the year, skillfully blended with the saints of his calendar. The cargo dreaded him terribly; his whip had very sharp iron tips and his arm was vigorous. You should have seen him strutting around on his boat with his white jacket, his white pants, his striped socks, his big straw hat, his cravat from India gracefully tied around his neck, his gold watch, his rings on his fingers, and his perfumed head. For he was *fashionable*, dressed in excellent style, good and sympathetic to the degree that he had three slaves exclusively for his favorite horse and a young Negro to give sugar to his little Maltese dog. Never had a Sultan cast a prouder glance over his mutes. He avidly enjoyed the pleasure of walking over bowed heads, making human creatures tremble and grovel in the mud, selling his fellow men, and striking, at his leisure with lashes of shiny, iron-tipped leather, the nervous black backs of his slaves.

That very evening as he traveled so voluptuously on the waters of the Mississippi, leaning off the edge of his raft, smoking his cigar and reading a few languorous verses of Dorat, a powerful hand tossed him ten feet into the water by his silk cravat from India, which squeezed his neck so tightly that he could not scream for help. He disappeared into the river in the middle of a ring which rippled into larger and larger circles, then reappeared swimming forcefully toward the boat.

"Help me, Dick, Mercury, Bill, help me, my children!" he cried out, floundering in the water.[7] "Help me, Dick, a hundred piasters if you save me from the water! Stop now, you others, row backwards, two hundred piasters, Dick, come on!. Half my chest, say, do you want to save your master?" And Dick, a large Negro from Guinea, six feet tall, looked at him without answering, with his arms crossed, shaking his head in a negative sign. "You don't want to, dog, well then, two hundred lashes and the iron collar for you!" "Shut up! you blaspheme," responded the slave, and he turned around to take his oar back.

7. "Floundering" is a pun because the expression *en se débattant* also means "haggling over a price."

Once more, "Save me! I'm ordering you to do it! You thieves, I'll have you hanged . . . I'm begging you, my children; I'm drowning; my strength is abandoning me. Stop!" He then hurled himself with so much violence toward the immense oar serving as a rudder that he succeeded in grabbing hold, but weakly. His chest shook convulsively, the water he had swallowed kept him from talking distinctly, and he mixed horrible curses with his threats and prayers. "Stop now, cursed demon! Stop, you in command of the rowers, or I'll have you quartered. Give me your hand, Mercury, or I'll have you cut into pieces and fed to the vultures."

"That's too strong, little white man," interrupted Mercury, "jump for your pain." Pushing hard on the other end of the rudder, he gave the planter such a jolt that the poor man was catapulted twenty feet in the air. On board, they continued to row. He reappeared, however, vomiting the water that was drowning him. Frightful contortions disfigured him, his red eyes bulging out of their sockets, his face made horrible by suffering agony and the excess of his rage.

"Oh, Kate, my beautiful Negress," he then screamed out, wiggling to regain his breath, breathing in these moments of pain like a dying ox. "Kate, you whom I wanted to make my mistress, throw me a rope, for heaven's sake. You will have your freedom, you will be free, you hear? I will send you back to Africa, Kate, you hear?" But Kate pulled her head inside without giving an answer to the white man, who began to sink under the waves. His strength was giving out, the current was terrible, the banks far, far away; swimming to land was impossible. "Kate," he started over again, making a last effort, "I'm dying." And a thundering voice, coming from deep in the hull, annihilated him. "Kate is my wife, filthy Englishman," roared the Negro from Virginia. "You wanted to sell me far away and steal her from me, take her like a toy only to throw her out of your hut afterwards. Die, then, with the instrument of your vengeance," and he lashed him harshly in the face with his own whip. The planter emitted a final gasp and exhaled water through his nostrils as he sank into the river.

He reappeared one more time, eyes dulled, arms and legs spread, and fists clenched violently. He gasped his last breath, but the stiffness of his members held him up, a floating cadaver that the waves pushed at their will. Less than an hour later, at an immense height above the dead body, an assembly of moving black dots formed, vultures laying claim to their prey.

They descended slowly, gradually, their movements calm and silent. Their black wings hardly moved his wet, sand-soiled hair as they glided so closely they breathed on him their fetid breath. One approached a bit closer, alighted on the shoals, ran skipping along, sniffed his odious feast, and with a cry, repeated by the whole flock, threw itself onto the eyes, snatching them out in huge pecks of its beak. Then the cadaver was surrounded by a whistling from hell, a noise of beaks and claws finishing off the task.

The hat of the unfortunate Englishman floated, and a steamboat happened to pass by, pick it up, and read the name of the owner written inside. The Negroes reached the Arkansas River, and after the women and children got off the boat, the leaders of the plot headed with the whole troop toward Little Rock where they encountered the garrison of the fort. The steamboat spread the alarm wherever it ventured and the soldiers of the redoubt pursued the runaways, none of whom knew the land, killing some, and taking some prisoners. Others drowned in the rivers or perished of hunger; perhaps some few escaped, but the very next day, the breeze from the west which causes the leaves and the flowers to be reborn in the forests of the Mississippi caused the black cadavers hanging from the limbs of the cypresses to sway in the distance on the edge of the forest.

Cabins

All of you who have descended the Mississippi will agree that a rage to jump to the ground takes hold of the traveler when he skims the bank so closely that his hand can reach the branches! You want to travel joyfully down the dark avenues and tread upon this new land, clear a passage through the cane, and sleep in the shade when the sun enflames its blue vault in the sky! When the boat stops a minute and the bell has rung on board, when the gangplank scrapes the bank, you should see every one jump off, vying with each other, leaping off the tops of galleries, and wandering across the forest like a herd of deer. Each day a new nature presents itself: new birds, which are even more brilliant with a lively, cadenced song, and new flowers that litter the soil, paving it with their sparkling corollas. Here, you may see a humid willow swamp where large marsh grasses grow and bend in the wind, undulating like waves, fading into the faraway shores behind which the river is again found with its colossal influence dominating everything. There, you may see a hedgelike dense thicket. I liked to penetrate such thickets timidly, startled by the least little noise of a trembling leaf or the passage of a chameleon sending forth a thousand colors on his changing mirror and fleeing the length of the trees more quickly than the glances that follow him. Next come the cypress groves, sometimes gloomy and silent in their own way, their aged heads abrupt-looking, harsh in their bizarre form, sometimes green and tender, with their black moss, sometimes sinister, overloaded with gray mosses ten feet long through which the wind passes and plays noiselessly. Seeing them flutter like this, you might take them for the worn-out flags of the chapel at Westminster, fluttering from a half-opened window like torn shrouds still bearing the coats of arms of their dukes now turned to dust. *Spanish beard* (common name for moss, *longmoss*) distinctly character- izes the southern provinces; there is nary a bush nor a tree to which it does not attach itself, nor a live oak that it does not encircle and cover with its gray veil, drooping down to the ground, letting the breeze scatter its flying seed. Thus each tree drapes itself in its own manner: the various cotton- woods, whose branches embrace a circumference of sixty feet, wear it in the middle of their tufts of down that they shed in the autumn and spread in the distance like flakes of snow. The pines themselves, dry and scraggly, hide their trunks under this parasitic mantle, while the prouder magnolias sometimes decorate their flowers, so large and fragrant, with it. The weak cuttings that we have transported to Europe reproduce them only imper- fectly, but on the banks of the lakes, in the marshes, even in the savannas, the humblest bushes drop their tired branches under the weight of the moss until, dried out by the winter frosts, it turns black, and unfettered like a horse's mane it drops off bringing with it the weak branch.

The first time I set foot in a cypress bottom, it was an autumn evening as the sun prepared to disappear behind the strand, leaving everything golden and sparkling. A caravan of flatboats was descending the river, disappearing from island to island until only one raft remained. A soli- tary man guided the shapeless heap of uprooted trees, sitting on his ca- davers of oaks and playing with a bear—a sad companion for someone who crosses six hundred leagues alone. Coming up alongside, I hesitated at the sight of the somber forests that stood up in front of me, frightening and sinister. I approached a monstrous sweet gum tree with dangling vines a hundred feet long starting from its base and suspended as if they had reached the top in a single toss, finely sketched against the sky like the rigging of a ship that connects one mast to another. Its roots were curved back, laced together, infinitely knotted among each other, woven of moss, and dotted with flowers and dried or green leaves. Upon shaking one such garland I heard a swarm of living creatures buzzing in the mass of greenery. Black, brown, and gray squirrels fled away, leaping and holding on by their tails to jump down lower or to snatch a falling nut as they were in flight. Cardinals flew away, tearing their red wings on the thorns, and painted buntings, spotted with scarlet, stuck their heads out of their nest held by two stalks of jasmine. Frightened hummingbirds, lighter than the moths in Europe, buzzed and disappeared, and a green snake, troubled in its sleep in the shade of the bushy branches, began to creep slowly toward the farthest extremity, to roll around and hide again under some flowers. As I advanced further to a pecan tree, thousands of parrots passed by with sharp screeches as strange as their swallowlike flight. Next I found the compact masses of cane that bears had already broken to clear themselves a passage. In the darkest places, flying squirrels hurled themselves lithely from branch to branch causing the membranes that served them as wings to whistle; crouched down at the entrance of their holes, they covered themselves with their silky tails. A sensitive plant—according to the Creole language, the "embarrassed" plant—withdrew at my feet. Fan-shaped palmettos fluttered around me and formed vast parasols similar to those of the Chinese. I leaned over a stream to see an enormous alligator spread out on the strand, snoring with a horrible death rattle, and row after row of tortoises, stretched out end to end on driftwood; at the slightest noise, they raised their heads and dove into the water.

I approached the bank of the stream, strangely surprised at all these novelties, surprised to the point of not being able to bring my ideas together. Our passengers tore off palmetto leaves which they cut elegantly into fans or braided into canopies. The sailors took turns swinging from a dangling vine which described an immense arc in the air, and the most intrepid were carried over to the branches of neighboring trees. Others gathered large quantities of walnuts, pecans, persimmons, and acacia seeds that the children ate avidly, while hunters shot pigeons, jays, crows, and opossums and one even bagged a wildcat.

On the riverbank sat a crude cabin constructed of badly joined cypress planks covered with bark of the same tree set on the river bank. The garden was no more than an enclosure of twenty square feet where sweet potatoes, *palma christi*[8] for the sick, giromond [pomegranate] for the cattle, and some stalks of corn, which serve for everything, grew haphazardly. A large family was gathered inside: three yellow, ghastly, skinny young girls who were barely dressed, four boys who were also struck by the fever, and some tiny infants stretched out on beds of moss. The furnishings consisted only of a large copper kettle for cooking food, some wooden forks and spoons, some plates that were also wooden, and some rusted guns suspended from the ceiling. Deerskin bags stitched with the sinews of a tiger cat held the other utensils.[9] The chimney was just a large flat rock onto which someone threw pine or sweet gum roots to light up the night.

The unfortunate family was fighting over a crane whose feathers littered the floor; a hunting dog, even skinnier than its masters, was gnawing on the feet and neck. They wanted to get up and give us the wood that we needed, but only one had the energy to rise and watch, the others were too ill. They had been established there for a year. When I asked them what had become of their mother and father, one of the girls gestured to me with her hand, and I went out under the plane tree where I found two wooden crosses enclosed by a fence. In six months, the fever had carried away the two heads of this nomad family, and the sad offspring were there without strength, without hope, awaiting the winter, so they might move on again, or meet death.

We would have been glad to have given them alms, but what good is money in the middle of the wilderness?

LOUISIANA

Although I had caught only an imperfect glimpse of these beautiful and impressive regions, I was anxious to leave so as to immerse myself in

8. "Palma christi" is the castor oil plant, *Riccinus communis*.

9. Pavie's tigers are bobcats, cougars or oscelots, frequently called "tigres" in Louisiana literature. In French, *tigre* refers to any cat born spotted or stripped, even raccoons. The Spanish also called all wild cats "tigres."

sparkling Louisiana, where I spent days too sweet to recount, and let my youthful expectations be realized, perhaps too profoundly for my own happiness! I must confess, Louisiana is the dream of all my leisure hours; my lasting memories form a separate place in my soul where I withdraw in moments of sadness and boredom. The reason for this is simple: tired of painful journeys after having wandered for a long time across the northern part of America, during the winter season I found in Louisiana an asylum where I retreated, craving for repose and friendship, to a village where I heard my name spoken, where I was received like the envoy of another hemisphere into the very center of my ancestral family.

In our temperate latitudes, life's habitual well-being lulls us into an astonishing apathy that makes us frightened by any extreme. In France the seasons pass by well marked, distinct: in the winter, we keep ourselves warm, in the summer, we open the window, and that is all there is to say. With few rare exceptions, this continuous cycle, over which accidents have no sway, strengthens even more that which is artificial in our lives. But in the southern climes of America, especially around the Gulf of Mexico, everything is extreme; at every step everything violates any common yardstick, nothing can be predicted, everything breaks the norm. It is an unbelievable mixture of good and evil, of abundance and sterility, of opulent cities and cabins scattered in the wilderness, of gentleness and cruelty, of happiness and misery.

During the winter, Italy has nothing that can surpass the purity of the sky of Louisiana. The temperature is invigorating, the days long like springtime in France, and a dazzling sky shines for entire months, its distances seldom darkened by frightening storms that rattle the forest, make the cities tremble, burn a plantation here and there, and spill torrential rains that inundate everything in their way, like a flood. In the summer—and its reign lasts two-thirds of the year—illnesses begin with the wind from the South, and then everything is deadly. Fevers spread with a vengeance over towns and cities, cutting down Europeans, Americans from the North, even Creoles themselves, filling the streets with coffins heading to the cemetery, funeral songs, and tears. Rich and poor, black and white—no one is spared. The recently arrived traveler feels a shiver run through his limbs, sits down overwhelmed, stretches out without energy, and the very next day, ghastly spots mottle his body. He gets up furiously, with a last effort hurls himself toward life which is escaping him, and falls back down dead. People flee from the cities, the sick ones flood back to the plantations, and the planters in their turn go to the pine forests to construct huts and to breathe, if possible, a healthier air. Breathless Negroes swarm to the plantation hospitals, sleeping in the shade and in the homes of the colonists. By day the youngest fans the master, who, overwhelmed by fatigue, stretches out under mosquito netting while the lilas shed an opaque shadow on the galleries, and the open-curtained windows call in vain for a healthful breeze; for, at that time, everything is dead, including the breeze. He who strays onto the beaten path at noon has no other shade than that of his wide-brimmed hat when a perpendicular sun burns down its rays. The forest is no longer anything but a refuge of filthy and deadly snakes, swamp mosquitoes that gnaw, and a thousand noxious insects. In the evenings, at the edges of the lakes, deer advance timidly to seek fresh air and roar in a lamentable manner, shaking furiously under the eternal bites of the mosquitoes; tigers roar, too, conquered by heat and fatigue. Rattlesnakes stick up quivering tails and indiscriminately wound wild horses sleeping under the dangling vines, wolves of the prairies, foxes and buffalo. Pricks from the most insignificant thorns must be burned right away lest tetanus rapidly penetrate the skin and circulate in the bones like a sharp barb, turning the limbs stiff, tightening the throat and mouth. Convulsions would follow, drawing out screams as piercing as the pain and breaking the most vigorous, like torture.

Few families see winter arrive without having to mourn one of their own, but the last rays of sun dry up the tears too abundant to keep flowing a long time. In a Creole, pain is swift, cruelly felt, but forgotten in the long run even though it might often reopen some badly closed wounds. Winter is the time of *la vie* for the colonists, for it is then that balls, parties, and games of all kinds follow one another in succession without interruption. Wealth sparkles in all forms: gold flows abundantly, harvests turn into sparkling jewelry, and boats abound. If you penetrate the interior of the forests, the lakes are covered with birds, ducks, geese, buzzards, Canada geese, whooping cranes, woodcocks, and snipes, which literally blacken the lakes from one end to the other. Deer run together in herds, bear return in packs from the cornfields to their holes in old sweet gum trees. The Indians come down from the prairies and trade with the Whites, exchanging furs for ammunition—gunpowder and balls.

An open and generous hospitality characterizes the people of Louisiana. If a stranger finds himself ill on a journey, let him knock loudly at the door of a plantation and he will find a place, attentive care, and friends who demand no recompense beyond his gratitude. Let him remain for the duration of his convalescence. In the evening around the fire or under the galleries, he will recount his travel stories to the joyful and attentive family, he will participate in all of the nearby celebrations where he will be the welcomed guest at the homes of all of his host's friends, and when he sets off on his way, it will not be without seeing their tears flow with his own. The Orientals are not more indolent during the hot season, the Russians are not more indefatigable in their winter hunting than these nimble and fearless Creoles, always on horseback, sleeping by turn on eiderdown and bearskin, infatuated with hunting and pleasures, always gay and of an independence of character difficult to find in Europe. And along the river: what lovely plantations, what pleasant groves of magnolias, orange and banana trees, what delightful hedges of yucca with flowers draped like Chinese lanterns! Cotton whiter than snow stands in immense fields, half-opening its black hands to spread abundantly its rich yield. Shiny green canes grow by sugar mills where syrups ferment, wheels squeal, and slaves and masters alike bustle around, busy at work, because each armload of cane is a *piaster* being minted. Sassafras, Chinese lilas, and palma christi in a parasol gracefully drape the huts of the Negroes, set out like tents. In the springtime, perfume suffuses the whole wilderness from the torrents of flowers shaking and swaying in the breeze; masses of purple corollas and golden lyres litter entire cities.

Come the season of pleasures and you will all be found reunited, happy inhabitants of Louisiana. You will be seen galloping within a ten-league radius to dance all night, and at daybreak, climbing back on your horses to return to your plantations: you alert young people with intelligent, proud faces, ebony hair, bronzed complexion, fresh young girls with mirthful faces, dark eyes like Andalusians, but less haughty than Mexicans, more animated than your neighbors in the north, French in the soul without thinking of it, good, sweet, as if you did not know that you are beautiful. Suddenly someone announces a flood—the waters have turned over *your* harvest, carried off *your* houses, drowned *your* animals; ruined for a year, and *you* keep on dancing. An epidemic kills your slaves, you become sad, silent . . . well, then! What do you regret, men or money? Here, I stop and I permit every one to reflect within himself. Slavery is there; slavery, the great vice of American society. You are rich, and these Blacks sweat blood and water for you, without a salary. Their life, their liberty, that is what you set yourselves as masters of, and the lashes of the whips and the iron collars. . . .

I shall present but one response to these accusations, which is that slavery is such a deeply rooted evil (which does not excuse it), so deeply entrenched, that the responsibility for it does not fall on the present generation. I do not defend slavery in any way, it had to come and it will be seen later, but I respect and honor those among the Creoles who know how to be compassionate with their slaves, and that is actually the majority. Even if any more of those monsters are found, as those I would point out for the people to avenge, I am happy to admit that I lived six months in a plantation without hearing a sigh. Certainly few nations are as generous and unselfish toward those who suffer as the people of Louisiana when it is a question of supporting an unfortunate being; they have a heart, a very tender soul, and in the care which they accord an ailing Black, there is more compassion and devotion, especially among the women, than fear of losing the price of the slave. Let us Europeans try to set aside our prejudices and judge clearly the degree of guilt we should place on the inhabitants of countries with a colonial culture. Let us first of all know what masters and slaves are, what are their morals, the respective defects and good qualities, and we will judge better, if not differently. Perhaps I have seemed too indulgent toward Whites, not compassionate enough toward Blacks; that is because I have lived with such gentle and virtuous families that it would be unjust to wrap in a common condemnation all those whose servants often differ from ours only in color.

CLEARINGS

On a lovely November evening at twilight we discovered the stream that separates Arkansas from Louisiana. On the left was still Mississippi, a blooming and fertile state formed in part from what used to be the Spanish Floridas, a large province that began, as we see it, at the *Meschacebé* and extended in immense savannas all the way to the shore of the Atlantic. Downriver, we sighted the Yazoo, the river from which the Indians living to the west of the mountains took their name, a powerful and numerous people that the author of *Natchez* numbers among the nations that conspired.[10]

In every direction on both banks of the river sizable settlements are forming; each day the Mississippi loses some of its silence, some of its solitude, and some of its original grandeur. Not being at all American, I will confess that the sight of these clearings was painful to me. I can already hear the colonists ballyhooing their vandalism. If I could plug up my ears enough not to hear their talk, their axes and their flames devouring the forest, I would do it. When a plantation functions on a great scale, duly established with its huts, gardens, and vast outbuildings, there is in this expression of human industry, carefully organized in the middle of a savage nature, something seriously beautiful that arouses admiration. But the fight is painful, and there is, on the part of man, an effort that reduces man and hurts. Driven by fury and rage within, he attacks these indestructible forests with iron and fire. In short, a clearing is a painful spectacle, which I will try to sketch here.

When a cultivator has chosen his site, he must clear the land of the grasses that obstruct it, then pull up, or rather cut by the root, the dangling vines entangled a thousand times from bush to bush, their stems haphazardly lacing together plane trees and oaks by mingling in their branches. Often fire takes care of this first task, causing the frightened serpents to flee in disorder: scorpions, chameleons, lizards, and otherworldly races of reptiles, as well as tigers and bears, all the creatures who for so many years have held peaceful possession of this portion of their promised land. When all is smoking cinders at the foot of the gigantic

10. In attributing Mississippi to Spain, the young author neglects to mention that France and England also owned parts of the territory. Though he similarly distorted somewhat the boundaries of Louisiana, Pavie knew that Chateaubriand, the author of *Les Natchez* (Berkeley: University of California Press, 1919), listed the Yazoo tribe as one of the tribes that conspired with the Natchez Indians to rid the region of European settlers. Bienville had built Fort Rosalie in 1716 on a bluff overlooking the Mississippi, approximately sixty miles south of Vicksburg. In 1729, the Natchez massacred the French settlers and garrison, prompting the French to retaliate by attempting to exterminate the Natchez (878).

trees, when the vines are swaying, blackened from branch to branch, dried by flames darting like an arrow to the summit of the old, smoke-soiled oaks and all around is the sad disorder of a vessel crippled by storm, when the leaves, equally consumed, fly as dust and swirl like the lava of a volcano, then the axe begins its toil. The Negroes come forward and strike, but not by the root of the tree, as it would take weeks to over-turn them and months to separate and chop up the trunk stretched out full length. No, they are content to ring it with a wide trench that reaches the heart and interrupts the flow of the sap so that the former king of the forests can only watch the progressive drying and rotting of the foliage that for so many springtimes had made up its crown of starry flowers with petals of gold. Runners of moss consumed by the fire cover the base of the tree with a haunting shroud, trembling with a sinister rustling, scaring away the blackbirds of a starving flock that disputes with the col-onist the premise of a first harvest. At this point the habitation consists of an enclosed field spiked with partially burned, barely extinguished stumps from which surge other dark and teetering columns of the former structures; when a storm rolls in, the tree thus ringed cracks noisily, crumbles, and falls into pieces, crushing here and there ears of corn, sug-arcane, a cottonwood tree, or perhaps a clumsy Negro who, were he not dead, would have been flogged for having so stupidly fallen asleep under its shade.

Thus each winter destruction and industry spread. What becomes of the Indian whose hut used to occupy the bank of the river, the protected cove ravaged by the scythe of the pioneer? Sad and preoccupied, he goes away, one more wrinkle inscribed on his forehead, and he weeps, for in the end his very life is hunting, and where will he find game when the sight of white men pushes the animals deeper into the wilderness? "Let them emigrate with the bears and the buffalo," respond the colonists, or "let them become involved in our work, let them throw away their bows and lead a plow!" Never. The savage life, poor and unfortunate as it seems to you, holds too strong an attraction for them; besides, they were born there, this earth was theirs perhaps, they alone were its masters for a long time. These thick woods that you are chopping down to make steamboats and to burn in tied-up bundles, these woods were the meeting place of the tribal councils of their nations. The shade covered a tomb that, although without epitaph, was not less than that of a medicine man venerated by his whole tribe. Could you value it someday? Industry is beautiful, noble, worthy of civilized man, but, for heaven's sake, let's not kick those whom we reduce to begging bread and water from far-off and inhospitable tribes and who, hemmed in between their still free enemies and ever advancing white men, become the prey of the Sioux, Osages, and Comanches. All land is not the same to an Indian who totes on his back the bones of his father and walks with this precious burden to the place where he erects his bone hut. His fatherland is not merely a word that makes him feel proud and vain without knowing why; the fatherland of the savage is his hut beside the stream over which lean persimmon trees, sycamores, and magnolias which he prefers to everything because they grew tall with him, the tree that furnished him strong wood for arrows, the plane tree from which he suspended the cradle of his children, and a thousand more things he has identified with himself, to which he has assigned names, and which he will mourn for a very long time.

Let us return to the clearings where the land gradually becomes purged. The blackened stumps fall and disappear, the grasses, pulled out relentlessly, no longer compete with useful plants for the abundant nutrients of this soil, fertilized by its proximity to the rivers. Little by little, the habitation takes shape; around the house flowers are added along with galleries where the inhabitants, who are surrounded by their crops, gather at dinner in the cool of the evening during the hot season. The huts of the Negroes increase in population like the herds whose lowing blends each evening with the song of the mockingbird, that faithful companion to man who will not have failed to build nests in the lilas nearest the door and in its favorite place on the chimney. Already, *pirogues* [dugout canoes] and skiffs travel the neighboring rivers, rowed by men who go hunting, camp on the rivers, and furnish game for their families. Neighboring land will be explored, trails established, and the colonist in his estates will become master—master and citizen, king and subject—until a new inhabitant comes along to establish himself next door and share with him the bounty which he, himself, had once appropriated freely, but now cannot abandon without regret.

The villages that one encounters in these parts—Petit Gulph, Memphis, etc.—consist of just ten to twelve houses or warehouses around which hurry wagons driven by Negroes, wagons loaded with bales of cotton, or with planters from neighboring habitations, meeting to sell their merchandise or embark on a steamboat. Memphis is a pleasant city, built on a rather high hill out of reach of the worst floods. We spent the night there, and watched the flame that serves as a signal to wood merchants spread a curious effect over these red and white plastered houses built in tiers on the hillside. So rapid and regular is the journey of steamships that newspapers and mail arrive almost every day in these tiny villages, even though they are two or three hundred miles from New Orleans. The colonists are as well informed of the least little news from Europe as most of our hamlets; that is the immense advantage of a river like the *Meschacebé*, navigable in all weather, covered with wood to feed the boats, extending like a great highway from the north to the south of this vast land.

HABITATIONS

If I could renounce forever the intellectual life that flows forth from the arts and abandon myself body and soul to this soft languor of which each has more or less his share in this world, I would retreat to some habitation on the banks of the Mississippi, there to sleep and there to dream at my leisure. The colonial appearance of the large plantations pleases me, for I love all that reminds me of the southern countries and the Orient. What an admirable scene the banks of the Mississippi present when the scorching sun spills its torrents of dazzling brightness on the vast, rich crops and outlines like a curtain the summits of the plane trees and the oaks fading into the distance! When the waters of the river are sparkling and golden in the middle of the yellow shoals, islands of greenness allow the gaze to wander from horizon to horizon until everything fades into the blue sky! Dazzling white fields of cotton roll on in every direction, here and there mottled by the shade of an immense live oak awkwardly swaying its moss as a bison sways his woolly beard. Or the barely ripe grains of extensive green rice fields may undulate in the rare, irregular exhalation of the dying breeze. Farther on stands the shimmering sugar-cane, crowded close together, as impenetrable as a cane hedge, as stiff as the prickly yucca whose tall stem is covered with white flowers that fill the evening air with such a sweet fragrance.

From the middle of the river [one sees] a black dot that recedes further and further and finally disappears. It is the wide-brimmed hat of a Creole who caracoles on his little unbroken horse, galloping at full speed his parasol aloft, his wide trousers floating like those of an Arab, and a dagger dangling from his red belt. Behind him a Negro carrying his master's carbine also gallops leaning over his copper-pommelled saddle. The Creole is racing to meet a hunting party, already awaiting him under the elegant mass of an isolated plane tree which casts its shadow across the route. They will mingle talk and laughter, scatter out into the forest, and gallop in pursuit of deer. If night surprises them, they will improvise, igniting a fire with a shotgun fuse to light up the whole camp. Their bearskins are spread out under the tent and the indolent Louisianans, grown as intrepid as Indians, will fall asleep contented near the flame that keeps wild beasts at bay.

Step for an instant onto this shore; follow the path between the rows of catalpa trees leading to the planter's dwelling, a simple and elegant home of wood, or sometimes of brick, raised a few feet above the ground and resting on four pillars of stone. Gracious white galleries [porches] surround and decorate it, and silk curtains hang softly at windows embellished by handsome shutters. Lilas, heavy with blooms, surround the windows, sheltering the dark, silent interior from the rays of the sun. Ah! How this cool darkness strikes envy in the breathless traveler when, covered in sweat and dust, he passes on the road.

Come closer still! Raise the blue bed curtains indiscreetly, and look. In a hammock of a thousand colors suspended from two handles polished to a shine by the swaying of the hammock's cords, an innocent, fresh young girl is sleeping, rocked slowly by a drowsy Negress whose ebony forehead occasionally dips to the tiles of the bedroom floor. An instant later, the young Creole awakens and pokes her laughing head out of the gauze mosquito netting. With a playful kick, she pushes her foot against the wall of cypress and swings herself some more; as the swaying slows, she is lulled back to sleep.

When the setting sun lengthens the shadows of the house until they stretch across the courtyard, everything comes to life. The garden's gates open wide and the young girl scampers down the path, darting nimbly into the orange grove where she picks at random some magnolia blossoms and a banana hanging under a leaf large enough to serve as a parasol. At the end of the stepping stones a fluttering, gleaming hummingbird plunges its beak into the chalice of jasmines and vanishes into the blue of the sky, swirling upward with a shrill, rhythmic cry. Under a clump of lemon trees a mockingbird sings from the edge of his nest and a pope flits about noisily, more brilliant than the rubies of Asia.

All of the family gathers under a canopy of green trees to retell stories told a hundred times before, rambling tales to fill the wide-eyed listeners' long winter evenings. Winter here is like springtime; the hot days are past. Fires are lighted in all the hearths: fire, a sight that distracts the Indian for whole nights through, fire, a necessity for the Negro exhausted by his toil, fire, which delights and attracts, fire, around which families gather to tell joyful tales that bring smiles to light up beautiful faces.

Now come back in January, when the sun no longer shoots perpendicular rays, so that its slanted light, henceforth oblique, contents itself with shading the brows of Europeans. The days are a little less long, that is all; as for flowers and leaves, almost as many remain. What has become of the cane, the cotton fields, the rice paddies? The fields are empty. Here and there flames devour piles of wood, producing ashes to enrich the land, Negroes stretch on the racks cotton grown whiter by the day, and in every direction mills rumble as the mules turn their wheels. Bales are formed under the cotton press, pushed toward the river bank, loaded onto the steamboats and carried away, all to the songs of sailors and slaves. Further away, a sugar refinery spits out torrents of flames and boils the cane crushed under the grinding stones. Cane juice fills immense cast-iron vats, spilling over from one to another, purified by the action of the fire. The barrels roll onto the shoals and cross the seas to be distributed in Europe, Africa, and the northern United States. This prodigious activity of men of all colors goes on day and night at harvest time, when the riches of the year are amassed in eight days. One hastens, one hurries, one must save time to spend it.

These imposing plantations, sometimes a mile in length, begin around Natchez, Mississippi. "Natchez" is a beautiful name, full of memories celebrated by Chateaubriand, known in Europe as the ideal Indian village. You who have read *The Natchez* must never go near this village if you want to keep your illusions. All that remains is a very tall hill piled high with shabby, crudely built houses with weeds sprouting from their walls. Whites brought the yellow fever which doggedly follows them step-by-step from the lighthouse. I could not even disembark; sickness still persisted in November. The village held a public festival that evening, and I wanted with all my strength to put the Natchez Indians back there. On the summit of the hill a fire burned that should have lit the meeting of a council of elders, but, alas! A balloon rose up to the cheers of the crowd, and all my illusions crumbled. Terrified vultures took swift flight toward neighboring islands, then headed deep into the forest, for the balloon was still following them.

Beneath the village at the bottom of a rocky cliff is a cavern, perhaps rather deep, that I would like to imagine as the sacred ossuary. Charming magnolias shade the valley. Some spoonbills hidden beneath the reeds lifted their sonorous voices at the approach of night, but the pelicans returning upstream took a wide detour from their route, avoiding those houses piled up on the hill.

Commercial Natchez emits an air of prosperity, with its numerous steamboats, rafts, and flatboats and rapidly expanding population. I do not like American cities when they are grafted onto the debris of Indian tribes. Change the name of this village or move it further away; respect what belongs to history and what has been consecrated by a burning imagination, otherwise the substitution desecrates the original.[11] After the large and powerful tribe of the Natchez, what could a hundred irregular houses mean in their place, thrown up at random without taste and without picturesque effect? You will never make anything out of it, not even a flat city stretched out in a line.[12]

THE RED RIVER

The sickness had not yet entirely died down in New Orleans and the Spanish, chased out of Mexico, had fled the mouth of the Mississippi where the fever ravaged them by the hundreds, to Baton Rouge, Bayou

11. Referring to the Indian village in Chateaubriand's book *The Natchez,* Pavie believes the new city should have borne a different name, as, for example, French cities built on Roman vestiges were renamed.

12. Pavie certainly underestimated the potential of Natchez, which disappointed his Chateaubriandesque expectations. Natchez was the richest town in the South at the outbreak of the Civil War.

Sarah, and even Natchez, dragging along in their trail the dying and the terrible scourge. I stayed in New Orleans only as long as necessary to find a boat to take me to the Red River, where I intended to spend the winter.

On the third day we arrived at the place where the Red River flows into the Mississippi. In the springtime the river inundates the flat land here, which does not yet support any settlements. Flatboats used to descend the Red River and travel back up again in fifty day cycles, stopping at this point for the navigators to camp and hunt buffalo; but today, when steamboats are spreading civilization and the destruction of forests everywhere, one would have to penetrate much further into Missouri to find a herd of buffalo.

The Red River, of little importance compared to the Mississippi, nonetheless would be the premier river in Europe; it travels nearly three hundred leagues (approximately nine hundred miles) in its course from its source in the Rocky Mountains. Its very low banks overflow with cold water almost everywhere following the thaw of snow.

During the summer, its flow is frighteningly rapid. Channeled between shoals and steep banks, it plunges impetuously into the willows leaning over the banks, uproots them, scalps them of their green crests, and leaves the forests dried up, isolated, emitting harmful miasmas.

During the rest of the year, the Red River is the Mississippi on a smaller scale, less grandiose and less imposing, but less melancholic, too, and more graceful in its details. Nothing escapes the traveler's eye: no dangling vine suspended in festoons from the colossal trees of the forest or strange plant passes unnoticed. Rushes and grasses grow so densely on the floating islands that alligators walk around comfortably and, after returning to their accustomed places as dogs do when resting, they fall asleep and descend with the flow, so well hidden under the leaves that timid egret embark on the same raft without detecting them. If I had not so often encountered these colonies of birds and reptiles navigating on the American rivers, it would be difficult for me to give credence to the tales of travelers; but anyone who has gone up the rivers of upper Louisiana—the Sabine, the Red River, or the Wichita—must have often noticed these marvelous oddities. Alligators are so numerous in the uncultivated places that I happened to shoot at forty in one hour, and on a solitary strand in a cove of the Red River, I surprised seven of them sleeping together in the sunshine. One could have taken them for a pile of silt, because the heat of the day had dried out their muddy hides and turned them the color of swamp mire.

The Black River, which the Indians still call the Wichita, empties into the Red River a few leagues above its mouth. Its waters are as black, as clear, and as sweet as those of the latter are red and brackish; however, once they flow together, they become potable. The town of Wichita, established for just a few years, makes daily progress in farming, and the depth of the river permits large boats to pick up the cotton and corn they harvest.

All the land on the right belongs to the district of Concordia, which extends quite far up toward the Mississippi to the Yazoo River. To the left spreads the much smaller parish of Avoyelles, rather populated in the interior, where it has some natural prairies on which numerous herds of cattle graze, but on the banks one hardly comes across three or four habitations.

On the third day of our journey, we stopped to spend the night near a newly built cabin. Since I was the only passenger, and no one on board spoke French, I was sent ashore to buy wood and get some much-needed provisions. The captain of the *Maryland* had never navigated the Red River and was as surprised as I was at the rarity of plantations and the singular appearance of the inhabitants, colonists from the prairies who apparently had never left their village of Avoyelles. Seeing me disembark they immediately put themselves on the defensive, alleging that we were bringing the yellow fever. Long negotiation was necessary for me to obtain permission to enter the cabin. Finally the adults let me into the house, but they obstinately refused to come on board in spite of the insistence of the children, who were anxious to do so, persuaded that a little sacred pouch full of herbs that they wore around their necks would protect them from all danger. I learned in the course of conversation that they had been established there just since summer, not knowing whether floods would force them to return to the interior. Their cabin was miserable, without utensils other than cane baskets woven by the Indians, a few crude chairs, some bags of skin from the young deer[13] (which are tawny like the deer of France, though in the first year, its hide is mottled with white spots, an effect that is agreeable to the eye, making these hides

13. Note by Pavie: The deer of Louisiana (*Cervus virginicus*).

always preferred) rather well worked, in which they put away their clothes, and some gourds for different purposes. They had to fight tigers that often came to carry away their fowl and destroy their herds, mosquitoes whose bites make this area intolerable to a European, and alligators who never fail each night to cross the courtyard enclosed by a wooden fence to get to the river. Already they have killed some ghastly ones with hatchet blows and gunshot, but several years' residence will be necessary for all kinds of animals to lose the habit of taking the route they have used from generation to generation. I do not know what a Parisian would think of such a life; but these planters seem happy, exempt from worry, and markedly without any desire to go live in more agreeable regions.

In the evening some Choctaw Indians came bringing venison and baskets. They camped on the shore, and their horses wandered untied into the forest to find nourishment. Then I left the family and returned on board where I found everyone sleeping. The night was dark, the shadow of the big trees added to the silence of the darkness, and the cabin lamp cast a doubtful glimmer that spread melancholy. I sat down at the table and opened a volume of Chateaubriand whose work, always full of enchantment, never had more charm than in this place. A thousand thoughts flashed through my mind: my memories, combined with the ideas given birth within me by *The Natchez*, oppressed me so much that I went back up on deck. Oh! delicious solitude! Everything was calm, happy around me; the colonists slept in their crude cabin, asylum for a peaceable and virtuous family, while on the strand rose the flame of the camp of the Choctaws, whose red skin, so different from the copper-colored Algonquins, recalls the oriental origin of all the peoples of the two worlds, nuanced by the sun and the snows.

Louisiana is divided into parishes and not into districts and counties like the other states. Upon leaving Avoyelles parish, we entered the parish of Rapides, whose county seat Alexandria is a newly established village entirely composed of Americans, where English is the dominant language. Built on the left bank, it has a neat street of brick houses with a plaza in the middle where the Court House and the Protestant church are found. We heard the falls gurgling when we arrived in the town: they are a quarter of a mile further up and often lend their name to the village itself. These rapids interrupt navigation during a large part of the year, and indeed caused us to abandon further travel upriver. On the opposite bank of the river one notices the cemetery all planted in cypress and lilas.[14] It is, with the Caldwell cemetery on Lake George, the most picturesque I have seen in America. Parasols of leaves and flowers blooming continuously from springtime to fall entirely shade the tombs. From far away it seems to be a garden laid out with exquisite taste, and when one approaches it, the white crosses, simple and imposing monuments concealed under the domes of green vegetation in silence hardly disturbed by hummingbirds and butterflies, recall the peace of eternal rest.

A violent storm broke out the instant I disembarked at Alexandria; the heat was stifling, even though it was the middle of November. Torrents of rain had rendered access difficult, and the path separating the houses from the river was muddy and treacherous. Harassed by fatigue and completely out of breath, I barged into a cafe and ordered a beer. Someone responded naïvely that since it was cold, they were not brewing any more.

The Forest

It was the thirtieth night that I had spent on a river since my departure from Pittsburgh, including the stays in Louisville and New Orleans, which were so short that I had decided it was not appropriate to spend the night on land. I confess that once I went ashore at Alexandria, I breathed like a bird who flaps his wings upon leaving a cage, and I could, for an instant at least, escape those terrible mosquitoes whose bites were bloodying my face and hands and endlessly disturbing my sleep. To reach my destination, I still had around thirty leagues of habitations and forests to cross. After an uninterrupted eight hundred and fifty leagues on steamboat, I set out joyfully on horseback across this beautiful land which always eluded me and tempted me so violently when I merely passed it by. It was the goal of my pilgrimage. At my destination awaited the repose of a joyful winter season with my own family.

I was still sleeping deeply when the steward, an intelligent and skillful

14. Note by Pavie: China-tree of the Americans, lilas of China, according to the Creoles: *Mélia-Azédarach*.

Negro, came to advise me that the horse awaited me, saddled and bridled, but not newly shod—they never shoe horses on the habitations. I took leave of the captain, with whom I had developed far more familiarity than is customary as I was the only passenger. I plunged into the forest, guided by the sound of the rapids. First I had to cross a plain of thick palmettos with strange trunks, oriental in appearance like those of palm trees, which the force of the wind and my passing jostled with a sonorous rustle. The sun had not yet risen, but I could see the forest on the other bank; the trees, in spite of the lateness of the season, still kept their leaves, tinged with that range of dazzling colors that autumn imprints in every country. I was alone on horseback, crossing this land that was new to me. How could this sweet sadness which bends the head nearer to the heart not cause a bit of melancholy to mingle with my thoughts? I had a premonition of some romantic accident awaiting me that might cut my trip short before I could sit at that hospitable hearth, the port toward which I had directed my journey.

Horses that are for hire in Louisiana, like those of Canada and Europe, have the bad habit of retracing their steps just as soon as the opportunity arises. Mine had the additional defect of stopping at every path, at every bridge, and in front of every human being he encountered, black or white. When the recalcitrant animal planted me irremediably in front of a Negro, I politely asked him to tear off a blade of the wild coffee that grows abundantly in this forest and whip the lazy horse until he set out again, and off we trotted until the next incident.

I was first struck by the abundance of turkey vultures, so fearless that they perched on fence posts and rooftops and mingled with fowls. From a distance, you would take them for domestic turkeys because of their red combs, brown color, and heavy, dazed appearance. Sometimes they came so close I had to give them a lash of my whip to get them to fly off; and, after a few flaps of their wings, they would end up twenty feet away, contemplating me stupidly with their mouths wide open. When they have eaten too much, which happens every time they find a dead animal, vultures can no longer fly, and you see them, half smothered in the great quantity of rotten meat they have gobbled down, running shamefully in front of the little Negro children who amuse themselves by tormenting the birds with lashes from a whip.

It was Sunday and no one was working on the plantations. From time to time I encountered slaves in twos and threes, trotting along, their legs dangling from a small horse with a long mane. They greeted me humbly, extremely surprised that I responded to their politeness, and when I asked them if I still had a long way to go before I got to their master's house, they never failed to say that it was "nothing but a jump"—a distance at least the equivalent of what the peasants of the Vendée call a "hop," that is, a good hour's walk.[15]

Parrots are extremely numerous on the banks of the Red River as well as in the part of Louisiana along the Mississippi. They fly with extraordinary swiftness, abrupt in all their movements. Passing like lightning within range of pistol shot, they all perch together on a tree whose branches dip down to the earth under the weight of these birds; then suddenly, at a single screech repeated a thousand times by the rest of the flock, they all flap their wings and take off, hissing strangely. They often followed me, jabbering away, seeming to take pleasure in performing their aerial acrobatics over and over again, endlessly dazzling my surprised eyes with their brilliant colors.

In the swampy cypress bottoms, creeper vines obstructed my path and I could advance only with great caution, surrounded by squirrels who jumped from tree to tree only to stop again to contemplate me from deep down one of these solitary paths, veritable cradles suspended over a lake.

Habitations dotted the land hither and yon, cut up and separated from one another by forest, natural prairies, bayous, streams, cypress bottoms, and marshes. I entered one such plantation for dinner. All of the planter's family were seated at the table. A Negro took charge of my horse, and they received me like an invited guest whose place had been saved. A slab of bacon, a slice of venison and some fried pumpkin made up this meal savored with a violent appetite. What surprised me was that at every meal, the heat of day and hot spices are abundantly mixed, which inevitably causes thirst. Nonetheless neither glass nor pitcher was there—anyone who wished to drink had to go find the "calabash,"[16] the common ladle that floats in a pail of water on the porch outside. Inhabi-

15. "Il n'y avait qu'un saut" is roughly the equivalent of "a hop, skip, and jump."

16. Although there were no calabash trees in the region, ladles from the ordinary gourd squash were called "calabashes" nonetheless.

tants of French origin do not wish to accept any compensation. Fortunately, the slaves, an unfortunate class working without recompense,
gratefully accept the tribute that the traveler owes the master.

My host, a respectable colonist, implored me not to set out at night
because of the extent of the forest that remained to be crossed before
reaching the river. He recounted to me several examples of imprudent
strangers whom the north winds had frozen after a storm. Freezing in
Louisiana in such warm weather seemed impossible to me, and certainly
the last danger I expected to encounter. Nonetheless, I thanked him for
his advice, even though I was quite resolved not to follow it. A storm was
gathering, however, so I spent the night at the edge of the forest in an
Anglo-American habitation where not only did I find neither the politeness nor the solicitous concern of my previous host, but they hardly bothered to give me the information I so badly needed. At least there, as in
every guesthouse in the world, I could freely release all my bad humor,
following the custom of a traveler wishing to give himself an air of importance.

Almost everyone was ill. Care of the house had fallen to three Negro
children, six or seven years old, dressed only in shirts and wearing at the
neck the same sachets that I had noticed in Avoyelles. It took them at
least an hour and a half to set the table on four legs, lay out the somewhat
ragged tablecloth, set out plates and food, and finally drag up chairs one
at a time for the guests. We ate solemnly and quickly, according to the
English custom, which is generally adopted by English-speaking Americans.

The one called "Doc" took off by the light of the moon with his shotgun to check the traps set in every direction for bears which frequently
attacked the palisades. As soon as I was settled alone in front of the fire,
absolutely alone, and the inhabitants had retired to their bedrooms, a big
man approached me. He was yellow and weathered, dressed in a blue
cape and leather leggings in the style of an old trapper. He came and sat
down beside me without abandoning for a minute his copper-butted rifle.
His severe physiognomy was as frank as his dress was unique. If he had
known how to read (but he told me that he did not), I would have been
tempted to believe that he was imitating all of his gestures and his look

from Leather Stockings:[17] the same facial expression, the same silent laugh, the same abrupt conversation, suddenly interrupted by the memory of some hunting expedition in a faraway country which he elaborates interminably, like a dog who searches for a long time until he finds the scent and disappears in the woods. I learned from him that he had come from the Pacific Ocean, free and without a salary as a traveling companion with an English traveler, Mr. Young. Mr. Young had also brought a Mexican servant. "He's there, if you want to see him," said the old hunter. Taking a torch, he headed for the porch where I found the Mexican with his head leaning on a richly decorated saddle, snoring, without having taken his curved sword or his pistols off his belt. We let him sleep. After a second conversation with the old man, who mixed his narrations with as many Spanish and Indian interjections as English words, I found my bed, and he went off to join the Mexican.

Lightning continued all night long. I stationed myself at the window, from which I could see a tree-covered hill, bordered by a cedar forest and cut off by an overflowing stream. The house stood in a spacious courtyard outlined in magnificent lilas; in the middle of the yard a monstrous black bear attached to a post lived in a shed leaning against a tree. He climbed up on the branches, furiously balanced himself, then returned growling to the ground frightened by the storm and pushed back by the water starting to invade his shelter. Little by little, streams formed all over, uprooting bushes, pooling together to form a river, then a universal lake in the middle of which the square house with its porches looked like Noah's Ark. As for the Mexican and his companion, they slept.

In spite of everything, I decided to leave as soon as the sun had chased off the clouds. Fortunately, I took along some food. As for my horse, I found him even more listless than the night before. Water swirled under the bridges and he stumbled with every step. The route was slippery and muddy; the holly oaks, very common alongside settlements, shook out

---

17. This offhanded reference to the hero of James Fenimore Cooper's popular novel *The Last of the Mohicans* shows how current translations of Cooper's works were among Pavie's family and friends. The American writer, living in Paris, frequented the studio of his admiring friend, sculptor David d'Angers, where he met the young Victor Pavie. David d'Angers gave Cooper a copy of his brother's *Souvenirs atlantiques*, which Crosnier reported, without a citation, that the American admired; "F. Cooper said 'There is in this book truth and sentiment. The author is a poet.' " *Théodore Pavie*, 66.

their long mossy hair on my head and inundated me as if the storm had started over again. I hardly entered the forest before lightning illuminated the horizon on all sides, and thunder pealed with such a dreadful clatter that I became frightened. Six months before, I had been in a terrifying storm off the coast of Virginia when a thunderbolt struck a hundred feet from the ship, but all I had heard before that moment seemed child's play compared to the horror spread through the forests of Louisiana by this terrible hurricane. I kept trotting along on my horse, but each mile I had to dismount to pass over a stream across some tree trunks as I held the bridle of my horse who was swimming. I rode about three hours that way, with the storm worsening all the time.

Not a cardinal, nor a warbler, nor a mockingbird, not even an eagle dared to show himself under such a sky. The beasts were deep in their lairs, and I was frightened to find myself alone in the middle of this world turned upside down, alone with an unfortunate, trembling animal, already stopping every minute. Finally, he refused to advance. Rain fell as if the clouds had burst open from one drop too many. Except for my walk behind Niagara Falls, I had never been so soaked; even my saddle was soaked through. Had I not gone to the trouble to cover myself with my coat? From all sides the creeping vines, like vast gutters, spilled rain onto my shoulders. Oh! I thought more than once about charming autumn evenings in France, just when the last rays of the sun embellish everything. Nevertheless, I did not lose courage. I began to sing loudly, more dead than alive, chilled to the bone by the cold, not daring to shake my limbs since a puddle had collected on each. I was still singing when my horse collapsed. I could not get off without being in water up to my knees. No hope remained of seeing the weather clear up, and just when I scanned the clouds for some sign of calm, a gust of wind delivered a thunderclap to my head. Lightning shredded the heavens with its fire, shook the earth, and fell in streaks of flame on an immense cedar tree ten feet from me. The top of the tree caught fire and it came crashing down at my feet in flames.

Fear took complete hold of me. I wanted nothing but to escape, to get out of the forest and find a habitation. Alas! Woods everywhere, cedar trees, pine trees, tree branches floating here and there, leaves and flowers snatched from the creeper vines, stuck on the thorn bush. . . . Everywhere the desolate earth appeared to have been struck by the anger of God. I do not know how many times I took off in an aimless stupor when, through the half-uprooted trees, I caught a glimpse of a human figure that seemed to be observing me with curiosity. Without knowing why, I cocked the trigger of my pistols and screamed out, "Who goes there?" The fatigue of this terrible morning had made me crazy.

A young Indian emerged from behind a tree, elegantly dressed in a deerskin cape, his head covered with a swan skin turban topped by an eagle feather. He carried in his hands a bow of yellow wood and an iron-tipped arrow from a quiver of cougar hide. The savage looked at me and burst out laughing. When I asked him the way to Natchitoches, his laughter doubled, and he made a sign that I was going in the opposite direction. I understood from his gestures that I still had to travel the distance of one sun, or one day's trek, so I set out again. The young Indian kept on giving me advice in guttural exclamations and in explanations making absolutely no sense to me, and I obstinately continued on my way. He started to laugh even louder and disappeared.

Night was beginning to fall when, confused and discouraged, I realized I was near the two beautiful magnolias that had sheltered me that morning. My false route had led me astray toward the Sabine, and I found myself reduced to being happy that my horse's habitual route had led me back there. By an unheard-of coincidence, this time I saw a rider coming toward me at full speed. He was taking the same route and hurrying to beat the nightfall, because he needed to cover this whole distance in which I had been wandering since morning in every direction. But my horse was almost dead and could go no further, while fatigue and hunger had exhausted me. The traveler shared his *cigarres du pays* with me, and we traveled along rather quickly because he took the precaution of placing himself behind me and whacked my nag mercilessly upon the rear. We rode along like that through a darkness so extreme that I had to keep calling my traveling companion every minute so that I would not go astray. In this manner, we crossed gullies, streams, and brush that entangled us, with no sign of a house. No light came to us, as it does in tales of fantasy, to put an end to our miseries!

Deep in a ravine, we were suddenly stopped by a long stream that was impossible to see, but whose murmur mingled with the sound of the wind in the forest. My companion wanted to look for a way to ford the stream, but everywhere the water echoed back a muffled sound when we threw in a branch, and in the darkness I could not move away a single step without running the risk of getting lost again. So the elements reduced us to spending a hopeless night, not on the soaked ground, but on our horses who refused to stand up and threatened constantly to roll over with us. It was impossible to light a fire with our pistols since rain had entirely soaked the powder.

At the cruelest moment of our day, a great consolation revived us once more: a distant bark resounded on the other side of Castor Bayou. When we yelled back, human voices responded. Someone lighted torches, but we still had to get over there. In a last ditch effort, we both dug in our spurs and, in a single bound, we jumped into water so deep that both horses and riders disappeared. We came back up to the surface, however, but the current sucked my unfortunate companion into the river, thrown from his horse, yet still clinging to it. He let out horrible screams and begged for my help. I tried to direct my horse, which was swimming vigorously, but the force of the torrent cast the traveler onto a shoal from which he got to the other bank before me. When I felt my horse's head bump against the bluff on the opposite side of the stream and his nostrils rip against the rocks of the bank, I was tempted to abandon the poor beast and jump to ground. The current still had him and his strength was giving out; I felt as if in one of those dreams where one keeps on going without ever getting anywhere. By chance a long branch was hanging over the water. I grabbed it, violently sinking all the rowel of my spurs into the exhausted beast. The resulting convulsive effort hurtled both of us onto the shore, but into a thicket so strewn with cane and creeper vines that the animal just stayed there, and I dangled by the ear three feet up in the air until I could pull out my knife and cut myself down from this horrible position.

The inhabitants of the cabin came toward us with torches, just in time to save us from their mastiffs which already threatened us. They gave us a slab of bacon and a cup of water for supper. We went to bed on a mattress between the two compartments of the cabin, leaving outside our water-filled boots, our coats, and the clothes we would have to slip back into in the morning. By 2:00 A.M. everything was covered with frost, but at least I was no longer in the forest. It would have taken very little for the cold to have frozen us for good. I could then reflect more maturely on the planter's advice.

Unable to find fodder under the water that bathed the countryside, our horses were reduced to grazing on our painted whale riding crops which we forgot near them.

We took up our trek again in biting cold, wrapped in frozen clothes. Though we suffered horribly until sunrise, it then turned too warm to allow us to go our remaining fifty-eight miles without fatigue and with no other nourishment beside the inevitable chunk of bacon.

Repose

I was harassed, exhausted, dying after traveling eighteen leagues [approximately 54 miles] in an evil land of enchantment, sometimes following along the river bank by shoals dotted with alligators and turtles, animated here and there by kingfishers, vultures, or *pirogues*, when the path finally opened up onto a prairie, with a village at its end, complete with smoke rising from the chimneys. All of the sensations of the day crashed down on me at once at the sight. I had grown out of the illusions of my childhood, ready to disappear before reality. Each step tore a layer from the veil.

At noon I crossed Cane River and, from that point on, I proceeded even more like a stranger into a country whose inhabitants were almost all known to me by name, names attached by all sorts of liaisons to the names of my own family which came to establish itself on the banks of the Red River. The closer we came to the village, the more curiosity we caused, I and my poor horse, so tired that he grazed every minute. Then someone whispered, and I turned around involuntarily upon hearing my name. When, out of simple curiosity, I asked the Negroes if I could find a place to sleep in some habitation, they always responded affirmatively, emphasizing the well-known generosity of their masters. Many times I glimpsed a remembered face through a window, and once in particular I was tempted to knock at the door, when I saw, inside the house, a fellow who once spent several days in France in my father's house. Only a child then, I never dreamed the day would come when I would bring my footsteps to his faraway land.

Having finally arrived at the plain, and then at the center of the village, I cast my surprised eyes all around the village. Although I was feeling impatient to be settled into the bosom of my family, I felt such joy at being at the end of my tribulations that I would have willingly postponed for a few more minutes the embraces I needed so badly. Suddenly someone stopped my horse by the bridle and made me dismount, for I was exhausted and weary. A joyful Creole supper, this time accompanied by an excellent Bordeaux wine, restored me. An hour later, I was stretched out on a four-poster bed surrounded by a gauze mosquito net, snoring. Oh! How sweet it is after so much traveling among strangers and being an obscure traveler tossed by each steamboat or ship onto an unknown shore with the rest of its cargo—a child escaped from his village, deprived for so long of that intimacy that nourishes a young soul—how sweet it is to fall soundly asleep, this time among my people, cradled in a friendship that is ready and waiting, and which asks in return only the profound gratitude that already fills the heart.

The next day I settled into the habitation. I loved to go to my own little cabin with a young Negro companion who accompanied me everywhere I went. I decorated this room in a special way, appropriate to my own taste. Above the little table piled high with books hung a rack of antlers; suspended from each point were artistically embroidered Indian garters and arrows tipped with iron and decorated with fish scales. An Indian costume also hung on this wall, complete with war club, a quiver, bows made from yellow wood, a mirror framed in an alligator head, and a tuft of feathers to place on my forehead. Above a little mirror, my double-barreled shotgun hung with my ivory-handled knife, a pair of snowshoes, and also some bearskins and tiger skins for sleeping in the woods.

The Red River flowed just a hundred feet from my window, with vast fields extending on both sides planted in cotton, high stalks of corn, and gracious parasols of lilas mixed with tufts of castor oil plant. A path led to the forest; right there a somber and mysterious cypress grove began, cut up by marshes with a charming fountain of clear blue water on the other side, so satisfying that a hunter could quench his thirst here in the worst heat without worrying. Frequently, in the evenings, deer drank here, and turkeys often wandered in among the papayas or wild lemon trees, whose white flowers as big as one's hand littered the ground shaded by persimmon trees and plane trees.

Three individual lakes formed a triangle around the fountain, one of which disappeared into underground springs in the river, but across woods so dense, so tangled in creeper vines and brambles that I was never able to follow it to the end without getting lost. The two other lakes abound in turtles, snipes, branched ducks,[18] and Betseys,[19] that enjoy the wild banks, their numerous flocks retiring during the heat of the day, scattering out into neighboring bayous, repeating their strange hissing sound which often interrupts the flight of a kingfisher scraping the water with his impetuous wing. I was never happier than when I could approach these lakes without being seen by the birds. Then, hiding behind a cypress tree, I followed all their joyful splashing as they plunged into the water which beaded into pearls on their sparkling plumage. As a European marveling at its primeval state, I admired nature in its harmony and repose.

On the other bank of the Red River I found another host of lakes, the largest being entirely covered with jonquils harboring a prodigious quantity of ducks, moorhens, otters, and alligators whose whole heads sometimes poked out through the reeds and whose two flaming eyes followed my every movement. As soon as I readied my gun, nothing remained. I surprised an alligator busy at building her nest. She was using her large tail as a mason's tool to cement together with mud a large pile of dried leaves. When the work was finished, it was as big as a cask. The animal deposited her eggs in the nest, and defended it courageously against the Negroes who eventually succeeded in dispersing her brood, though some of the adequately formed ones scampered to the lake as soon as they saw the light.

Hunting was as easy as it was plentiful. We paddled in pirogues to set up on little islands, three feet in circumference, scattered in the clearings. One hunter made a trip around the lake. Either he surprised the ducks, killing ten or twelve at a time, or he scared them off without shooting at them, in which case they flew off above the rushes. Being disoriented,

18. Note by Pavie: A kind of brilliantly colored tufted duck having webbed feet, but with claws like ground birds; he frequently perches and nests in trees. [William Dean Reese identifies the "branched" duck—probably referring to its branch-perching habit—as the stunningly beautiful wood duck.]

19. Note by Pavie: Another duck whose head is decorated with a black and white tuft, known as a Louisiana duck, monk duck or nun duck. [From Pavie's description, Reese surmises that the Betsey is a hooded merganser.]

they hesitated a long time choosing between going to the right or to the left, a delay that left them exposed too long to the floating gunmen, so that a certain number of birds always fell. In the evening, we harvested our crop in a skiff, and, even if we lost a certain number that were only wounded, the hunt was quite satisfying.

The Brulée River flowed a mile further and joined the Red River, making a parklike island, abundantly populated with deer. One day during a hunting trip with hounds, I took up my post between the headwaters of two lakes with my horse tied up twenty feet away. Just as men's voices caused the deer to approach the spot I occupied, a fantasy took hold of me, and I left my station to go admire the ducks which were just as splendid and golden as in the watercolors of Fielding.[20] Once there, I so completely forgot my duty that four young fawns passed within pistol shot and it never entered my head to shoot. Moreover I was and still am such a bad shot that I always preferred to go along on a hunt as an amateur.

One hour, two hours went by, and I remained there listening to steady gunfire in the distance, so constant that in any other case I would have taken it for a skirmish with Indians. I set off at a gallop through the cane, and what was it? My companions seated tranquilly in their saddles shooting pigeons. The wood pigeons, stunned to see their ranks so thinned out, flew from tree to tree, finally taking refuge on the tallest branches where the shot could only hit one at a time. We went on back without deer, each one having instead a beltfull of pigeons.

I said that the Red River ran a hundred feet from my window. The winter evenings in my cabin seemed as lovely as autumn evenings on the shores of the Mediterranean. What charming parties took place in the village, sending bright flashes of social life into the heart of this imposing solitude! Two thousand leagues (approximately 6000 miles) from Europe melodious female voices accompanied by guitar echoed the most beautiful lyrics of French music and the sublime harmonies of Rossini in their native language. Residents here read and understand literature of all peoples: Shakespeare, Dante, Tasso, Byron, Cooper, Walter Scott, Lamartine, Victor Hugo—all of these glorious names blended harmoniously with the silence of the forest, and all the poetry that great men have divined grew even greater in the bosom of this nature. The author of

20. Newton Fielding. See note 1 of Part II.

Atala was my faithful companion, whether I directed my course to the banks of Lake Natchez, picking my way through tombs over which brambles were growing, or, seated on a vine swinging from the summit of a sweet gum tree or climbing to the crest of a plane tree, I remained a few hours to read and reread these sublime pages, balancing myself voluptuously like a bird.

At night, by the light of the moon, I slowly rode the current downstream in a pirogue. One time, I landed in a remote savanna amid which surged up tall pecan trees laden with nuts and persimmon trees full of fruits fought over by wild cats. Another time I paddled upstream and, lying down in my light dinghy, I felt a sweet joy, a feeling of well-being, of gentle laziness in allowing myself to ride waves bearing the reflection of the moon, shiny and silvery, as if the queen of these forests. Then I returned to my cabin and listened to the songs of my Negro companion, whose sonorous, harmonious voice lulled me to sleep.

So passed my days. Could anything have been more beautiful for an eighteen-year-old, given that one lives with a brilliant parade of illusions at that age? At that age, everything looks rosy; what sadness other than a gentle melancholy could accompany the journeys of one who is merely a bundle of physical and mental energy, of hopes, enthusiasm, and life? All one could hope and dream could be called up and satisfied with a wish, all that could quicken a heart in which pain was still unknown, all that could cause a melody to resonate in an ardent soul.

I fully enjoyed this complete independence for which every man thirsts, but without knowing it, because happiness is so rare in this world that it often slips away unperceived, and like the grains of sand in which gold rolls along, these rare parcels shine only a short while after the wave has passed. Unfortunate is the one who felt the happiness of liberty too early, for he began life where he should have finished it. He ages early and dries out at twenty, already the prisoner of regrets. He devours life, drifting along haphazardly trying to recapture some glimmer of youth: his homeland, the simple pleasures he shared so long with his childhood friends, episodes scattered further and further through a tranquil existence, the peace of not knowing, all prizes he will no longer find. Like an exile in this world, like a plant lost from its sun—sad, isolated, mistrusted perhaps, his long remaining days will be spent in boredom.

INDIANS

The village of Natchitoches is the oldest settlement in Louisiana and the farthest point in the immense desert[21] extending to the Pacific Ocean. Today it remains a lost sentinel of civilization in the middle of the Pascagoulas, the Caddos, the Coshattas, the Cherokees, and all of the Indian tribes that have been dispersed. They have degenerated from their primitive power, but still conserve, if not their indomitable ferocious ways, at least the wandering habits of a nomad life over which American institutions hold no sway. Plantations flourish, rising up almost without interruption on both banks of the Red River displaying a luxury that gives such picturesque habitations an oriental aspect, in sharp contrast with the vestiges of solitude and of virgin America spread here and there in the path of the traveler. The village may be of little significance, but the environs offer delicious promenades: across the cedar forests crowning the hills with green and blue tints blending into the sky, or along the banks of the numerous streams over which branches and creeper vines cast bridges of flowers endlessly laced together, or from its solitary lakes to its deep dark bays where in the evening a pelican lifts its prophetic voice or pink spoonbills sparkle on the still waters like the flames that dance on the marshes in the evening.

The Indians come here to trade from every direction in the forest. You see them coming down the hill, leading fur-laden horses that they follow on foot, carbine under arm and bow over their shoulders. Around them dart the children; bored with the serious and solemn march of the warriors, they scatter among the woods, pierce with reed arrows the brilliantly colored birds, whose feathers they pluck to decorate their own foreheads. Next come the women, loaded down with baskets, sifters, and leatherwork to sell, their tiny nursing infants sleeping peacefully in the folds of coverlets slung over their shoulders. Arriving at the plain that stretches across the village and down to the river, the caravan comes to a

---

21. *Desert* is generally translated as "wilderness"; Pavie, however, probably got this word or concept from J.F. Cooper, who took with him to Paris a copy of Stephen H. Long's topographical report to President Jefferson which initiated the desert myth. See Goetzmann, *New Lands, New Men,* 110–26. Here, therefore, Pavie apparently had in mind the desert in the American sense of the word.

halt. Horses wander freely or roll under the acacias making their little cracked bells jangle, while the Indians gather behind the bushes to get themselves ready: some open haversacks where they store the silver rings they hang from their noses and ears, others paint their faces red and black, dividing one cheek into blue squares with bizarre characters and slathering the other in a different color. They lift the tuft of hair on the top of the head and mix in eagle or swan feathers, bedecking themselves with brilliantly embroidered headbands, garters [armbands], bracelets decorated with porcupine or sewn with parakeet heads or the beaks of black woodpeckers. With a tomahawk at the waist and a bow in hand, they march proudly toward the village making their cougar quivers rattle as the tail sweeps the dust. The women also decorate their foreheads and cheeks, wash their long hair in bear oil, tattoo the children, dangle wild seeds around their necks, and timidly follow in the footsteps of their warriors, the whole band walking single file in the invariable order they observe across the narrow paths of the forest.

The Pascagoulas settled between Natchitoches and Alexandria, while the Choctaws spread from the Red River to the Washita as far as Lake Ponchartrain, at the mouth of the Mississippi, and the Caddos, longtime friends of the Whites, became familiar with the American ways. The sight of a habitation or a store where their eyes covet a thousand abundant objects no longer surprises them, but they retained an extraordinary instinct for deciphering the face of the newly arrived traveler at first glance. No Indian has failed to recognize me not only as a foreigner, but as a Frenchman, and it is to my being French that I owe the kind reception they have always extended me, still keeping an indelible memory of our former domination in America. Americans scorn the savages: they detest them enough to take away their lands or, at least, to chase them off of them. The Indians bear a great friendship and also a profound respect for all that is French, as well as an inveterate hatred of all that is American, of those whose power they have seen grow so swiftly for half a century. As for the Spanish, they laugh at them, attack and pillage their caravans—a natural result of the little power held by the inhabitants of Mexico, whose villages are scattered apart by eight and ten days of travel.

Several times I met Indians reared among Whites who, at the age of fifteen, had fled the settlement to give themselves over to the indolent yet painful life of the forest. The more fearless in combat and staunch under torture a savage is, the lazier and softer he becomes after burying the war hatchet. You can see them spend days on end squatting down, head in hands, hands on knees, motionless, watching the river flow by. Are they pondering? I believe so, although many people say no. Every day flames ravage their forests, steamboats disturb the solitude of their rivers, white people sell their lands and divide it up into parcels, then into planta-tions—are those not rather sad subjects for meditation by the one who reigned as absolute king over a world? This half-existence they lead, shamefully wandering through forests and villages like dogs without masters on public plazas, this precarious life humiliates the soul of the Indian—proud and indomitable in his self-respect. He who is so indepen-dent, who crosses woods and plains, rivers and mountains, with no more worry than a deer for his evening meal and a place to lie down and sleep at night, he who carries all his worldly possessions in his quiver and bow, who travels without compass from one pole to the other more surely than we do from field to field with our eyes to guide us, he, son of the forest, knows by instinct that this life is ephemeral and that everything on earth is devoured by time, as his hut is carried off by a storm.

The incomparable virtue of the Indian, which he alone possesses, is knowing when to be quiet. He demonstrates this in the smallest things. One evening, as I dreamt at my doorway, a Caddo happened by, com-pletely attired in his native costume. In his own language, I inquired about the price of his gear. The skillful Indian permitted me to admire piece by piece what I soon came to covet, and, with the most profound indifference, he put all his strange regalia back on when I already consid-ered it bought, rejected the money, shook his head, and disappeared.

Eight days later when I was reading, a sonorous voice summoned my attention. I turned, almost frightened, to find the same Caddo. He had entered so quietly that I had not heard him. His costume was the same. Leaning on his sturdy bow, he crossed his legs with nobility worthy of Hercules resting; I had never seen a man so finely formed. "There are the weapons you asked from me; give me the money and a glass of rum."

I longed to enter into a conversation with the savage whose faultless French contrasted strangely with his tattooed face, his red skin, and his weaponry. Another Indian of the sort with the burlesque dignity taken on by certain chiefs had come to listen to us. This big, gaunt fellow, clad only in a long piece of flowered calico fashioned into a loin cloth, had the habit of solemnly walking about, hands behind his back, leaning on a cane ten feet high, trying to imitate the bearing and conduct of whites. His frequent visits annoyed me, and I asked this other warrior of the same tribe about this strange person.

"He is just a poor Indian like me, an ignorant man who has never seen anything. If I am wiser, it is because I have lived with white men who have read to me from great books. Do not laugh at him; he is a brave man, respected by the tribe. White men reared me and I love them for that, but for the rest, I prefer my wandering life. I took off their clothes and put on my moccasins and a tomahawk. My skin is red, is it not? You considered me a savage with no experience, because I said nothing. I had business to tend to in the next village and I wanted to appear there armed. Farewell, it is time for me to leave; I am awaited at my hut."

"Why do you not have any firearms?" I asked.

"My weapons are reliable and do not make any noise."

"But where will you find your route?"

"Oh, do not worry, night or day, it matters not, I am going there, see? Where you see that cloud. Farewell."

Indian peoples venerate tombs. Each year at the same time, relatives of the departed come to shed tears and cry in anguish over the earth containing the remains of those dear to them; they leave flowers and provisions, and listen to the noise of the wind in the neighboring trees, persuaded that it is the voice of the dead speaking to them. If some major occasion—a great hunt, the general games, or a war—keeps them with the tribe, they charge a stranger with going to the tomb to fulfill the sacred duties and, in recompense, give him some rich furs.

All major events begin with a sacrifice: warriors and women participate according to the nature of the invocation. Priests and medicine men are generally feared, even by the chiefs; their faces are tattooed differently, some even shave their heads. Two spirits divide the world: a good one, to whom it is useless to pray since he only does good deeds, and the other, the author of all evil afflicting humanity. Each Indian throws into the fire in honor of the latter the tuft of fur that grows between the horns of the buffalo, the best portion of deer, the first ear of corn, in effect, the firstfruits of all hunts and harvests.

Years they divide into "moons," and moons, into "suns." On their New Year's Day, which falls between the second and fifth of February,

Indians pass through the villages in great numbers. A cane flute pierced with a single hole on one side, or making a prolonged drum roll on a piece of board with two sticks of wood—this is joyous music to them, to which are blended the voices of women and children, all intoned on the same note repeated in octaves in perfect pitch. Two young people march in front with flags of feathers, and the first white man they find at his door receives their New Year's wish, with more or less pleasure since they produce an infernal racket requiring a gracious response, a smile and some small coin. We read in the *Conquest of Mexico*[22] that this festival, celebrated with the same traditions, fell at this same time of the year for ancient peoples of great power; we also find the same divisions of time and a host of other curious similarities, leading us to suppose a common origin for all the inhabitants of this vast hemisphere.

Chateaubriand, in *The Natchez*, speaks of the tribe of Mobilians, who kept the sacred fire. Some traditions of this venerated people remain today, though the people themselves have completely disappeared. The language of the Mobilians, incorrectly call the "Obilians" by the inhabitants along the Red River, is the best proof, as it is generally understood by ten or twelve tribes spread throughout the American West.

In *The Natchez*, the author of *Atala* gives an exact and poetic description of the solemn games, still celebrated sometimes in the great plain of Natchitoches, the racquet game being the one that attracts the largest number of Indians. They arrive a long time in advance from the four points of the horizon, spilling forth from the forests by a thousand different paths. This offers surprised Europeans the most curious spectacle. Here, an exhausted family sets up camp, chopping wood, cutting the branches to make its campfire, spreading out the bearskins and bison blankets while horses neigh, rolling in the grass or mixing with the Mexican steeds of a neighboring hut. There, warriors gather around the flames silently to smoke the peace pipe each one passes around the circle. Then they prepare racquets and balls and oil their nervous arms to increase their suppleness.

22. This book was not in the library of Mme Chouan's in 1996, when I assisted in the before-the-sale inventory. Therefore, it is not possible to determine which versions of "The Conquest of Mexico" Pavie is referring to. Numerous renditions were available at the time—even in the form of opera—as the story of Cortés held great interest for the Romantics.

Everywhere are camps where women prepare the evening meal, or the children imitate in joyful movements the important games each Indian is preparing. Bows, arrows, quivers, and carbines hang from the lower branches of cypresses, a thousand puffs of smoke fly away in swirling clouds above their summits, gathering here and there on the tufts of moss which long harbor the vapor of the flames, then exhale it in the sunset as a network of purple. Then the village comes to life; the inhabitants, less numerous than the hoards of savages, close their doors and set up a state of defense without admitting the mute concern which adds even more to the solemnity of the festival. In the streets at every step, warriors deliberate, talk loudly and disperse, returning to the vault of plane trees to emit piercing cries, repeating the sound as if to assure themselves that the forest has not lost its echo, that no other voice would dare to respond to this provocation.

Finally, just before sunrise, the games begin. Already the warriors are assembled in the plain, the feathers on their foreheads undulating like the waters of a lake, like stalks of sugarcane. Posts mark off the conventional distance, the nations take their spots, a general silence reigns. Sacrifices begin when the high priest throws the sacred sacrificial objects into the flames and jousters dance three times around the fire, then repeat the spinning war dances, pierce the air with their whoops, make the blades of their axes sparkle and the steel of the cutlasses glitter. The spell works; the evil spirit is appeased, and the chief sits down, exhales four puffs of smoke from his pipe to the four corners of the horizon, and gives the signal.

Then comes an exclamation in a single voice, a roar that shakes the woods in their deepest solitude. Frightened, the swallows flee swiftly and the bullfrogs interrupt their sinister croaking. Twenty nude warriors are deployed at the same time to catch the ball in narrow racquets in order to hurl it into the air and bounce it off the head of another Indian who falls unconscious, or strike the stomach of another, wounding and killing him so that his blood reddens the dust. The ball wounds, kills, and keeps on bouncing; it is hurled again and again without stopping, hissing as it cuts through these waves of red heads. Everywhere women encourage the men by striking them with sticks while others, young and old, armed with gourds filled at the river, water the sweaty, panting, wounded Indians, who return to the game with renewed fury. The game continues and feathers litter the earth. Victors trample the fallen underfoot, in vain they lift up their heads and try to stand up in the middle of the crowd, their hands work the soil, grab the foot of the passing conqueror who in turn stumbles and loses his victory. On top of this moving pile entire teams of players writhe, their legs cross, crackle, and break, blood flows until one of the two nations throws the ball to its post, and all is finished.

Some have gambled their horses, their weapons, and all their possessions. The vanquished retire and the triumphant tribe remains master of the battlefield. For several days, chanting follows the dances as the women care for the wounded or bury the dead, until finally the crowd disperses and returns to the forests. Deathly silence hovers over this vast prairie, arena of dust with scattered bloodstained grasses; the only debris remaining from the festivals a handful of drunken hangers-on sleeping in the edges of the trail.

In the contest that took place in October, the Pascagoulas, a weak tribe of the Red River, gained victory over the combined Choctaws and the Caddos, but almost all were wounded and several succumbed afterwards as a result of violent blows received in the heat of this exercise for which they carry a passion. Later, when hunting, I came across one of them limping through an Indian camp with the help of a stick. I recognized in him the winner of the racquet game. He had me sit on his mat and smoked with me; he took such glory in his triumph that he was hoping to be killed in the next festival.

Cherokees, Miamis, Shawnees, Chickasaws, Tahatees,[23] Coshattas, Delawares, and Creeks all meet each year at a certain time to compete in the games. The Osages, Karankawas, Comanches, and other bellicose Indians from upper Arkansas and the northern provinces of Mexico live so far from the plantations that their ways are little known; in fact, the latter tribes (with the exception of the Osages) are all nomadic. Their hunting consists of following a herd of buffalo down to the last one; their combat is often little more than skirmishes with Spanish (Mexican) caravans they can easily rob but attack only when success is a sure thing.

23. In the *New Texas Handbook*, vol. 6, Thomas N. Campbell identifies the Tahocullake Indians (Hogologe, Tahogale, Tahogalewi, Tokogalgi), a small group of Yuchi Indians who apparently accompanied the Cherokees from Tennessee to northeastern Texas in the early part of the nineteenth century (193). Pavie names the chief of the same group as the source of a fifteen-node rattler sent home in his trunk.

When it is a question of a battle among nations, one of the two must be almost annihilated—the Osages recently made a raid on the Sioux from which they brought back seventy-seven scalps.

CAMP

Before sunrise, the horses equipped with copper-pommeled Spanish saddles, await us attached to the galleries; then comes a pack mule, its packs completely full, the skins stretched over the folded tent, with pots, ingots of lead, and a barrel of powder dangling from each side. Spurs jangle on the boots of the mounted hunters as the caravan advances.[24]

Our little band meandering through the forest made a pretty sight. A stocky Negro with a carbine over his shoulder led the way, mounted on a tall, dappled horse with a long mane and flaring nostrils, a large Labrador retriever with droopy ears leaping at his side, followed by the mule with his little bell, jangling as he trotted down the slopes with his heavy load, then steadying as he regained his usual gait. Two Negroes carrying our carbines came next, and we closed out the ranks, wrapped in our coats, each one with two bottles of rum suspended from his saddle, in our pockets a tinder box and some delicious Cuban cigars.[25] After five

24. Charles Pavie and his brother-in-law took Théodore camping at the end of December. From his letter to Victor of December 12, 1829, we know that the site had been inside the Neutral Ground from 1806 to 1819, because he states that it was in Texas before the last boundaries were established: "campement fait sur les bords du lac Espagnol, jadis dans la province du Texas, avant les dernières limites" ("the camping trip taken on the banks of Spanish Lake, formerly in the province of Texas"). The property could have belonged to one of Charles Pavie's brothers-in-law, probably Francisco Rouquier, or it may be the 640-acre Arroyo Hondo tract (claims list #188), still held in common with Charles Nayrit at the time of Charles Pavie's death. This land was belatedly entered into the inventory of his property on August 27, 1838, as 320 acres at 50 cents an acre (Book of Successions, 1838, p. 225); 320 acres on Bayou Pedro [Bayou Pierre] were adjudicated to John Laplace at $1.26 per acre for a total of $403.00.

25. After the "slave rebellion" in Santo Domingo (today Haiti), some six thousand French refugees went to Cuba, where they remained about twenty years. They were forced out of Cuba when Napoleon went to war with Spain; most resettled in New Orleans. Natchitoches and Cuba exported the finest tobacco.

hours of riding through the forest guided by the instinct of the Negro, who stopped from time to time to recognize the flow of a stream, the moss in the trees, the incline of some tree branches—always thicker toward the east—we began to see the vast clearing formed by Spanish Lake, then we advanced on foot. Cypress knees[26] poked out through the soil, and the mud that hid them made the route difficult for the horses who took marvelous precaution stepping beside these sharp points.

The summit presented us a truly delicious view of the half-caved-in lands surrounding the lake, a pure and primitive Louisiana, with not a cabin, not a house other than the temporary huts of hunters whose carbines resounded in the distance. Echoes prolonged this rumbling a hundred times, provoking the swift, dense flight of thousands of ducks, setting out in a single mass. In the evening, bands of bustards[27] let their shrill voices burst forth here and there in a silvery clangor, creating a general whistling on the waters which weakens as their triangle disappears on the horizon. A spoonbill, always solitary, glided over the reeds mysteriously and imperceptibly; once it has found the rocky strand where it likes to bathe its long legs, it became so completely immobile that I remained a long time considering it in mute admiration, sharing the religious respect accorded spoonbills by the Indians of Mexico.

A cabin, or rather a cypress bark shed, served as our shelter the first night. We cut down some trees and set them alight to warm us and cook our provisions. I confess, when I returned from an excursion by the lake to have my share of the supper, the spectacle was so new to me, that my companions noted my surprise. From a slightly inclined pike hung in front of the flames was suspended a skinny, black, half-roasted teal from which we were each to rip off a member. With what? I knew nothing about that; but happily, I soon made a fork from a piece of wood. We had brought bread in the saddle bags, but the water was brackish, so we were obliged to wait for a Negro who had gone to find fresh water. He brought back some water-filled gourds into which we mixed a little rum, and, the meal finished, we went to bed. At night it froze even under the

26. Note by Pavie: The locals call the abundant cypress roots growing around the trees *boscoyos;* they make the trek of pack animals extremely dangerous and painful.

27. Note by Pavie: Louisianians give the name of "bustards" to hyperborean geese; twice as large as ordinary geese, they weigh up to twenty-five pounds. [Reese identifies the hyperborean goose as a Canada goose.]

shed, and our coats hardly sufficed to keep out the cold, even more pene-trating because the heat had been as intense during the day as it is in France in the month of May.

We still needed to cross the lake to establish our camp on the other bank, at Capalca point.[28] A Negro escorted the horses back to the habita-tion along with the kill, divided into three pirogues that were so narrow that hardly a half inch remained free and one false move of the paddle would have caused them to tip over and spill our haul. A wind, rather violent, but favorable, with the help of our coats transformed into sails, pushed our flotilla gracefully among the ducks who divided as we passed, then closed back over our trace. So numerous that the water became tur-bulent from their dives,[29] their thousand colors sparkled in the sun like the flowers of the prairies of Opelousas. We crossed in two hours, pulled the canoes to dry land, and the hunt began.

Each hunter goes where it seems best to him, but most preferred to follow the banks of the lake, often in belt-deep water with feet enveloped in light deerskin boots, a handful of moss stuck up the barrel of the gun, a game bag from which to take the lead without measuring it, and a pow-der horn made from the horn of a cow or a buffalo. Sometimes when I had lined up a band of ducks surprised while crawling on my knees, then advanced in the rushes with extraordinary precaution, I would sink up to my neck in an alligator hole and feel under my feet the scaly back of the still reptile. When the water recedes, one sees them stretched out, be-numbed by the cold, and with an ax, one may cut into the monsters sleep-ing so lethargically that they die without giving the least sign of suffering. A hunter returning to camp, relights the fire with dry branches, suspends his game on a rack resting on two trees, and returns to the hunt until eve-ning. Everyone gathers and general supper often extends well into night. Someone must always remain in the camp during the daytime to keep away the birds of prey, always on the prowl and ready to carry off every-thing found on the rack.

28. Note by Pavie: Creole or Indian name for Catalpa.

29. Note by Pavie: the *canard-cheval*, the most prized of the Louisiana ducks, gets its food from the bottom of the water, at ten or twelve feet; it has ashy white wings, and its head and tail are black.

After two days of abundant hunting, we had exhausted the supplies of bread and liquid. The bad quality of the water kept us from drinking it straight, so we sent a Negro to the village to take back the game and replenish the supplies that we lacked. He had hardly left when the sky took on a menacing aspect, a frightening darkness spread suddenly, and thunder clattered. Our camp lay outside the shelter of the large trees, at the foot of two clumps of honey locust that sheltered us from the wind, an advantageous position whose usefulness we recognized as everything gave signs of a terrible storm from the north. We doubled the stakes for the tent and dug trenches all around it to prevent the rain from inundating the interior. Once such precautions had been taken, we pressed close together in silence to await the hurricane whose ever-increasing roar arrived with extreme rapidity. Crackling trees, branches ripped away, and the roar of wind in the lairs of the forest marked its passage; it exploded above our heads even more frighteningly, and all that long avenue where herds of deer took refuge, all that graceful clump of catalpas that embellished the point where we camped, all that was ripped up, broken into pieces, uprooted more quickly than those castles built of cards children enjoy erecting just to blow down. The tent resisted; there was a moment when we felt it cry out from its stakes, and stretch up, ready to fly away with the leaves of the lataniers whirling around in the air. Acacias groaned and bent over to the ground; but the first phase of the storm passed away as quickly as it came, and we took a deep breath. I hazarded a glance outside the tent and saw the lake bubbling like the crater of a volcano, shaking its head of froth on which flitted bluish flames, sharp like the blades of double-edged swords. The storm continued the next day, as violent as the torment that litters the Channel with the shreds of red sails snatched off the *chasse-marées* [fishing luggers]. For us, tranquil under the tent, lighted by a branch of cedar stuck into a cane pole, we spent a part of the night discussing a thousand memories of Europe, smoking cigars, thoroughly enjoying the pleasure of hearing the rain fall in large drops on the canvas, of being protected by a simple shred of cloth used against this universal uprising of troubled nature in its most solitary retreats, raising its plaintive voice from everywhere as the water streamed around us, inundating the bank up to the canoes. All prejudice had disappeared; the Negroes shared the same shelter with their masters.

But one worry still remained for us: the slave loaded with our supplies might have set out across the lake before the squall. If so, he would never have been able to reach the bank in his frail skiff. Before daybreak we left to check; two eyes shone brilliantly facing the fire; and I grabbed my rifle loaded with a ball. The creature pulled back in front of me, and I still kept advancing imprudently into the thick underbrush. Then it stood up on its feet and I saw a lynx stretch out its agile flanks, jump over the hedge, and in one leap, roll under the willows. The prime burned without firing, and I remained defenseless twenty feet from the furious animal. A rifle sounding in the distance, shot from the tent to signal the other bank, convinced him to leave, however, and I realized I was shaking all over, one hand tightly grasping my dagger. I returned to the camp, to find the Negro had just arrived with refreshments—milk and, above all, the bread whose lack had caused us to suffer cruelly; we had been reduced to boiling vegetation in the brackish water, stalks of *herbe à chevreuil* and *baumier*, a drug that is bitter but extremely healthful for the hunter who has spent a day in the marsh.

The area surrounding the lake looked desolate. Two strangers joined us; the storm had overturned their camp, leaving them exposed through the night to all of the fury of the tempest. The waters swelled and threatened to flood our point soon. Frightened birds allowed one to approach them easily; and a good shot bagged twenty-five ducks in one evening, and two swans (*cygnes*) fell at the same shot, breaking some heavy tree branches with their fall. But this place no longer held the same attraction for us. Everywhere we struggled over damp earth, saturated with rain or, in some places, entirely submerged. Bustards flew off, no longer finding the shoals they prefer over other types of soil, birds of prey fanned out with renewed ardor over the reeds to hunt for some sleeping prey—wounded geese or squirrels lying belly-up in the willows.

We decided to break camp. Little birds threw themselves, twittering, onto the circle of clean, fresh grass revealed when we removed the tent. Once out in the open, rowing in our canoes with joyful rowers' songs, we saw vultures take possession of the abandoned spot, jumping competitively onto the animal debris hung on the thorns, and a lugubrious circle formed like spirits of the night whose cloven hoof traces a circle of dried flowers in the middle of the prairies.

THE BEAR HUNT

Louisiana is, as we have seen, crisscrossed by a multitude of dispersed lakes on whose banks the inhabitants establish themselves during hunting season and provide abundant kill for the rest of the year when all they can do is flee the mosquitoes, the sun, and the snakes and insects teeming in the forests, and search in a thousand ways for shade and sleep. Spanish Lake, which remained for a long time inscribed inside the border of the Mexican territory, flows into the Red River twenty-five miles from Natchitoches. No plantations are found beyond that, just grazing land here and there in the woods, with immense herds entrusted to the care of Negroes, cornfields of meager yield, then some clusters of rather sad houses of honest, hospitable old inhabitants, living in small groups, away from the noise of the world, isolated even from the rest of the colonists. The slightly brown tint of their skin indicates that the wives of the soldiers-turned-planters descended from the Indians.

The only way to travel by water is to paddle in pirogues. About forty leagues from the village, navigators encounter the *Grand-Embarras* or the Great Raft, a stretch of several miles, wherein innumerable tree trunks, especially cedars coming from the foot of the mountains, so obstruct the river that its course disappears from sight. One can walk on this immense raft without realizing that a deep river flows under one's feet, pressed down by the floating wood that it tows along, fighting against this dike, a barrier so strong that in the winter the river submerges it without being able to break it up. A company was formed to lay out a route for steamboats across this nearly insurmountable obstacle; but so far all efforts have only resulted in detaching some tree trunks from this great body of logs, only to have them collide with new logjams downriver and interrupt previously free-flowing navigation.

Not far from the Great Raft, another bizarre freak of this powerful nature strikes the traveler's attention. The village of the Caddos, composed of huts elegantly arranged in a circle in the midst of a clump of trees, is reflected in the lake whose blackish waters can be seen at its feet. Here and there tops of ancient cypress, beech, and sycamore sway in the middle of swampy waves, a ferruginous color silvers its surface and mottles the surrounding grass up to the bark of the magnolias shooting heartily above a cool shady place. Indians report that they used to live on this site, today buried under the water. The earth trembled, opened up, and swallowed the beautiful forest that protected their huts, up to the tree tops; today this lake carries the name Lake of the Caddos.

The savages of this tribe have had their vicissitudes: when the French established themselves on the Red River, they divided the Indians into repartimientos, as did the first colonists of Cuba and Mexico. They continued this practice a long time; one still sees old Caddos who remember having been slaves. Today they are free, and the Africans, fated always to moan in chains, take their place. In spite of the barbaric injustice they suffered for so long, the Indians preserve (though I do not know why) a great friendship toward the inhabitants of the plantations, and the Great Chief will sit at table with several distinguished persons in the village. He orders his wives and followers to retire, seats himself in a chair without appearing too uncomfortable, and in his speech his hearers discover a wisdom above that of an Indian, especially when it is a matter of the respective concerns of the two nations.

All other tribes concede that the Caddos are great hunters, and regardless of their relationships with Whites, they continue to use their bows. Prodigiously agile, rather short, robust, and well built, there is something generous, intelligent, and pleasing in their lively and frank countenances, in their beautiful builds, in their faces—less rigorously tattooed than the others. With them, there is visible progress, however little reckoned. They probably owe it to their chief, whose ideas are remarkably elevated.

The same can be said for the chief of the Pascagoulas. A government decree once threatened to deprive him of the miserable portion of land he occupies at the foot of a lovely wooded hill, fifteen leagues from Rapides. He went to find the judge and, proudly showing him the courtyard of his own home where Blacks, horses, and cattle stirred about, in effect everything constituting a fine residence, said to him "Well, Brother, if I told you that you had to leave all this right this instant, what would you do? You do not have here the bones of your fathers and it has not even been twenty springs that you have sown, twenty winters that you harvested since you abandoned your home on the other side of the great lake of salty water—now we, the Pascagoulas, who owned all this land between the Natchitoches, the Shawnees, and the river, we must flee our village and see our forests and our huts burned. Listen, you are my brother, go tell those who command you that I have here one hundred young people ready to defend their homeland!" Men who speak with such energy, if they were educated, would be capable of acting on their ambitions.

Let us return to the Caddos and to their excursions. In the winter they spread out in the forest to hunt bear with no other arms than bows of yellow wood[30] and arrows three or four feet long tipped with iron, fish scales, or even stone artistically crafted into lance points. Each hunter's belt holds a hunting knife and a shiny hatchet they call a *casse-tête*, (a tomahawk or head smasher) intended to open and skin game birds, to chop branches to make fires, to smoke, to fight in hand-to-hand combat, and finally to scalp the head of a dead enemy. An Indian never goes out without his precious tomahawk, formerly made with the same kind of stone used to arm arrows. He wears a simple costume: unornamented garters cover the top of the thighs and the feet are bare, deerskin covers the shoulders, and on the head wave some duck feathers, which snag on the bushes and are torn to shreds after an outing, with the rest of the gear.

Besides lakes and rivers, every mile one finds bayous, deep streams in tortuous courses, sometimes dry, sometimes rapid and overflowing like the rivers that feed them. Hedges of cane cover the banks, making it impossible for any to cross them save a wolf, tiger, or Indian. One must penetrate these bayous to hunt bears in the winter when they retire, warmly sheltered by the cane, and sleep on a bed of moss that a weary traveler might envy. Once the animal gets going, it trots, grumbling, through the reeds whose crackling allows you to track it, it jumps furiously into more open wood, swims across rivers, ponds, or the wildest streams, crosses the fields of cotton and even the courtyards of houses without ever looking back and without attacking anything along its route, unless aggravated by injury. Misfortune, however, befalls him whose shaking hand alters his aim or the inexperienced hunter who loses his composure; the bear will not loose his trail. Standing up on its hind legs, opening its shaggy paws, the bear throws itself onto its prey, suffocates him, crushes him in a hug, and looking for the head of his victim, digs in its sharp claws, which rip open the skull and break it, killing as quickly as a bullet.

---

30. According to William Dean Reese, the yellow wood is that of the bois d'arc, also known as Osage orange, whose Latin name is *Maclura pomifera*. It was favored by Indians and settlers alike for making bows.

Sometimes the hunter must cover more than ten leagues across the varied forest, in turn swampy, impenetrable underbrush, or thorny triacanthos, but the Indian never errs in his observations: a leaf overturned by the foot of the beast so that the morning dew no longer gleams on it, an uprooted weed, a withered flower crumpled in passing, by such signs he tracks a beast. In the evenings, even at night in the blackest darkness, the native hunter will return to his tent, guided by his instincts. A foreigner, exhausted from fatigue, accompanied a Caddo on one of his excursions; at midnight the traveler, barely dragging himself along in the footsteps of his guide, despaired of ever finding his tent. He wanted to stop, to light a fire and camp, but the grave Indian, weary of his complaints, continued onward, like a ship moving on the faith of a star. Finally the foreigner sat down and warned the hunter that it was time to light a fire; the hunter took charge of lighting the fire, and the first spark lit the face of the Indian laughing mutely in the manner of Leather Stockings. On the second flame, the Indian was no longer there, and the desolate European already lay stretched out on the moss when the voice of his guide screamed out, "What are you doing there? Can you not see that I was merely playing? We have returned." And he came out of the hut with a flame that illuminated, as if by magic, the rest of the hunters asleep on their buffalo hides.

There exists another kind of bear hunt, which is more ingenious and less fatiguing, though it demands long treks through the cane. Indians carefully examine trees with holes for evidence remaining on the bark and when they find recent scratches on a trunk, it is certain that a bear has taken refuge in the hollow tree to spend the winter. The hunters lash together several poles, one to the end of another until the height of the hole in the tree can be reached. Then they light a short cane stick that is attached to the end of the pole and thrust into the opening an enormous lighted wick that falls on the prey. The bear, awakened with a start, infuriated by pain, roars and devours the burning reeds which fill him with fire and smoke. He then bursts forth from his cavern, but the Indian is watching with his bow stretched and his eye on the arrow. He follows all of the movements of the animal which is now bounding more swiftly than a deer surprised alongside a stream, as he slides down the treetrunk as a sail with a broken halyard descends a mast. Suddenly the bear stops and turns cowardly, stiffening all four paws, and hanging in the air. The vibrating arrow reaches its target, nailing the unfortunate bear to the trunk of the plane tree. With a great effort, the bear succeeds in breaking the fatal weapon piercing his entrails. The beast rolls over and bounds back on its feet, but the Indian grabs it by the tail and, so as not to spoil this beautiful fur, he plunges his hunting knife into the frothing mouth.

THE SABINE

It had been six months since I had crossed Lake Ontario. It was July then; yet the north wind stirred up the waves on this sea, and its glacial blast would have made one believe that the thick clouds clustered on the horizon were hiding snow in their sinister flanks. Now, in January in the forest of Louisiana, we found a clear sky, starry nights, somewhat chilly, but gentle and fragrant like an autumn evening. We mounted our horses at the first cry of the wood pigeon, and I pushed myself cheerfully toward the route to Texas, impatient to explore southward over all of this sequence of united republics that I had just perused.

We were trotting along, and the forest repeated the sound of our footsteps and our joyful chants. I had on my saddle two robes [pelt blankets] for sleeping in the woods, a traveling bag, and two immense pistols in holster. Provisions, cigars, and a powder horn dangled from the pommel. I wore other smaller pistols and a Mexican dagger on my woolen belt, embroidered near Quebec by the Algonquins. My traveling companions were also armed with all that was necessary, and we were feeling this power, this ease that one feels on a beautiful morning in the middle of the forests, especially when one feels well armed.

After several miles we let our mounts drink at the Hondo River, a delicious stream that long marked the boundary of the two powers. We noticed two admirable magnolias near the path, the most beautiful trees in all the land, on which travelers customarily wrote their names on the bark. I looked there in vain for the name of Chateaubriand, which nonetheless should have been there according to the local learned ones. When I dismounted on the bridge to carve the five letters of my unknown name into this consecrated tree, I found a young alligator on the route. It did not dispute my way very long and plunged into the bayou, playing in its silvery waves.

Our first encounter was with a Mexican caravan. Beside a stream rose up a vast parasol of palmetto leaves, and under this canopy was seated a Spanish lady with a Negress. A few steps away, horses and mules were grazing with saddles and supply packs on their backs, and the "hire-lings," a type of salaried servants who spend their lives escorting travel-ers, were resting under a tree—some lying down, others smoking or keep-ing watch. All had pistols and daggers, while from their buffalo-hide saddlebags were attached long cavalry swords. Their arms, along with their beribboned flat wide-brimmed hats, green jackets and wide belts lent these Mexicans the appropriate character for singing quite naturally "Yo que soy contrabandista,"[31] although by nature, they share with Indi-ans their dark and severe faces, the leather chaps to protect their legs from brambles, and the triangular bearskin scrap strap that hangs down in a triangle and holds the stirrup. This little troop looked so strange, so new to me, so different from the rest of the scenes I had witnessed in America, that I stopped, perhaps impolitely, to contemplate it. I beheld Spain, pure and simple, as today's young writers depict it, with the addi-tional American slant of wild and imposing nature against which civilized man casts himself to best advantage: solitude and silence in which the sound of a voice resonates in accord with an inexpressible harmony.

Occasionally through the trees of this almost imperceptible route, slow convoys of wagons pulled by oxen or horses go down the paths and slip from view like the chariots that the vigorous pencil of Decamps[32] knows so well how to place in perspective. The wagoneers sing their songs—an interminable succession of refrains. They are of mixed blood,

31. This was the song that signaled the slave uprising in Saint Domingue in 1804. It is doubtful that Pavie actually heard the Mexicans singing this song; it is more likely that he included it as a tribute to Victor Hugo, who wrote in *Bug Jargal*, "One day as I entered he took no notice of me; he was seated with his back to the door of the cell, and was whistling in melancholy mood the Spanish air, 'Yo que soy contrabandista' ('A smuggler am I)' " (31).

32. Alexandre-Gabriel Decamps (1803–1860) displayed paintings of Oriental subjects in 1826, 1827, and 1828 (the latter salon Pavie attended), and published an album of litho-graphs in 1829. He was probably a friend of Victor Pavie through their mutual friend Alex-andre Dumas. His biographer classes him as "the head of a subdivision of the romantic school." Pierre du Colombier, *Decamps* (Paris: Éditions Rieder, 1928), 22.

some Mexican and some American, strangely dressed, more or less in the
style of the Indians, always wearing at their narrow deerskin belts the
long pointed knives that serve a thousand uses. When we passed near
them they interrupted their trek, and, leaning over the horns of these
powerful oxen, whips over their shoulders, they exchanged some insignificant words, saluted if they were Spanish, or gladly accepted a swallow
of grog if they were descendants of Englishmen. Half-sleeping heads
poked out sometimes from between the covers of the wagon. When the
retinue had caught its breath, when the impatient horses shook their
manes and stamped their feet, then a "good-bye sir" or an "adios señor
caballero" ended the exchange. Axle and yoke ground once more, the
wagon master took up his song again, and silence returned.

From mile to mile we found traces of camps, whether of wagoneer or
Indians, the former distinguishable by their vast encampment, by the
holes from the pickets of their tents and the grass grazed by their oxen,
whereas the savages' stopover left only a little fire of wood stumps placed
vertically so that a less heavy smoke rises directly into the air, not perceptible from a distance. Beautiful deer antlers almost always lay near the
ashes, too common for one to bother to gather them. Indians found their
directions by these, although Europeans' eyes found them impossible to
decipher.

One evening, we knocked at the door of a cabin where we were received cordially. We had to take care of our own horses, and placed our
weapons and bags inside the house and the provisions under the
porches—great rooms of bark held up by posts. The inhabitants served
us dried venison, cornbread, and a thick black beverage that they expected us to take for coffee, but that was impossible! In place of candles,
as the flame of the fireplace began to diminish perceptibly, an enormous
Negress, as disgusting as a Hottentot, placed herself near the table with
a lighted branch of cedar tree. This moving flame circled the cabin
spreading a lurid light; when it fell on the face of the Negress it excited
our hilarity, followed by a repugnance approaching horror. The family
let us eat supper, and afterwards all of them went to bed on the floor
helter-skelter with the exception of the grandparents, who took over a
bed. We took advantage of the other two beds. After tossing and turning,
coughing and sighing for a long time, the children fell asleep. The fire-

place only rarely emitted a flame, and soon a general slumber reigned in the cabin.

We travelers, all three French, continued to laugh and chatter until the scenes of this strange night led us to a profound sense of admiration. This cabin, like the other blockhouses, was built from tree trunks stacked rather regularly one on top of the other, but no one had bothered to plug up the six inches of daylight between the logs. Near midnight the moon peeked out across the treetops and suddenly cast its magic rays between the bars of the cage, randomly lighting the disheveled head of a child snoring on the floor, a tanned and wrinkled forehead of a hunter dreaming of bears and buffaloes, or the fresh face of a young girl dreaming peacefully beside her sister, whose breath played with her black hair. What were they all dreaming? What were their hopes, their fears? Such gentle tranquillity of repose told us that ambition had never caused its nightmares here.

Outside the hut another spectacle greeted us—a brightness so clear and so limpid that it dazzled. Plane trees, reduced by the clearing flame to hideous skeletons, jutted from the neighboring field; from their summit flew heavy circling owls whose round wings projected opaque shadows when they passed in front of the moon. The cabin itself seemed swallowed up in sleep. Toward the east the baleful cries of jackals and lynxes arose from the depths of the forest, while the chants of an Indian tribe camped in the prairie a few miles north pierced the vaulted archway of trees and mounted gravely into space like the faraway smoke of a fire that alternately dwindles and flares up. We led our horses to the bayou; their resigned hoofbeats resounded weakly on the dead leaves. When they drank the cool water and their reflections smashed against it like a forehead against a mirror, a circle of waves escaped from their nostrils, extending to the shore. A passing breeze answered from tree to tree, so gentle and trembling that one would have called it the timid dream of a young girl.

Back in the cabin the faraway sounds of Indian chants, the voices of wild animals, and the flight of birds of the night reached us as the mute murmur that buzzes in the ear of one who sleeps. The day broke and we had to leave.

Only ten leagues from there, we passed near the American fort established to contain the Indians and make them respect the border.[33] On the left, we saw the village of the Adaes, inhabited mainly by Spaniards, before we began to enter the marsh that borders the Sabine. Palmettos and prickly pears or Indian figs give this place a completely Mexican look. During the winter, water covers all of this swamp, and travelers and their mounts must resort to rafts, improvised with the help of axes, to cross the river. At the time when we found ourselves there [February 1830], the Sabine was very low, and we explored it on foot after emerging from the underbrush where the horses got tangled up more than once on vines. We hailed the ferry, and I stopped to contemplate the other bank which, like everything new, immediately tempted me. Impatiently I jumped down to the ground, or rather to the sand, and I greeted the land of Fernand Cortez!

THE COSHATTAS

About twenty years ago the road was traced from Natchitoches to Nacogdoches, that is if you can give the name of "road" to a foot path that is difficult to follow even in daylight, without running the risk of getting lost. Before that time, it was a dangerous trip. The two banks of the Sabine served then, even more than now, as the refuge of thieves and murderers from the two nations, who only had to slip across the narrow river to find themselves protected from the arm of the law, when the latter

---

33. Hubert Howe Bancroft mentions an 1826 letter from General Gaines from Camp Sabine (*Works*, vol. 13, p. 164). Powell A. Casey describes a "Camp Sabine" and the "Camp on the left bank of the Sabine River" (188–9), the site for making and maintaining the Neutral Ground agreement. According to Casey (93–4), in November 1820, Secretary of War Calhoun referred the 1819 request of the Louisiana governor for a small fort with garrison on the Sabine to protect the settlers, to Andrew Jackson, the commander of the Western Division of the Army. Jackson advised the War Department that no military leader would invade Louisiana from Texas, but a small fort near the Sabine would keep the Indians in Texas from troubling the settlers in western Louisiana. This encampment or its function eventually evolved into or became conflated with the site which took the name Ft. Jessup in 1832 (93–8). A restored Fort Jessup can be visited today outside Many, Louisiana. Powell A. Casey, ed., *Encyclopedia of Forts, Posts, Named Camps and Other Military Installations in Louisiana, 1700–1981* (Baton Rouge: Claitor's Publishing Division, 1983).

deigns to awaken from its deep slumber. But one must excuse the law—pursuit into the woods is so stiflingly hot! And then it is vexing to encounter the trail of the guilty party just at the moment he has put the waters of the Sabine between himself and you. Peacefully planted twenty-five steps from the border, he mocks the law until a new offense obliges him to cross the river one more time, and he will do it fearlessly because no one dares hold him responsible for his past actions. It so happened that we found ourselves eating at the very table of a man known throughout the country as a murderer forced into exile in Texas. While shaking his hand in the American way, I experienced an almost uncontrollable repugnance; his stare, falling on me, made me shiver, and his shiny carbine mounted above the chimney seemed haughtily to proclaim the blood it once caused to flow.

Let's get back to the Sabine. Low and swampy on the Louisiana side, as we have just seen, the Texas bluffs are higher, sandier, and dry, with tall grasses growing here and there among the scattered pines. In a word, Texas is a whole other country, with nearly new vegetation and a more arid climate, which is, consequently, healthier. Spanish moss no longer drapes the trees, and scraggly oaks, barely as tall as sassafras trees, replace the maples, persimmon trees, and all of those elegant shrubs from the woods of Louisiana. The Red River, already dominated by the Mississippi, then loses all its power, and this new land, although flat and consistent like its neighbor, anticipates the mountains of Mexico.

In the flank of this steep embankment, a little to the right of the place occupied today by the shack where passersby stop, two well-armed men camped, squatting near a small fire. Behind them stood the packs of the horses you could see grazing freely under the cedar trees. What were the two travelers doing there? Little or nothing; they were waiting for the river to flow normally, for it was currently overflowing its banks, and its overpowering current was folding over the trees of the marshes and uprooting the palms and the cane. Meanwhile the wind from the west was stirring up muddy waves with so much violence that it would have been dangerous to try to cross the river on a raft with horses laden with cargo. The rain had stopped the previous day, but the torrents dug beds into the crumbly rocks of the right bank, surrounding the camp with two natural moats. Thus our two travelers, each seated on the trunk of an inclined juniper,[34] cast bored glances across the muddy black river, from which protruded a multitude of treetops, some green and flowering, some withered, which had been uprooted by the floodwaters and now ready to surrender to the powerful flow. This rather sad spectacle varied in the morning by the sun rising above the distant forest in the east and in the evening by the last rays of the setting sun momentarily casting a purple tinge across the various planes of this vast tableau.

After waiting eight long days, they returned to their tent, satisfied to see that, according to their observations, the waters showed signs of subsiding, albeit slowly. Having deliberated on the construction of a large solid raft with poles, they selected wood from the forest appropriate to their design, and axes soon resounded in the silence. The work went rapidly: vines lashed the trunks together as easily as cables. Four great cedar trees formed the mass of the raft on which they generously spread branches of laurel and large-leaf magnolias.

It was almost completely ready to launch when the sound of distant voices rose up in the west, carried on the breeze that continued to blow across the water, but this murmur quickly faded when the breeze died down. The travelers suspended their work and, from the highest point on the riverbank, tried to figure out where the chants were coming from, but they had stopped. Just a few minutes later, we heard the same voices again, but more piercingly and more distinctly, and then they seemed to get lost among the numerous twists of the Sabine, only to start over and die down again the third time among the clumps of trees littering the islands. What remained for them to do? Uncertain whether danger approached or moved away in the opposite direction—if indeed a danger existed—they packed everything inside their tent, hid the tent under leaves, sat down beyond their extinguished fire, and waited. Anyone within range of pistol shot could not have found the least indication of a hut, even a deserted one, among the underbrush. Two large juniper trees crossed their branches in front of it, preventing even the most penetrating glance from perceiving this mysterious hiding place. The riders turned their attention to what would follow, more from curiosity than from concern.

34. In the South and Southwest, the juniper (*savinier* in French) is also called "cedar" or "red cedar." This is the Spanish *sabina* from which the river took its name.

Suddenly chants arose from downriver and a rapid beat marked the cadence of a thousand paddles beating the water in unison. A slender pirogue [a canoe fashioned from a single tree trunk] emerged from under the trees, then a second, then a multitude of others in single file, rowing with frightful speed, each powered by eight Indians leaning forward, heads immobile, eyes fixed on the prow. Had you seen them, you would have seen a movement more precise than the wing of a wood pigeon: they gripped their short paddles and, in a single thrust, plunged them into the water, creating a frothy eddy under the keel. No rowers on the Thames, whitehallers from New York, nor sailors from Quebec ever made a craft fly with more grace or speed. Their tattooed heads, red as the lava of a volcano, made their thousand sparkling feathers stand up on the water, and a cry of joy rose up from the first canoe, repeated by this long parade of boats snaking its way along with the meandering of the river.

These were valiant Coshatta warriors returning from hunting buffalo in the prairies dominated by the Rocky Mountains. Each pirogue moved under the weight of rich furs, as rowers celebrated their happy excursion with victory chants. Joyously, they moved down the river toward their village of pyramidal huts, still standing today at the place where the Opelousas trail crosses the Sabine.

The flotilla was passing at the feet of the strangers whose startled eyes were checking for the end of the parade of skiffs. A part had already passed when their frightened horses whinnied and bolted. Instantly, more than a hundred Indian faces turned toward the riverbank, and each pirogue came ashore one after the other. Ferocious cries resounded through the forest, and from everywhere came the response of a sharp hiss like that of a snake. The travelers fled. Soon you could see the savages searching about with that scrupulous attention from which nothing escapes, colliding with each other, jumping lightly above the underbrush, then glancing back with inexpressible delight toward this mass of pirogues attached to the banks and whose lovely cargo was held in balance by the waves. One Indian sprang onto the juniper trees, and, like a deer, bounded to the edge of the camp; the others gathered around him, and in one second uncovered the equipment and provisions.

The horses' cargo of necklaces and firearms transformed the Coshattas into vultures. They screamed as they pillaged, and soon knives sparkled, since brawls over booty make blood flow quickly among Indian tribes. The fury grew and heightened, when suddenly the last canoe appeared. Their chief stepped off onto the rocks and, with a single word spoken in his stentorian voice, suspended the pillage. His face, still red from anger, seemed inspired; he cast his sparkling eyes over his warriors and each and every one of them lowered his head.

The chief reprimanded them and had the trembling strangers brought forth. "Excuse me, white men," he told them, "my children are poor and ignorant. Instead of fleeing like women, you should have called in the great chief. Open this leather bottle and leave." Each Indian advanced timidly and received a swallow of eau-de-vie, as he deposited his share of booty from the pillage at the feet of his tribe's elder, got back into his canoe, and continued on his way. "Now," added the chief, "bring my furs," and the rowers painfully went up the hill with sacks of richly embroidered buffalo hides. "White men, take these as compensation for your losses and remember to return to us justice for justice."

The bewildered strangers gathered up their things scattered on the sand and mechanically saluted the extraordinary savage who, with a single word, had prevented the loss of everything they owned. They had guessed at his speech rather than understanding it, and they watched in wonder as each skiff detached itself from the bank and took its course back up in the same order. When the last one set off under its paddles, the chants started up, but quieter and more sadly. Ashamed, the warriors no longer lifted their scarred foreheads, and one might have said that the wind inclined their haughty heads like the grasses in the marshes. Two minutes later the chiseled stern of the most beautiful canoe plunged under the branches of the trees, carrying the seated chief, leaning over his spear, an eagle feather decorating his white hair, his powerful voice intoning the victory hymn. Then, all disappeared behind an island in the Sabine, without any other trace than the frothy wake, soon erased by the current.

The next day a heavy raft painfully crossed the swollen waters bumping against the submerged tree trunks. When it arrived under the cedar trees despite the difficulties, the riders remounted their impatient horses and galloped back into the heart of the beautiful forests of Louisiana.

Texas

When, on a cold and rainy December night, seated near my fire, I hear in the street a beggar's wooden shoes clatter sadly, it brings to mind the delicious morning that I spent on the banks of that poetic river yet untouched by the paddle of any steamer. When I close my eyes, the sun appears to me as before, sparkling through a great magnolia stretched open like a parasol above my head, and the dark waters flow by my feet silent and free in their rapid course; then comes a whisper of memories that awake, foment, and finally end when I drop off to sleep. I hardly dare believe in them!

We were trotting along across the tall grasses, on a path so narrow that its tangled blades hid it from our view. Herds of deer bounded all around us not thirty feet from the road, greeting the return of dawn, hardly bothering to concern themselves with the noise of our passage. The oldest shook their heads crowned with spectacular antlers, fleeing beneath the dried cedars embracing the long avenues. We watched them for more than a mile, bounding freely, so rapid that their white tails looked like wings of birds. All of the pines bore traces of flames; sometimes it is the Indians who leave fires to multiply weeks on end in the forests, other times it is wagoneers, camped on the banks of streams, who, before they leave, burn the grasses half eaten by their team, so they will be able to find a fresh crop when they return a few months later. Thus each evening we discovered among the new growth of the forests a white tent around which swirled smoke. Cows wandered nearby, some lying down and chewing their cud, and horses and mules with sonorous little bells which alerted us from a distance to the presence of a wagon train.

The countryside no longer looked the same: regular hills rolled on for mile after mile, interspersed with prairies extending as far as the eye could see on both right and left, while forests again crowned the other summit. When night falls and the north wind gusts impetuously from the far side of these prairies and whistles through the channels of the woods, the cold becomes so sharp that you have to cover your ears with your coat. Horsemen stand out against the horizon like sails on the ocean. Weary eyes lose themselves in this endless succession of undulations blending with the sky, which is itself but a distant glimmer swallowing up the presence of an animated being in the bosom of the wilderness. The heat of the day seems to intensify the horror of this infinite space, and it is with an inexpressible joy that the exhausted traveler sees the forests rise up in rounded domes, offering hospitable shade at last, and a shelter for the evening.

We stopped at a certain habitation, one of several along the route, of a very unusual new kind of construction. It takes the form of a regular square raised up four or five feet off the ground and divided into four bedrooms separated from one another by a large corridor open to the outside; you get to the bedrooms by a catwalk, a plank used like a drawbridge, which needs only to be raised to put the house in a state of defense against animals.

One of our horses had injured himself by stepping on a knee of cypress root in the marshes of the Sabine. Our host took charge of getting another one, and for this purpose, he disappeared into the forest. Some moments later we heard a ringing of bells, and more than twenty horses dashed into the courtyard, bucking. At least there was a choice. Most looked handsome enough, but bites from wood ticks disfigured several; the insect gnaws on the cartilage in a horse's ear causing it to sag like a dog's.

Further on one comes across the hamlet of American farms on the Ayish Bayou; it is said that since their establishment, thieves have disappeared from the whole region. I know nothing about that, but in truth, if they have gotten rid of them, at least they should not have kept their thuggish physiognomy. I saw there the most wretched faces that I have seen in my life. A group of these good, worthy people gathered together, mostly armed, and when one of us ventured politely to collect a small, somewhat overdue debt, their faces darkened so much that, on our return, we avoided crossing the settlements of the Ayish Bayou. Three weeks later, in the waters of the Bayou Toyac [Attoyac], an Indian discovered a floating corpse. A few leagues away lived a rich American planter, very generous toward travelers, who opens his door to whoever wishes to enter, but I would never advise anyone inclined to love mankind to set foot inside. His slaves serve at table nearly nude, Negro men and women whose bodies present a web of wide lines, which are nothing but scars from lashes of the whip.

If my words came to the attention of those involved, they would accuse me of judging them too severely, but I am only speaking of the facts; however unimportant my words may seem, I would never risk defaming for my own amusement even someone completely unknown to me. In this region, no one knows exactly where, lives the famous assassin nicknamed "the brigand of the Sabine." I'll omit his name, even though it's rather poetic. No tangible proofs of his crimes exist, but he himself boasted, in front of a judge with whom he had to deal on a civil matter, about sinking his dagger into the heart of a man with the same amount of pleasure as into the steak of a deer. Today he's an old man, his hair all white, his long beard, also whitened by the years, lends him an imposing air, respectable even, but this does not disguise the fire in his eye. Seven sons, vigorous young people, lead more or less the same life as their father—they terrorize the land. A lost traveler once asked them hospitality for the night. He casually threw a bag of money at the door and dined with feigned tranquillity in the middle of this family that he recognized only too well. The house was clean and richly furnished, and whether by luck or by generosity—for outlaws can be generous in New Spain just as in Castile—not only did he wrest his head from the jaws of the wolf, but they even asked no payment of him and sent him on his way.

Several years ago, the _____ (I said I would omit their names), "the outlaws" I'll say, were taking an excursion, a sentimental journey toward the Arkansas territory. Did they go to admire the wild nature of these deserted forests? I don't believe so. They had been traveling for a long time without encountering anything besides bears and waterfalls, when they saw a cabin. Some Negroes who claimed to be free lived there, and they must have been so, certainly, because they had been established in that place for perhaps ten years, precisely the conditions that should have delivered them from slavery. The outlaws persuaded this family that if they wished to follow them and abandon this miserable existence, the family would find with them fields to cultivate, without losing their freedom, purchased at so dear a price. The Negro family listened to this proposal: without firearms, without communication with anyone besides Indians, they vegetated miserably. This life overwhelmed them, because of the solitude, spoken of so easily by those who know it not. In this frightening isolation, they watched their children grow up half-savage, and slavery threatened everywhere. This solitude oppressed the unlucky Negro. Memories of Africa tormented him endlessly in his isolated cabin; therefore, he believed just one more time in the promise of the white man.

Once arrived at the outlaw settlement, he saw his wife sold to a neighbor, his children enslaved and scattered, and he, as man, father, African, enraged, cried bitterly and complained to the one who had robbed him of everything. "You bore me. Shut up!" responded the outlaw. The Negro, becoming more and more hysterical, sobbed and rolled around on the ground, enraging the outlaw. Snatching a heavy pistol from his belt, he shot his slave point blank. The unfortunate Black let out a scream and reddened with his blood the very earth that he should have watered with his sweat.[35]

Since then the Blacks of the region consider the outlaw a kind of werewolf. A panicky terror seizes them as soon as someone utters his cursed name. If anyone spreads the rumor that he's coming to seek vengeance on the rest of this family, free at least for today, the people of color flee through the forest, hide in the islands of the river, abandoning their homes. They hardly dare believe their eyes the next day when they see their shingled roofs still standing where they expected to find nothing more than a heap of ashes.

Thus it was with great joy that we arrived very late at the home of a decent colonist who received us cordially. His children, all dressed in deerskins, overwhelmed me with questions about the wagons I had encountered a few miles down the road. They scarcely took the time to throw our horses some rice fodder and some corn husks, before making me accompany them, in front of some wagons whose heavy axles we soon heard turning. Supper dragged on late into the night as we tasted whisky and tafia moonshine, spirits newly arrived. The next day, after two hours of rest, we looked forward to bridling and saddling our mounts, to reach the village of Nacogdoches, the destination of our journey, by the same evening. Already we were hearing Spanish spoken in homes, and instead of English saddles which hardly cover the horse's back, instead of riding whips and narrow hats, we saw dignified horsemen with large sombreros, their wide brims turned up, pushed back on their heads, red-tasseled horsewhips, and enormous spurs, sonorous and shiny like those of cavaliers of old. In a word, England, imitated by all

35. Thanks are due to Archie McDonald, who suggested that the outlaw might be John Murel. Don C. Marler's Dogwood Press of Woodville, Texas, has reprinted *A History of the Detection, Conviction, Life and Designs of John A. Murel, the Great Western Land Pirate*. His version of this story, not published until three years after Pavie published *Souvenirs atlantiques,* is given in Appendix B. In personal conversations, published scoundrel specialists Jean Epperson and Jack Jackson suggested that Pavie's outlaw might also be a member of the Yoakum gang. The "decent colonist" may have been Milton Garrett, whose house still stands near San Augustine.

Americans, was giving way to Spain, in the form of the Republic of Mexico.

Nacogdoches

It was night when we crossed the bayou, almost swimming to the other side where the village of Nacogdoches rises. In the darkness, made even darker by the dirt walls, we could distinguish nothing but two immense fires whose flames leapt a great height, in front of which opaque bodies came and went, like sails that pass in the evening across the disk of the setting sun.

In the depths rose up a tall shed capped by a half-Gothic, half-Spanish bell tower, strangely illuminated by a flickering light which intermittently extended long fingers of flame across its chiseled contours, or penetrated into the interior and reflected on the drums, the pavillon chinois[36] and the guns of the military barracks there: the guard house, the hospital and the church. This was the camp of the foot soldiers who were hunkered around a fire. A sentry marching in long strides in front of the entry blocked the light coming from the interior with his regular passage and seemed from a distance to be the pendulum of a clock. The central plaza extended to the forests on the left and on the right to the barracks of the soldiers, who were standing around proudly draped in their blue coats which fell down to the rowels of their spurs. Horsemen clustered in groups, talking in loud voices. On the side rendered inaccessible by smoke sat two Indians of the ancient tribe of Delawares, which formerly occupied the banks of the river of the same name and counted its huts on the site that rich Philadelphia covers today with its hundred steeples. The savages smoked stone pipes; the cavalry, cigarettes of corn. Such was the unique sight offered me by this village of Nacogdoches, miserable outpost keeping a garrison of a hundred foot soldiers and eighty cavalrymen of whom ten, at the most, own horses. They escort the wagon trains on

---

36. A military percussion instrument consisting of a staff with bells that jingle when the staff is struck against the ground. Also called a "Turkish crescent" or "jingling Johnny."

trips made as dangerous as they are difficult by the cannibalistic Indians of the interiors.

We lodged in a hostel kept by an American,[37] because foreigners make up all of the active part of the Texas population. It was necessary to climb a ladder to get to the sleeping room where a dozen beds of moss were spread out, covered by heavy buffalo hides, more heavy than warm during the cold nights of January. Because the attic was open all around, it froze almost every morning, which did not keep the noonday heat from making this space unbearable during the rest of the day.

Nacogdoches comprises forty buildings, mostly stores where English is spoken, the rest are more or less dirty huts with no other floor than the ground, on which Spaniards stretch out skins and multicolored rugs which also serve them as coats. As for the Mexicans, they do nothing, absolutely nothing but warm themselves in the evening around the fire, the men well wrapped up in their coats, which they never take off, the women covered in their manner with a mantilla tied under the chin to permit smoking. In the summer they cultivate a little garden where they grow corn, tomatoes, peppers, and large pumpkins from which they prepare with strongly peppered eggs, a reddish colored meal that only a Mexican mouth can stand to eat. This farming busies them little enough to permit them to sleep two-thirds of the day, always with the eternal coat which, like the one of Jupiter's statue, serves in every season. In spite of this apathetic indolence, Mexicans have in their look a Castilian fire which lends something distinguished to their appearance, a pride missing from the republicans of the United States. The children, dark and yellow like their fathers, also have big black eyes with wide outlines, and strong, well shaped heads which reminded me immediately of the beggar in Murillo's painting.[38]

37. John Durst was then living at the Old Stone Fort, originally built by José Antonio Gil y Barbo and today reconstructed on the campus of Stephen F. Austin University and serving as a museum.

38. Pavie had seen at least one of Bartolomé Esteban Murillo's paintings of Spanish urchins on display in Paris before he sailed for America. This description suggests that he saw *The Young Beggar,* property of Louis XVI. Other Spanish paintings in the collection of Louis-Philippe were displayed publicly during the July Monarchy. Pavie later became an amateur art critic; his father published several of his articles on Spanish painters in the 1830s.

The colonel [José de las Piedras] lives in a hut just as crudely constructed as the barracks of his soldiers, with a beautiful buffalo skin, the gift of some Indian, as its only decoration; however, a corporal is there to serve as orderly and a sentry stands posted outside his courtyard. A Creole from Vera Cruz—trained, distinguished, and extremely cordial toward foreigners—the colonel comes each day to sit down on the gallery of the hotel and talk with travelers, for whom he gladly provides an escort when they must cross Texas by the interior route. The cavalrymen who saw us chatting familiarly with him never hesitated to take off their hats in front of us, and on every occasion they impressed me with their extreme courtesy. Three of them stationed themselves with their mandolins outside the guardhouse every evening, and their truly melodious voices blended so harmoniously with the sound of the Moorish guitar that I expressed my admiration to them. They would have gladly continued all night. The guard changed three times a day at morning, noon, and sunset, at which time the chaplain recited the prayers to which the entire company responded in an orderly manner with arms and packs. They played this music on various drums, fifes, and trumpets; the drum majors, like the corporals and sergeants, carry in their hands long rods that they never put down, which replace the staffs of English sergeants.

One evening we had gone to the main gate of the encampment. The colonel was talking with his aides, handsome horsemen, each leaning on a large, curved sword, wearing a belt of buffalo hide, spurs with a layer of silver on a red background, pants open to the calf and decorated with loops and golden buttons, and the bottom of the legs covered with a piece of well-tanned leather, tastefully stitched. The chaplain was there smoking his cigar; the guard was circling the plaza which the infantrymen swept with brooms made from branches of wild coffee bush. When they arrived in front of the colonel, they stopped and announced the playing of "Viva la Libertad," the national anthem of the new Republic of Mexico. Each one stood up and removed his hat as a sign of respect. A religious silence reigned among the assembly. Suddenly a great noise of horses arose from the direction of the forest, and sharp screams pierced the plain, and we saw, marching along to the noise of instruments that they never stopped playing, a hoard of Cherokee Indians, all armed. As they advanced, they continued their noisy acclamations, repeating their military maneuvers until nightfall.

They brought along with them a young bison captured on the prairie. Their Great Chief, an old man with a long white beard and a noble and imposing face came with two of his wives behind him, decorated in ribbons and necklaces. At the head of the rest of the band, four warriors proudly carried the remains of some Comanches killed in the latest encounter. There was a cougar skin quiver full of poisoned arrows, lances with stone tips, clubs and one carbine with its stock trimmed with the neck skin of a horse with its mane attached. But their most beautiful trophy, the one they displayed like a banner, was the silky, well-braided scalps of enemies fallen in combat. The chief especially strutted about, shaking these horrible, still bloody spoils at his knees, at his belt, and at his spear decorated with bundles of vulture feathers.

Several of the savages displayed wounds, one of them having received an arrow in the forehead which split open his skull leaving a scar that disfigured him completely, but which seemed too glorious to him for one to dare to pity him. His face was tattooed in blue and black and his hair pulled back like a hoopoe's tuft exposing the top of his head to better display the scar. They spent the night celebrating their victory and returned to camp in the forest, reappearing the following day at daybreak to busy themselves selling furs. I bought a black bearskin for four shillings. Indians of different neighboring tribes, Shawnees and Delawares, departed somewhat disgusted by the Cherokee victory celebrations, rites in which all of these tribes indulge from time to time on similar occasions, but which displeased them coming from someone else; they will not acknowledge the victories of others since each nation believes it should take precedence over the others.

A horse race was announced for the next day. The Mexican commander arrived in full dress, with aides in dazzling uniforms. Their chaps, covered with pieces of leather artistically embroidered with porcupine needles, enclosed the legs of the horsemen and joined together at the waist, thus protecting the lower body. When the chaps are opened, they hang down to the bend of the horse's hind legs, and the sun glistens on their elegant decorations, the spurs shining so brilliantly they blind the eye. Feather-trimmed hats, a pair of pistols and an ax complete the equipment of the horseman whose gold- or silver-handled saber clatters against the stirrups. Officers also carry a dagger, a deadly weapon in the hand of a Spaniard. The chaplain and the surgeon accompanied the colonel; their double-bit harnesses decorated with bells like the mules of ancient monastic priors. I followed the crowd and, at a distance of two miles, we arrived at the plain where the race was to take place.

It was necessary to clear the arena of the trees that covered it: each horseman applied himself to the task with his axe, and soon, with the help of the spectators, and especially the children who screamed noisy "hurrahs!," they dragged the immense oaks deep into the forest. Two horses were brought in: one, a beautiful English thoroughbred ridden by a lithe, alert American done up like a jockey with top boots and spurs, the other, a young Mexican steed with ardent nostrils and a long mane (*crinière*), vigorous like all indomitable steeds that Texas nurtures. A Spanish corporal rode the Texas horse; six feet tall and almost naked, his athletic form responded with each stride of the animal. He had neither boots, nor spurs, a Spanish scarf covered his black hair, and in his fist hung a horsewhip. The two antagonists started off on foot. At the colonel's signal, the two racers plunged into the arena. Screams of the spectators rose no more quickly than the clouds of dust in which the racers seemed to fly. Near me I saw Indians, mouths agape, who watched stupefied, repeating, as in *The Last of the Mohicans,* their guttural exclamation: "Ugh! Ugh!" At first the English horse took the advantage, but the Mexican steed whistled by in front of us like an arrow, leaving the other far behind and carrying the winner into the forest, his long legs responding to its furious movements with so much grace that general applause arose. On seeing the noble steed's white tail (*crinière*) disappear under the branches of the forest, the children jumped for joy, crying: "el blanco caballo!" (the white horse!)

A distressing event caused trouble in our hotel. Everyone was poisoned with the sole exception of myself, who by chance had only a cup of milk. Around midnight, the twelve inhabitants of the attic awakened me with their frightening convulsions, cursing the cook and crying for help. The less vigorous balanced between life and death for two days; one in particular was in a deplorable state at my departure, and I haven't heard word of him. I fear also that the Negro cook was hanged.

Among the motley crowd from all nations who met each evening around the soldier's campfire and spent the night sleeping under the stars,

I noticed a young Indian from the Cherokee tribe. He was a handsome young man, about eighteen years of age, of a frankly savage physiognomy, who nevertheless had something graceful in his deliberate walk distinguishing him from his compatriots. He followed me around hoping to get cigars; tired of his pestering me, I engaged him in a conversation about the wandering life of his tribe, their beliefs, and even the topography of the region. The Cherokee suddenly took on a serious air, reflecting before responding to me about all these things that he had never before considered seriously. It seemed as though his ideas took at a stroke a direction that he could not account for. Then, sitting down on the sand, he made a sign to me to come sit beside him.

After a silence of several minutes, the Indian took his tomahawk and, with precise gestures, began a speech in rather good English in which he elaborated, with a charming naïveté, the happiness of this primitive life which he would not have left for anything in the world. I invited him to follow me to France; this proposition plunged him again into deep reflection. He seemed to weigh the idea, so much does the idea of France offer wondrous possibilities to the imagination of the sons of the wilderness. "Well, then," he replied, "does one find deer and bison and bears in France? Does one find huts on the banks of the streams and trees to chop down to make you warm? Don't the white men pursue the red men, our brothers? Are the forests secluded and full of game? For I don't like it when I am sleeping on my bearskin and I hear the footsteps of the white hunter around my fire." Then, as if he had been awakened from a dream, he looked straight at me and said, "the chief of the Osages did what you are proposing to me. We never saw him again—you killed him. No, I will never go! And the great lake has no shore! No! No! No!" And crossing his arms, he looked at me with a melancholy air that seemed to say, "And you? What are you doing here?" "See," he continued explaining to me and tracing with his tomahawk a twisted line representing the Sabine, "see on the left the forests; on the right, the forests, always the forests, the prairies, and the great lakes where it snows. All of that belongs to the savage; everywhere he goes the forests open up in front of him, and the Whites do not dare go except in troops. Here," and he made dots in the sand, "here are our huts; farther, the Shawnees; there, the Comanches, who eat their enemy. Show me the same way your country on the sand. Mark for me the villages of your nation."

The same evening, the Cherokees who came in off the prairie went back out, as was the custom. Only the priest or medicine man (jongleur) remained, and one warrior in a state of complete drunkenness, an odd pair who took turns following me around to get cigars; stuffing their pipes and maneuvering me to a spot between them, they showed me a gratitude I would have gladly forfeited. They got so close to the fire that no one else in the hotel could get warm. All explanations being useless, I got up from my place and added my exhortations to those of the other travelers, but as the Cherokees understood only their own language, it became necessary to take them by the shoulders and show them to the door.

I accompanied them to keep them from deciding to come find me. The medicine man joined to his declarations of friendship a gift that I was forced to accept: the bowl of a stone pipe decorated with a turtle, some fish, and some other hieroglyphic characters. I intended to lead them to the fire of the cavalrymen and escape quickly, because as soon as an Indian, excited by ideas of victory, by generosity, and a little whiskey, attaches himself to your footsteps, it is almost impossible to get rid of him with anything short of a rude, and impolite act—that is, by shamelessly chasing him from your presence. So I crossed the plaza with my two Cherokees, catching sight of an open building with light and some glasses. They entered without ceremony and took their places at the counter of the store. The storekeeper, a rather foppish young Englishman, snatched the lighted pipe out of the mouth of the drunken old warrior and, instead of returning it to him to pass around and smoke in turns as the Indian was expecting, he blew all of the burning embers into his eyes. The old warrior cried bitterly, and the medicine man stood up very angrily. I became quite concerned when the little Indian of whom I spoke earlier rushed brusquely into our midst from the far side of the plaza where he had seen everything. Seizing his shiny hatchet, he pushed me back with one hand and ordered me to stay put, and with the other hand brandished the tomahawk like lightening around the head of the Englishman. He threatened his ears and his chin so closely with the blade of the weapon that the wretched European, as pale as a corpse, trembled all over. Then, after a minute of this frightful menace, the tomahawk took aim at the skull of the poor Englishman. I cried out with fright as I envisioned his head split open down to the nose, but the Indian suspended his blow and, with great composure, returned his tomahawk to his belt, shook my hand, cast a threatening glance at the merchant, and vanished with his two friends.

After a few days of rest, the chief of the victorious tribe longed to return to the forest, but he had first to distribute gifts to the colonel and the important people of the village. The quiver of poisoned arrows went to an old retired soldier,[39] the preferred friend of the Cherokee. As for his spear and his scalps, the chief never wished to give, exchange, or sell them, even though his furs would not have sufficed to pay for the bracelets and firearms that he was shopping for. So he gave the merchant a note written on parchment with which they provided him, in which he promised, himself (here was his name), Great Chief, etc., . . . to pay in the moon of . . . , so many buffalo pelts, so many beaver skins, deer hides, etc. This simple sample of the writing of a Cherokee was traced in characters similar to Hebrew, without any distance between the words beneath it ran a literal translation done by an interpreter from the troop. The owner of this note will probably derive profit from this item only by selling it as a curiosity, because an Indian almost never bothers to pay his debts.

Everyone in the village seemed happy at the departure of the Indians—their nocturnal dances and chanting disturbed the public peace. Not having anything left to observe there, I directed my steps toward the bayou, whose abundant and excellent-tasting waters furnished the post and the rest of the population.

In general the water is delicious, even though rather rare, in this part of America. Marshes are no longer found in the interior of Texas; the land is arid since it almost never rains.[40] The climate is also healthy even though the region shares the same latitude as that of West Florida, itself so deadly in the summer. The territory around Nacogdoches is pleasant, with its riverbanks covered with lovely magnolias on which small parrots like to perch. Sometimes parrots are more numerous than leaves, and make the branches droop down to the ground. One can approach them

---

39. I would like to thank Jack Jackson for setting me on the trail of Peter Ellis Bean, whom he recognized in Pavie's description, and for subsequent advice regarding Pavie's encounter with Piedras and Bean, which is described at length in the introductory notes to "Le Lazo" and "La Peau d'ours" in *Tales of the Sabine Borderlands.*

40. Note by Pavie: In January, it had not rained for six weeks.

rather easily and, once their wings are clipped, it is easy to tame them as well. One finds them in almost all of the Mexican homes.

On one of my walks, I got lost. I knocked on a door and, not getting a response, I dared to enter. A young girl was sleeping in a hammock. She woke up at the sound of my footsteps and came toward me, offering me a seat. I found the situation uncomfortable, but she familiarly took the cigar I held in my hand, lighted hers casually, and guided me back to the path. Such are the simple and naïve ways of the Mexicans.

FOREST FIRE

After an agile boat powered by twelve men bent over their oars, after the headlong, airborne course of a ship under sails, nothing pleases me as much as to feel under my knees a frisky horse, chomping at the bit. Whether the rain is falling, the wind blowing, the sun casting its fires across my brow or the snow striking my thick coat with its flakes, or whether the burning dust is flying into the nostrils of my steed or his breath exhaling as smoke into falling sleet, it does not matter. I trot across prairies and crevasses, free as the air we breathe, my horse and I; I dream, I forget, I am happy. Once more, I prefer the adventurous life of a traveler to all others, and I can never remember without a deep sense of longing the day we set out for the Red River behind a pack mule.

When the time came to stop for the night, we allowed the horses to roam in the woods and we slept with our heads against our saddles, under a cover of buffalo hide, sheltered from the wind by a cane hedge. Everyone slept until the shrill ring of the bell at the horses' neck two hours before sunrise—a signal as precise as the crow of a rooster, when one is certain of seeing in the East a red tint rise little by little across the sky. In the distance the intermittent cry of the large birds that rise before daybreak resounds. The neighing of horses seems to awaken all of slumbering nature; stoking revives the fire in the camp, then the heavy saddles, the holsters, saddlebags, and supplies are put in their customary places, the noisy lashes of whips echo through the forest, and the caravan departs. Is all of that not better than a heavy carriage with its six horses bogged down in the mud, its drivers cursing as twenty glazed, sleepy heads stare out the windows beside the door without even knowing what is happening?

Our route the second day proved yet wilder and more deserted—not even a wagoneer near his tent, nor a Spaniard with his big hat. We saw just one Indian dissecting a deer, a portion of which we shared. This respectable savage sat in front of a little fire, hands on his knees; beside him on the grass slept an old dog who started to bark, but his master whistled softly and he went back to sleep. A rusty old carbine, a bullet pouch made of bearskin without ornament, a smoke-stained powder horn, and clothes even simpler than this made up all his possessions. He wore a crow feather in his white hair, and two blue lines crossed his forehead and joined under his nose. Something noble and seemingly not of the present appeared in the physiognomy of this Indian—you might have said that he tolerated us near him like a man accustomed to seeing one thing replace another, year after year, century after century.

"Of which tribe is your father?" asked one of our group in the language of the Caddos. "Of which tribe?" echoed the old man. Waving his hand from the east to the west, from the south to the north, several times he repeated the negation *"eccho,"* and we understood that his tribe had vanished from America. "And your wigwam?" *"Eccho"* intoned the old man, fixing an unflinching gaze on the immense prairie, extending to the horizon, where the antlers of frolicking deer appeared above the grasses like the fins of porpoises on a calm ocean.

"Where are your sons, your wife, those for whom you hunt and who will care for you when your legs can no longer carry you?"

The Indian said nothing. He leaned his chin on his hands, his eyes closed, and he receded into his thoughts. Immobile, his chest raised only with effort, his hair fell onto his forehead, and his crow feather fell out like a rice bird on the snow.[41] He looked to see if we were still watching him, and, astonished to discover my eyes still fixed on him, the Indian understood from this that I was a foreigner. His face kept its melancholy sadness even though it lost a bit of its hardness. He ate quickly, whistled for his dog, and went away.

41. Note by Pavie: *Vulg étourneau,* often confused with *l'étourneau* (starling) of Louisiana; in English *rice bird,* which spreads out in numerous flocks on the rivers during the cold months.

I learned from the colonists that he was the last member of his tribe—the very last. "He's some kind of fool," they added, "and the Negroes amuse themselves by shooting seeds at him with a peashooter when he passes by." As for me, it seems that the last man of a nation, whatever nation it might be, a sickly old man ready to bury the name of his people buried forever with him in his tomb, if indeed he has a tomb, gives us more reason to ponder than to mock. If I were an inhabitant of Texas, I would want someone to lead me to the place once occupied by the huts of the old man's people, so I could make every effort for him to live there in peace, and when his death came I would like to build a mound for him, exactly following the instructions he would have given me, above which I would write "Here lies the last warrior of the tribe of the Nacogdoches!"

A few leagues further, the route snakes through some scraggly oaks near a stream. Against the bank I discerned the form of an elegant, lithe young Indian, fully armed, as immobile as a statue. You might have thought he took root in the middle of the fig trees opening on all sides around him. Was he watching the fish play in the crystal clear water? Was he contemplating his reflection? Sleeping? I do not know, but I believe he was listening to himself living. He made a pleasant sight with his brick-red legs, his reed arrows on his shoulder, his bow in hand, beautiful like a god of the ancients in the bosom of his empire. An Indian in his forest wears an indigenous expression marvelously appropriate to him alone; whether he fights, hunts, or sleeps, he is to the wilderness what Quasimodo was to the Cathedral of Notre Dame: he is its soul.

We crossed the Sabine again. Once more treading on American soil, I felt a sweet, pleasant sensation, as if returning to my second homeland. Even now, in February, the heat felt intense, the maples, cypresses, and poplar trees were already beginning to put on new leaves; the evergreen mimosas and hermosas were putting out the buds, which eight days later opened so deliciously into feathery plumes and fragrant blooms. As we left the marshes, several sinister faces and carbine barrels glinted through the slits of an abandoned cabin. We loaded our pistols at the same time those inside prepared their arms, but they probably felt as frightened as we did, and with no reason to be. Night soon fell, and a cabin came into view. Hunger tormented us. What happiness to find a hospitable roof, a slice of venison, and a calabash [gourd dipper] full of fresh water. But, alas, the cabin was deserted. Both horses and riders started back on their way again, quite saddened, and we had to trudge six more leagues before finding another.

If the path had only been complete, even tortuous, or at least negotiable—! But our horses sank up to their knees crossing a marsh, with tree stumps, bushes, a thousand little intersecting trails, and bridges formed of half-broken branches of cane sticking up like walls that stop the rider, cut him open, snag his legs, or hurl his hat thirty feet away—all this in pitch darkness. For music, we heard the growls of a wild cat, the screeching of owls, the roar of cougars—a rather uncomfortable position! Allowing our horses free rein as their instincts rarely failed them we were trotting along in the darkness, silently, harassed, mud-covered, and famished, when suddenly an extraordinary brightness amazed us. We stopped and cried out in surprise and admiration.

Another wilderness event astonished us, a variation of its magical decorations—a forest fire, but on such an enormous scale that it deserved to be compared to an ocean tempest. With smoke and flames everywhere, the poor horses whinnied and we ourselves could hardly breathe; our eyes closed, tears of pain flowed down our burning cheeks. We stood on open ground, and from both sides of the wide route rose burning tree trunks like columns of fire in a Greek temple. Green leaves crackled, with a terrible echo, and at long intervals, old sycamores in the distance shattered into a thousand pieces with a noise that echoed in the forest, followed by a rain of sparkling embers, lightweight violet and blue lights swirling in the wind. When the flame, swifter than the frightened deer, devoured the dry grasses, one could see it spread and hear it nibbling away, devouring its prey like the foam of a rising tide swallowing the sand of the beach. The liana vines, whose new flowers vied with one another for the space to bloom, yellow jasmine, red jasmine, and new vines all hung withered and sad above the sea of flames roaring at their feet, until a spark carried by the seething swirl of flaming embers reached a vine embracing a tree trunk like a snake, and with a hiss shriller than a poisoned arrow's, everything disappeared, swallowed up by the fire.

Tigers, surrounded on all sides, roared with fright as they leapt over the burning embers, and bucks fled so quickly that one could hardly distinguish their opaque bodies among all the inanimate objects that no longer had shadows. The wildcats did pirouettes at the summits of the poplar trees, chased by the furious elements; their eyes burned more brightly than the fire on the ground, sending forth bolts of lightning. Their furious roars, their scorched fur, already singed by flying sparks, intensified the sublime horror of the spectacle. On my right, an oak tree, almost entirely consumed, held on by the roots on one side, but so feebly that I saw it tremble. I hardly had the time to give the mule a vigorous lash of the whip when the tree rolled so close that I thought the mule was lost; it had entirely disappeared in a cloud of ashes and smoke. More intrepid than its master, the animal lunged over the immense log at full speed, without hesitating. Thus we kept on moving, always faster and faster. Smoke suffocated us; little by little the fire consumed all the sap of the forest and we could hear nothing besides the victorious flames roaring like a victorious army, masters of the battlefield, when the dying have ceased to groan and, the work being done, the conquerors murmur ominously, drunk with blood and victory.

I admit that I breathed more easily when we emerged onto the plains. One league more and we found a stream where we could quench our burning thirst or bathe the frothing mouths of the horses. I started to gallop at full speed, whipping the pack mule in front of me. In my impatience to arrive, I passed the American fort so quickly that I did not even see it. Moreover, our smoke-filled eyes, blinded by the flames, could distinguish nothing. "Who goes there?" cried out the sentinel, and I kept on riding. "*¿Quién está aquí?*" and I made my whip crackle. For the third time, "Who goes there?" cried the same voice and raised his musket. Fortunately I saw something move in the shadows, and I answered back, "A traveler," just in time.

A half hour later, we lay stretched out on a good mattress, as far as possible from the fire with no great desire to renew its acquaintance. Twenty leagues, fifteen hours on horseback, a very meager lunch twenty-five miles before: what a supper! What a night.

Perhaps you will ask what could cause such a fire. I would be at a loss to know the answer, and no one in the land bothers to find out. It is a curious thing for a foreigner; the most beautiful spectacle that could strike the eye of a European. Perhaps a wagoneer burned the grass to renew it and chose too dry a day, perhaps an imprudent hunter burned a tree to smoke out a rabbit from under its root, perhaps an Indian merely wanted to amuse himself!

THE VILLAGE: NATCHITOCHES

Those who have a Finley map of America before them need only to follow the Red River upstream: in the midst of several streams, and a multitude of lakes and bayous, you will find Natchitoches on the left bank. Considering the names of the surrounding places, you would expect to find nothing but impenetrable wilderness, marshes, and lost forests, the haunts of wild beasts and wandering brigands, tempting you to pity anyone reduced to living so far from the cities, two thousand miles from Europe, scattered over the banks of rivers, hemmed in on all sides by woods whose outer limits are unknown. Yet, how many happy families spend peaceful days there, leading an independent existence where neither political troubles, nor civil wars, nor the deafening roar of the agitating masses ever arise! It may take a long time for a foreigner to grow accustomed to the deep calm of such a peaceful world; solitude weighs on one who does not understand it. But let that person plunge back into the volcano of revolutions, let him be tossed about by this incessantly roaring tempest, let him feel crumpled, slain by the shock of so many bitterly varying opinions—only then will he learn to recognize the price of his lost repose, or even know whether he will miss it. For in the end "to flee from this world is not to hate it," Lord Byron said, "not all mortals are suited to share the agitation and work of their brothers." I am no misanthrope; he, only, deserves this label who disdainfully pushes aside the oppressed, whose only crime in his eyes is that they belong to the human race he has sworn to hate. But I never felt the strength to fight the masses hand to hand, nor the pride to hope someday to regenerate my country, still, if my opinion is nonetheless the best, it has not been proven.

Let's come back to the village and its surroundings. Two miles west extends a sad and gloomy lake called "Lac de la Terre-Noire" because of its murky waters.[42] My favorite promenade was there. In the desolate appearance of this liquid plain dotted with trunks of blackened cypress trees, covered with even blacker moss, in the countless turtles sleeping on the rushes, in the cry of the solitary cormorant deep in the cove, in the

---

42. Lake of the Black Earth; today, Sibley Lake, according to Natchitoches historians Bobby DeBlieux and Carol Wells.

piercing eyes of an alligator ambushing its prey on a water lily, in the pensive attitude of a pink flamingo[43] on one foot, in a cloud of pelicans balancing loosely in a spiral and randomly emitting a hoarse sound that seemed to come out of the clouds, in all of that, I found in the midst of silence an inexplicable charm, a voluptuousness that I would not know how to describe. Happy are those who have felt it; for me, the picturesque, infinite harmony of nature is everything. In the evenings, a thick smoke rises off the lake, turning the waves darker still; one would think it an extinct volcano breathing in its sleep, or the large number of trees standing up in the middle of the lake might lead one to believe that this lake, like the Lake of the Caddos [Caddo Lake], resulted from an earthquake.[44] The streams, or rather the *springs* that feed it present a ferruginous color and a sulfur taste, though the nearby magnolias seem more beautiful than anywhere else, and thousands of little flowers humbly litter the moss-covered soil; a sweet spot on which to sit and dream.

Following along the edges of this sheet of water, one sees numerous trails leading through the underbrush where rabbits sleep and land turtles withdraw on returning from depositing their eggs on the shoals. No pirogue has ever created ripples in the lake. Swallow-tailed kites with their white heads and forked tails plane above the waters—masters of all their expanse—or land proudly on the branches of the cypress trees' gray heads. After an hour's walk, one hears the murmur of a waterfall, as the waters of the lake shoot under tunnels and rush through the hoops of blooming liana vines into an arm of the Red River [the Bayou Pierre], which subdivides into two other narrower arms. Just above, the branches of willows and jasmine cast another sequence of natural bridges, a marvelous effect for the eye of the seated spectator. A sawmill[45] also turns there, and one may return to the village following the course of the river,

43. Pagès identifies this "flamant" as a woodstock, whose presence is confirmed by Wells. Audubon placed roseate spoonbills in the locale occasionally. For the absence of flamingos, Ron Tyler refers us to *Birds of America*, vol. 6, p. 173. But, spoonbills, Audubon says, may be found "occasionally in summer up the Mississippi to Natchez." Vol. 6, p. 76.

44. The Lake of the Caddos may have been formed in 1812 by the New Madrid earthquake. According to DeBlieux, the lake Pavie describes here was formed by the overflow of the Red River because of the Caddo tribe's logjam between Shreveport and Grande Écore.

45. Eliza Bludworth's father, James Bludworth, also the brother-in-law of Charles Pavie, owned a sawmill.

shaded by old poplar trees left untouched by the colonists, lilas in the prairie and two tufts of rosebushes on the left, retreats for mockingbirds and hummingbirds, the last vestiges of an abandoned habitation.

This place faces the head of a very long island (Ile Brevelle) opening its triangle near a logjam anchored to the bank by the water's force; from here, for about ten leagues extend, scattered on both banks, the most brilliant habitations on the river, proudly competing with their numerous outbuildings, brilliant gardens, countless herds grazing in deep bays, and interlocking one into another in even more sparkling forests, green savannas of palmettos, and imposing cypress. All this part of the island has kept the name of *la Côte-Joyeuse.*

Two leagues from this point one finds the little Lake of the Natchez, entirely covered with rushes so thick as to be almost impossible to penetrate in a pirogue. Woods surround a large portion of it, and in the evening one hears the tiger cats roar on its banks at the hour red-winged blackbirds swoop down in flocks more numerous than the leaves of the trees, to twitter with deafening noise in the moss of the acacias. While strolling one lovely evening in February, I saw the immense poplar trees of the savanna all ablaze, lit up as when the fire devoured the forest; the reflection of these phosphorous fires cast dazzling tints on the surrounding leaves, and the lake waters reflected the immense torches, always burning, never consumed. This phenomenon of American forests, quite rare in Europe, has frightened more than one superstitious traveler. One month later, the Negroes set fire to these sublime remains of primordial nature, and the roar of trees tumbling to the ground and the smoke of flaming poplars extinguishing themselves in the waters announced that this devouring light would not be followed by the magic brightness that changes a forest into a palace of fairies.

Climbing the path above the river to the hilltop where the old cedar tree stands alone at the summit since the wind uprooted the magnificent sycamore that grew near it, in which buzzards nested, affords another beautiful spectacle. At one's feet lie the red waves and shoals of the river with its cane, and sometimes its alligators! The village and the pine forests unfold on the plain to the right, blue lines on the horizon and other distant forests marked by clearings carved out of the plantations, and on the left, prairies, savannas, fields of cotton and corn, galloping horses, and herds that bellow and moo. On an autumn morning near the time of Indian summer when the sky is cloudy, when everything flies and stretches out under a dome of diaphanous vapors, drifting or stationary, the bell of the village pierces the fog, Spanish huts scattered on the back of the hill stand out clearly with their garlands of large-leafed vines where heavy gourds hang, and their shutters are closed like sleeping eyes. Here and there sounds a little bell at the neck of a horse or the horn of a colonist as he calls his slaves to work, and little by little troops of Negroes move onto the plantations. Plows do their work, and indigo buntings set off joyfully from the summit of the catalpas, repeating the rhythmic chant that bursts forth with each flap of their blue wings, as brightly as the morning lark's.

Oh, delicious village, peaceful retreat! I loved you because your inhabitants are loving, hospitable, and sensitive. I loved you for your streets planted with catalpas, acacias, and wisterias, whose flowers give off a sweet fragrance. I loved you because, when seated on my bearskin by my window, I could see the Indian camp at the edge of the woods. I saw the savage by his fire, and I heard his voice blended with the mournful cries of wood pigeons and the croaking of a million bullfrogs from the bottom of the lakes. I loved you because, at night, the Pascagoulas and the Cherokees danced in a circle and sang at my door. I loved you because the herons, swans, and flamingos cast the shadows of their wings across my window. I loved you because each morning the birds of the wilderness came to wake me. I loved you because at any hour I could see wagon trains meandering across the hill among the fig trees to disappear under the canopy of pines with the noise of spurs and the crackle of bells. I loved you because the hurricane raged across the shingles of my roof, and I remembered the nights spent under a tent. I loved you because the winter rains flooded the countryside, and the waves rose up around me and made tree branches float at my feet. I loved you because I found here old people who once knew my ancestors, who told stories from their youth, bringing back to me memories of names I held dear. I loved you because in the shadow of your bell tower lived a family that was mine . . . I loved you for a thousand things more!

The Coast

Winter passed and I had to leave. Farewell to adventurous outings, picturesque hunting trips on the riverbanks, and wilderness tribes scattered across this old world like the ruins of buildings now vanished. Joyous pennants wave at the mast of the ships; the cannon booms—farewell!

He who sets foot on a boat for the first time and sees all of the beloved things with which he has lived and identified himself, all things included in the sacred name of *patrie* [homeland] receding toward the horizon— that person, I say, experiences an uncontrollable heartache, an undeniable weakness, a mental and spiritual anguish without earthly expression because "a first departure is a bitter lesson." But when one has spent months or years on foreign soil without realizing it or having anticipated becoming attached to it because it is not his own, when unaware that he has already made such an attachment he takes off cheerfully toward the open road, dazed by a thousand thoughts of return, only then a sudden, unexpected, unbelievable jolt awakens him that one would never have anticipated. Then the traveler feels a painful dejection in his senses, something so deeply sad that, in truth, he deserves great pity. He feels as if an invisible genie, like the angels that accompanied patriarchs in the wilderness, after having sustained a man through brave excursions, abandon him, returning to the celestial regions.

Once on board, I sat at the foot of the capstan. The boat tugged impatiently at its mooring cables, the wheels, testing their strength, intermittently agitated the frothy waves around the keel, and the smoke belching from its stacks poured forth black flakes over the blue of the sky. Through much insignificant noise and many preparations in which I took no part, I fastened my gaze on my door—henceforth closed—on the deserted garden and the quiet, lonely house, and on the earth I wished to tread just one more time. A few friends yelled good-bye and wished me a happy trip; the trembling voice of a young Negro who had followed me on all of my promenades kept repeating to me "Farewell, Master." I heard nothing, I saw nothing, my eyes still fastened on my favorite catalpas . . . truthfully, a traveler so proud of braving storms and thousands of dangers, nevertheless a weak being who reports his personal feelings self-servingly.

Now, it is the beginning of May, when the floodwaters change the appearance of the countryside: gone all the shoals, replaced by a flowing river full to its banks, and ten feet of water in the dried-out bayous, the forests long since returned to green and full of sap. Cypress trees, wet by the waves, seem to rejoice in the evening wind in this ubiquitous lake. Squirrels traverse the highest branches, fearing to soil their silky coats;

opossums hang by their tails from the stems of liana vines and spy on frightened rats and snakes, chased from their nests. Deer retreat to high ground to bathe themselves peacefully far from the busy rivers; the Indian advances toward the prairies, called by the bison and lynx. In the savannas, so beautiful, fresh, and lush a few days prior, an immense alligator, as big as a tree trunk, snores horribly, his snout half opened, his paws spread open like iron grappling hooks, until an unusual noise forces him to dig in further away. All land not cultivated or protected by dikes or levees, sandy land covered with cedar trees, in other words, all land nourished from the river's alluvial silt which each year yields a triple harvest of flowers and wild fruits, all that is just a sad and dark sea, marshy and debris-littered, a true flood—interesting for an instant but soon deplorable to see. Ducks and winter birds fly north, followed by the hummingbirds, dazzling parakeets, and egrets in their first down. Everything on the water and in the woods takes on color, is reborn in a more extreme form, more powerful, more grandiose. Little by little the waters retreat, new growth covers the planted earth, young birds put on coats of a thousand sparkling colors, songs begin again more joyfully, and the harvests grow more beautiful, but then the fever appears, instilling death and mourning in the cities.

Navigating the river offers us a special distraction: hunting for herons, which are easier to shoot because the river is narrower, and, especially, hunting for alligators, which one may then approach as closely as twenty feet. At floodtime, these animals fill the forests in unbelievable numbers. Their prodigious size makes a European tremble, even though one knows they only attack dogs and calves. I have even seen Creoles bathing in waters infested with alligators, happily scaring them away during the swim; they come back but, as soon as they recognize the presence of men, they leave again. Hunters use a simple and interesting technique, filling a cow's bladder with water to make it float, so that the alligator tries in vain to seize it, following this prey as someone pulls it toward the shore. From there one can kill it with a ball [bullet], provided you hit it in the eyes, missing the impenetrable shell that envelopes this kind of salamander like armor, making them seem, in moonlight, to be enameled with plates of silver.

In two days we reached the Mississippi, which I can never see without admiration, swirling at the feet of enormous plane trees, proud of the power of its new waves. On the left, we passed the Bayou Sarah, on the right, the enormous plantations of the Pointe Coupée where an old Frenchman "possessed of" a fortune of a million five hundred thousand piasters had just died. He kept from twelve to fourteen hundred slaves on his immense plantation.[46] Here a beautiful jetty extends, calculated to exceed the highest flood level by only one inch protecting in profound security the numerous opulent dwellings that so graciously decorate the banks of the Mississippi. They spring up in the shadows of lilacs and fragrant orange trees, amid a white sea of cotton and an ocean of sugarcane, reflecting in their fiery windows the burning rays of the sun. I spent several days on the coast of West Baton Rouge with a French planter who offered me, in the name of a nearly extinguished friendship, the most touching hospitality. I tasted in his home the sweetness of a night on the banks of the Mississippi, enjoying the suave harmony as the melancholy chants of the forests blended with the grave and solemn voice of the great river. At the foot of two flower-laden lemon trees, where a mockingbird placed its nest, we came and sat so as to see, passing by on the route, colonists on horseback whose herds of cattle bounded around us. We heard the faraway murmur of a steamboat a few leagues away and watched a coasting vessel struggle to sail against the violent current.

Multitudes of biting swamp mosquitoes made the marshy interior unbearable, and almost all of the forest is marsh. Fire attracts them in the evenings along with little black gnats that get into the eyes. One must move the light to the farthest extremity in the apartment. The forest is almost entirely marshy. When horseback riding, one must frequently step over enormous treetrunks fallen across the paths, and the horses' jumps splatter mud. Flying squirrels, river rats, and wildcats seem more abundant in wooded places, but blackbirds join them to ravage cornfields. Raccoons uproot the plants before they grow, in order to eat the seeds.

---

46. Probably Julien de Lalande Poydras (1746–1824), who came to New Orleans and became a successful peddler in the Mississippi Valley after British captivity and a stint on Saint Domingue. He is known to have offered a cash prize to any woman who would marry him, but no one claimed it. At Poydras's death, he owned six plantations and five hundred slaves. Fred Daspit, *Louisiana Architecture, 1714–1830* (Lafayette: Center for Louisiana Studies, University of Southwestern Louisiana, 1996); *Dictionary of Louisiana Biography,* vol. 2, 661. I am grateful to Carl A. Brasseaux of the Center for Louisiana Studies for helping me identify this character.

In the farthest plantations on the high side of the river, bears devour the seeds. At night when the moon shines, they can be seen sitting down to open stalks of corn with their paws; the planters must send some young Negroes with whips, and the frightened animal flees from the clatter and its echoes, whereas it would probably attack an armed hunter who dared pursue him.

On horseback we crossed the triangle that West Baton Rouge forms. In my opinion this gives the noblest view of the forests with the most colossal vegetation of the whole river. The imagination could not conjure anything more magical. Coming to the road on the opposite side, we hastened to cross at a gallop so as to have a little cool air and avoid the nearly perpendicular sunrays of the plain. For nearly a league, we rode in palmettos up to the bellies of the horses, and I shook from fear upon suddenly seeing a serpent poke out from under their shiny, satiny leaves.

At the corner of the street of the village, now perceptible across the river the traveler can distinguish the Court House. What a strange sight to find there, upon leaving after so much solitude, a court, lawyers, jury, and guilty people. They plead cases in the two languages. Hidden by two large columns, I happened to overhear an English speech pronounced in a voice familiar to me, and I recognized at last one of my traveling companions who came to Pittsburgh on board the *Trenton*, indeed the one who had been so solicitous toward me.

Negroes from along the coast, from the Bayou Sarah to the end of the river, may succumb to a dreadful mania: eating the earth. When this unique, inexplicable mania takes over, no edict or punishment can prevent it. Little by little they perish: their shiny black color grows dull, they become ghastly, leaden, they grow blind and die. I even saw some little tiny infants kept in the cradle until they were two years old, who feebly extended their arms toward the earth to scrape it up with their fingernails and devour it.

On the east bank lies the village of Baton Rouge, undeniably one of the most picturesque villages in the whole United States, built on the slope of a low hill, with wide, well-laid-out streets entirely shaded by magnificent linden trees whose feathery flower-laden tops hide all but an occasional rooftop. Vast square wooden barracks with two white-painted porches house a few companies of regular troops; the interior, planted with a row of chinaberries reaching up to a surprising height, offers a view right over the Mississippi to the opposite bank. Vultures are so familiar that one sees them skim the plazas, alight on trees, along the streets and the fences of hen yards, or even on the palisades of the enclosure where the troops practice their maneuvers. No one interferes with their flight, indeed the locals respect them because of their usefulness; as soon as a dead body begins to rot, they devour it in a minute, thus sparing the country from the unhealthy stench of so many domestic and wild animals that perish forgotten in the woods.

The left bank bears the name "Acadian Coast," the same name of the country, English today, that the French cleared to the west of the Saint Lawrence, and from which the cunning, tyrannical politics of the conquerors chased them in such an horribly odious manner. Further down lies Donaldsonville, an important village that will one day become the capital of Louisiana, at least, the provincial government plans to transfer to Donaldsonville one day, as New Orleans does not need this resource to be one of the most flourishing cities of the two Americas.

In the midst of familiar gigantic trees, I noticed a charming kind of mulberry tree with elegant, oblong fruit hiding behind each leaf and whose pyramidal form was tucked elegantly away beneath the thickest domes of old sweet gum trees, live oaks, and the liquidambars. Mulberry trees grow rather commonly all along the coast. During the mulberry season, thrushes arrive in such a large number it is impossible to chase them away. They are so fond of the intoxicating seeds that neither gunshots nor scarecrows can force them to abandon the trees. In a habitation with two such trees at its door in the most beautiful location, the property owner thought up a system of bells, one at the end of each branch, and gave a Negro the full-time job of ringing them.

NEW ORLEANS

Oh! If the sun could satisfy itself with casting only an oblique ray of light on this beautiful Louisiana which it devours, and would stop its burning course in May; if the elegant reed marshes would keep their deadly August vapors for serpents, chameleons, their alligators, turtles and the scourge of the colony, mosquitoes, if the *Meschacebé,* less proud, would not overflow its banks each springtime to deposit, along with the seeds of powerful vegetation, those of even more powerful fevers, then New Orleans would be populated like a European capital, as rich as a city of India, as joyful as an Italian town, and as brilliant as an oriental one. Imagine a vast crescent crowned with houses, regular but not monotonous, dotted with white rooftops and many-hued canvases, outlined with bell towers and trees in pyramids like minarets, with an active murmur day and night: songs on the quays, songs on the plazas, songs on the boats, and in the evening a thousand lights reflected in the waters. Were this a painting, imagine in the foreground, like open lacework, like a transparent forest, a triple line of three-masted, heavy-boomed ships gobbling down sacks of sugar and bales of cotton, around which half-naked Blacks hurry with their red sleeves, muscled arms, and raucous voices, and brigs, American schooners, proudly unfurl their thirty stars on a field of blue alongside heavy English vessels, green like the ocean, with narrow main yards, grinding chains, and the red flame traversed by the white cross of Albion! The cannon groans: all sails filled, lively like a bird, rose-colored like a flamingo, from a distance a brigantine from Cuba exhales its perfume of bananas, pineapples, and oranges. Next comes a shaking steamboat, her enormous mass turning proudly in front of the quay, boastfully displaying her decks teeming with two or three hundred passengers, her silk-curtained back room where women stroll as if on display, its upper deck from which rise a thousand deafening cries in a single voice, for those moving dots are five hundred Kentuckians who, having sold their harvests and rafts, return to their harsh forests to steer once more the other rafts that descend and never return upstream. Look again toward those humbler woods so immense in expanse that one would take them for a sea, as a violent effort resounds like a sigh, and four or five heavily loaded boats advance without apparent motion, without sails, growing ever larger between the two portholes until at last the vast tug pushing them appears, vomiting forth a wave like a sea monster. An hour later it rests in port, but the waves still quiver with agitation, and frightened seagulls turn their flight upward as far as the eye can see. And all of that glistens amid a blue deeper than the Ocean; the sun which enhances every object gilds the waves of the river, silvers the decks of the ships, the tiles of the streets, the roofs of the houses, and shimmers on the foreheads of Blacks and bronzes the thin faces of Europeans. If you raise your dazzled glance heavenward, you will see, blended with the uniform sky, the haughty eagle which soars, rocks, and seems to sleep in regions unknown.

In the middle of the city, unfolding between its two neighborhoods like two enameled wings, extends the "Place d'armes," a square [plaza] of perpetually burned green, vainly trying to shelter puny young elms, scorched, smoky and reeking dust. Opposite, the rather beautiful church, the Catholic cathedral, dates from the time of Louis XV. On the right stands a house with iron grilles, doors with heavy iron locks, some kind of gendarmes [police] and ghastly pale black and yellow faces pressed against the iron grille—the prison, the jail, where they lock up runaway slaves, and scoundrels. When the door opens to the sound of chains, the rebellious slaves emerge, balls attached to their legs, covered in rags and tatters, accompanied by armed men and followed by an officer, whip under his arm, escorting them to their task of sweeping the sunken streets, flooded by storm rains right up to the sidewalks. One Negro yawns and acts bored until the blow of a stick on his nose awakens him; he wipes the flowing blood, laughs or bellows from degradation, opens his mouth—as large as a shark's—and picks up his broom. Elsewhere a brazen black hussy wears an iron collar around her neck, its four points rising higher than her head. She threatens the guard, attacks passersby, lies down in the street, and once again gets whipped. Then she roars, rolls in the mud yelling, tears open her wound, rips into shreds the cloth bandage barely covering it, and remains, mute with rage and pain, at the feet of the prison officer. Joyful and laughing, two proud Mulattas pass, their teeth white, their ivory foreheads enhanced by red silk turbans rolled in the style of the women of Havana. Perhaps a look of pity will stop them at the sight of these unfortunates twice deprived of their liberty, twice reduced to brutes by double irons, for the rest of their days awaiting beatings they do not understand. But no, a free and elegant Mulatta, who does nothing, may stroll and enjoy the privilege of being important enough to see herself protected, just outside the insurmountable barrier, strengthened by prejudice, between her and the white man.

Let us leave this foul mire and cast our glance on the well-aligned streets, cut at right angles, shaded by roofs that spread a delicious darkness into the depths of rich shops. It is impossible, especially during a stifling day in springtime, to pass in front of these cool vaulted cafes without being tempted to pause a while, read some newspapers, and enjoy a glass of chilled punch, soda, or beer smoking a cigar marked with little black spots—a real Havana whose fragrance wafts down all the streets and all the public places. To find shade at each step invaluable, and it is especially delightful to find ice, which is brought in by sea from Boston, Philadelphia, Providence, and elsewhere.

The city is built perpendicular to the plain. Streets parallel to the river divide the city, cut up in their turn at right angles by similar streets so that the blocks of houses form regular squares, often ravaged by fire. When fire catches, it almost always destroys the affected blocks completely. New Orleans, quite lively, especially in the evening with the shops brilliantly lit, is most alive on the quay, where the foreigner gets an idea of the immense commerce of the Louisiana's capital, from the western end where steamboats, rafts, and boats, to the butcher market and the boats of *caboteurs*,[47] which are so clean. The quays display an unbelievable variety of languages and costumes. Here the noisy laughter and animated conversation of Frenchman whose lively dialect bears traces of Santo Domingo interrupt Americans and English, serious in their speculative discourse; there, the song of a Spaniard or a Mexican in a gaudy colored coat and big hat does the same. Sailors carry on their disputes, each swearing in his own language, from the blond Norwegians to the dark Portuguese. In the midst of the tumult and affluence of twenty nations, this commercial activity which agitates and rumbles like a volcano, a serious, impassive Indian from the wilderness sits on a rock with his bow and arrows unmoving, dividing the waves of people like a piece of rock separating the waves of a waterfall.

In the evening, when the sailors return to their shores, the Negroes to their huts, and the savages to their teepees, the strollers come outside. Orange merchants light up their canvas boutiques and the illuminated cafes fill with people. For the person who likes to judge a city when it is sleeping—or rather when it is dreaming, for nothing that happens at that hour counts toward daytime life—or for the one who likes to daydream on the riverbank, facing an anchored boat, when the murmur of waves replaces that of men, this levee makes another delicious promenade, with its lilac-

---

47. Vendors or peddlers who travelled the rivers in their own boats, selling an array of merchandise; their markets disappeared with the spread of steamboats.

lined walkways, especially the neighborhood that follows the course of the Mississippi. One after another, gardens unfold: bowers of blooming orange trees, hedgerows of jasmines, tall magnolia trees and laurels, and, further toward the west, immense forests as far as the eye can see, blending with the starry sky! I know nothing more beautiful than the look of a bustling city become silent before infinity. For this reason, cities, villages, hamlets, even the simplest settlements in America evince a grandiose character all their own; one feels surrounded by an unsettled atmosphere of primitive nature, something indefinable washes over one on earth and heavens—M. de Talleyrand said that, there, the seasons themselves never stopped.[48]

Behind the city, a basin and canal dug into the interior linkup with Lake Borgne and Lake Pontchartrain, creating the shortest way to the Floridas, the route taken by little boats bound for Pensacola to pick up building bricks. Today fishing and boating parties rendezvous on Borgne and Pontchartrain, the two great lakes that the English covered in armed sloops to accomplish their debarkation for the battle of New Orleans. On the banks of Lake Maurepas, the lake farthest inland, wandering Indians conduct a part of their sad existence on the city dump; real dogs without masters, they fight over the remains of a bone in the street and indulge in the most disgusting excesses. People chase them off by throwing buckets of water on them, but they content themselves with hiding their heads in their hands believing thereby to escape from stares.

New Orleans boasts a well-attended theater, even sending a traveling troupe north in the summer to present plays, but people of color, who have separate seating even in church, cannot even enter the pit or the main floor of the beautiful, large, richly decorated auditorium, . . . and Americans say "Liberty and Equality"! A young man may receive a brilliant education in Europe and show himself rich and well dressed, or a beautiful, monied young woman may display a careful upbringing, but it matters not, not even when sometimes they are even whiter than those

48. Charles Maurice de Talleyrand-Périgord (1754–1838), Bishop of Autun and confessor of Marie-Antoinette, was excommunicated by the pope for revolutionary activities. He traveled in the United States from 1794 to 1796 before aligning himself with Napoleon Bonaparte, whom he subsequently disavowed. Talleyrand exercised an immense influence over foreign affairs under Louis XVIII, then served as French ambassador to London under the July Monarchy.

who scorn them; their ancestors were slaves. They bought their freedom with their own money or perhaps even by performing some impressive action, but it matters not; they descend from an African, snatched away from his native land, sold into chains consequently, ten generations bear the dishonor, so much so that a bankrupt European fleeing prison, branded, cannot decently seat himself beside such beings!

Regardless of what Bostonians say, the militia for the city and the area are the handsomest in all the United States. The artillery especially has an extraordinary reputation: the grenadiers wear fur hats in the French manner. I had the pleasure of seeing a mock battle in the Marigny Plain,[49] which extends a great distance behind the city. The helmets of the cavalry, rich planters from the coast wearing the uniform of dragoons, sparkled in the May sun, swarms of butterflies fluttered on the foot soldiers' bayonets, and buzzards assembled in advance, as if for the carnage. French commands were repeated in Spanish for the company of *tiradores,* and in English for the regiment from the United States and the riflemen. Riflemen, with shirts of ticking, powder horns, and Tennessee riflemen's leather pouches for lead began the attack from behind palmettos that completely hid them, and the regular troops responded with rolling fire. Discharges rapidly followed one another, cannons boomed, the cavalry came forward, and the grenadiers advanced at the run with mounted bayonets, producing a cloud of smoke that concealed at least four thousand armed men. After the parade, the whole army lunched at the general's expense in the shade of the willows along the canal.

This canal also bears the name Marigny because it was dug while Marigny was governor. Its purpose is to drain off stagnant waters and decontaminate the city. Marshes surround New Orleans and, in the flood

49. Marigny de Mandeville (1785–1868), whose mother was a member of another leading Creole family, the d'Estréhan, was an aide-de-camp to Governor Claiborne during the Battle of New Orleans. Marigny was a real estate entrepreneur who subdivided his plantations to create the Faubourg Marigny and the town of Mandeville. (*Dictionary of Louisiana Biography,* vol. 1, p. 548). He is best remembered by the French for his generosity toward Louis-Philippe and his brothers when they came to New Orleans in exile during the Restoration. Louis-Philippe repaid the Creole's generosity when he became king by hosting him at Saint Cyr for three years. Marigny returned a cavalry lieutenant with equestrian knowledge and skills. Simone de la Souchère Deléry, *Napoleon's Soldiers in America* (Gretna, La.: Pelican Publishing Co., 1972), 154.

season, the city lies some ten feet below the level of the river; if the dike broke, everything would be irretrievably flooded. Flooding raises boats up higher than the houses, and roaring waves threaten the beautiful gardens of the residential area as the Mississippi rolls in its flow trees, snatched from forests upstream, at the height of the tropical flowers' blooming stalks. A steamboat wheel or even the least little wind raises the waves to the height of the jetty. If such a hurricane, very common in the summertime, started to blow in this season, you would see the vessels lifted up into the streets and shipwrecked as far as the center of the plaza.

It does not have to be a hurricane—sometimes an ordinary rainstorm spills two feet of water in the city, so that alligators wander in the gutters [beside the streets], and snakes, into shops. In 1829, with the Spaniards chased from Mexico dying by the hundreds, torrential rains disrupted some of the funeral processions, and once a floating cadaver slammed against the sidewalks, forcing a priest and his assistants to flee.

ATTACK ON NEW ORLEANS

Let him come!

The Britain expedition, or rather, the Britain defeat, is an event so important and so intimately tied to the events of Europe and to the French spirit—a spirit still throbbing in these inhabitants, who did not forget their fatherland in the few intervening years—that I believe I must discuss it. On the very site an eyewitness, [the author's uncle, Charles Roque Pavie] and what is even better, a soldier who played his glorious part in that bloody day, communicated to me the precious details about it. A child of the French Republic, in turn sailor and combatant on the Ocean, in the colonies, and on the continent, his language accented with such energetic truth that seeking to imitate it would be to risk distorting it, therefore we will let him speak for himself.

"Since the months of October and November [1814], the English and French newspapers, personal correspondence, and then the mysterious murmur that spreads alarming news so hastily, had led us to fear an invasion. However, it seemed that by a profound tranquillity, a quiet assurance, we could set this danger aside; for no measures were taken, no help summoned, and no call-to-arms issued in the interior to counterbalance the worrisome rumors brought to us by sea. Legislators did name a Defense Committee, but, for lack of money, its hastily adopted plans remained unexecuted. Besides, the Creoles, always difficult to move, still waited to be ignited by that fire, that energy that animates them when the moment comes to act. Still the moment had not come and yet, the storm kept on gathering and gathering.

"Around this time, General Jackson, today president, had just won a great victory over an army of Creek Indians. Surrounded from the base of an Appalachian mountain to its summit, they were forced to surrender. Jackson, commander-in-chief of the Louisiana Militia, arrived in Louisiana with astonishing swiftness. In proclamations translated into French by [Edward] Livingston, he explained the danger. His example ignited a population finally wrested from its lethargy by the sacred cause of liberty.[50]

"Irishmen, Creoles, French, Spanish, and Americans instantly forgot their old quarrels, shedding all their pride to enthusiastically embrace the defense of American rights and way of life. Each man flew to arms, manufactured pikes, took up carbines again, melted balls; the women prepared remedies for the wounded, relief for the fatigues of a war whose cruel consequences justifiably concerned them. It reminded me of my youth; reinvigorated by the climate of Louisiana I found the energy I had at twenty years of age. We found ourselves surprised, we old European

50. The Battle of Horseshoe Bend took place on March 27, 1814, on a horseshoe-shaped strip of land on the Tallapoosa River in what is today Alabama. Ostensibly vengeance for a massacre of two dozen whites, this battle was near genocide. Some eight hundred Braves died; only a handful of Creeks lived to surrender to Jackson at Fort Toulouse on the Tombigbee. Jackson's Choctaw ally, Pushmataha, joined him again at the Battle of New Orleans, where he and his men fought bravely for the man who called him "Brother." Pushmataha died of pneumonia in Washington D.C. Some six hundred Cherokees also assisted Jackson at Horseshoe Bend, including Sequoyah, the inventor of the Cherokee alphabet. This was the opening volley of the skirmishes which eventually led to the expulsion of both friendly Choctaws and Creeks from the Alabama region, and the Seminoles from Florida. Even those who helped rout the British from New Orleans and Pensacola in 1815 took the Trail of Tears. The military display that the Pavies attended on Marigny Plain in 1830 was the gathering of troops bound for Florida to accomplish that expulsion. A Louisiana attorney whose father negotiated the Louisiana Purchase, Livingston served as lawyer for the Laffites and as Jackson's secretary of state.

soldiers, to be so ardent, but hatred does not rust away, and fighting Englishmen again stirred us. Moreover, were we not fighting for the most
sacred of causes?"

Here the veteran stopped, haunted by a thousand recollections of glorious combats and atrocious *pontons* [hulks of boats used as British prisons during Napoleonic wars]. I quietly allowed him to go back over all
of those years which were so full of memories. Respecting his silence, I
contemplated his high forehead, his still black hair, and the outline of his
eyebrows burned by the fuse of a cannon—once, [aboard a ship] about
to be boarded, he found the cannon had no wick so he lighted the fire
with his cigar!

Soon he continued:

"Someone signaled the arrival of the English squadron, and the look-
out, blinded by fright, reported uncountable numbers. A few more days
and they took our gunboats, and the way before them open to enter, the
English become masters of the lakes! Then martial law was declared, and
every citizen, from 16 to 50 years of age, flew to defend his home. At one
terrible moment, a dreadful crisis, we saw that we would have to abandon our wives and our children in the midst of a multitude of Negroes,
whom the enemy's infernal vengeance was quietly working up; this stupe-
fying idea seemed a danger a thousand times greater than the first [the
English].

"I summoned my servants. All appeared as usual, nonetheless, I believed I could discern on their submissive, devoted faces an atrocious joy.
'The first one who moves,' I shouted, drawing two pistols from my belt,
'the first one who moves is dead! Every evening I will leave the camp and
keep watch on you.'

"After this speech, I began to run through the streets, excited by the
spectacle of the general enthusiasm. But in the midst of such agitation,
such incredible activity, consternation painted many a face: who among
the inhabitants, except veterans like us, had ever heard the whistle of a
ball? And the promised reinforcements, what had become of them? We
had clamored for them. General Carroll was supposed to have left Mobile with his cavalry; fifty leagues of a wretched trail (steamboats did not
exist then) separated them from us. They crossed this span in two days.
A coalition of five hundred men joined us, comprising the total force with

which we opposed 15,000 Englishmen calling themselves the invincible ones, the conquerors of Europe and Waterloo![51]

"For two days we did not know the enemy's position, as our forces were insufficient to form observation corps. Suddenly, we heard that they had marched so precipitously and in such security that a scant two leagues separated the enemy from the city. Our first reaction was to question the news, as no one wanted to believe it, but Jackson hastily called to arms, or rather assembled those citizens enflamed with the desire to fight. We met on the plaza where a venerable priest blessed the flag of the Republic, and our trembling spouses, touched by so many diverse feelings, mixed their prayers with their tears!

"A handful of *braves*,[52] 350 men from uniformed companies and riflemen, 500 soldiers from paid troops, and some cavalrymen threw themselves in front of the English, attacked them with ardor and unbelievable fierceness, and succeeded in halting their march. Both sides fought desperately, and, after an hour of combat, each of the two armies dropped back to reestablish its position. A horrible disorder reigned during this attack—our line infantry, cutting through the forest, opened fire on our militia, we killed each other point blank—but fortunately the error did not last long! English forces captured one cannon piece from us, but soon Savary's brave Mulattos recaptured it, like real *braves*, with their bayonets. An eighteen-cannon schooner, the *Caroline*, harmed the English most, allowing itself to be dragged along by the current to take the enemy in the flank and make large breeches in its tight battalions. Oh! How nobly the *Caroline* behaved! At each volley, she trembled from the keel to the tip of the masts, spitting fire as a battle horse spits its froth.

"Jackson thought it a false attack, and had all the militia file down the path toward Gentilly, which leads to Chef menteur, where we waited. As for me, I was the sergeant of the grenadiers, and I commanded the most

51. The Battle of New Orleans took place January 8, 1815. Napoleon's first abdication was April 6, 1814, but the Battle of Waterloo was not until June 18, 1815. After Waterloo, Creoles gradually forgot the chronology and began to say that the Battle of New Orleans had avenged Waterloo. After all, the surviving English troops headed to Waterloo very soon after their American defeat.

52. Napoleonic veterans like Charles Pavie and the rowdy Humbert were always called "les braves." It would not have been lost on young Pavie that warriors among Indians and Napoleonic troops bore the same name.

advanced post. We spent the night with guns on our arms, exhausted from fatigue, and more than a little worried!

"I was the only Frenchman in my little troop. To cure our boredom and make the day slated to deliver us the enemy break sooner, I thought of playing *ombres chinoises!*[53] We had no tents because the extreme cold made the frozen ground too hard to permit driving in stakes, but the Creoles skillfully braided palmetto leaves into some improvised huts; in ten minutes, we pulled up 50 arpents of fence to make a fire, and the fields offered no more defense in the whole expanse that could block our view.

"If the English had attacked the next morning, they would most certainly have taken the city; our line could not have held. Fortunately, the intermittent fire of the night before, each man shooting helter-skelter, the diversity of commands, uniforms, and maneuvers, everything contributed to making them believe that they were dealing with seven or eight thousand men, and they thought it would be better to strengthen their primary position and wait for the rest of their troops because all had not yet landed.

"And we used this precious time well. We called up the Louisiana militias *en masse.* We dug a hole in the jetty protecting the city, a little below the outskirts, but inundating the cypress grove only permitted the enemy to transport its supplies more easily. During the night preceding the attack, some old Frenchmen built a rampart of stones and earth, several militias followed their example, and Jackson, taking advantage of this idea, craftily requisitioned for this work all of the Negroes, relieving some of our keen worries about their large numbers, and when we judged that this line of fortifications could receive cannons, we established a battery there."

"And where could these cannons come from, since the city was without resources?" Théodore asked his uncle.

"I forgot," continued the veteran, "that by giving them amnesty, all of the corsairs of Barataria [Jean Laffite and his men], had joined the ranks of citizens. Two recently captured Russian ships loaded with cloth furnished tents for the land around the marshes, and 24 marine cannons we put to use; the corsairs took charge of them and accomplished it admirably. Then, right in front of the enemy camp, we erected another battery

---

53. Chinese shadow shows are done with backlighted hand motions.

that sent bullets into enemy territory night and day, harassing them without stopping. During the night of January first, they tried to erect a battery within cannon range to regain the offensive; our line silenced it in short order by blowing it up.

"Finally the eighth of January arrived, the memorable day of the grand assault that decided the fate of Louisiana. At daybreak, the attack began against the Tennesseeans, backed up by a few cannons. A part of their column strayed into the woods, but only the center gave way. Soon the two armies attacked, amid general confusion. The disposition of our lines, sometimes concave, sometimes cut at sharp angles, naturally lent itself to crossfire, and the English fought with a powerless rage against these 'brass spiders' which blasted them from all sides. Finally they saw that they had to give up to keep the carnage from being even more terrible. The commanding general, furious at seeing his disciplined battalions thinning under our blows, ordered the reserve to advance. 'Hurrah! boys,' he cried, 'This day is yours.' 'Not yet, sir,' interrupted a rifleman, and with one shot from his carbine, laid him out stiff. . . . This event decided the battle: the Englishmen, without a leader, turned their backs, and the rout was complete. . . . And those were the formidable troops who were supposed to enter the defenseless city victoriously and who had already divided our women and our wealth among them.

"In truth, they fought valiantly," the storyteller continued, "And one must acknowledge that a special Providence was watching over us. We could hardly believe in such an unexpected and complete victory. In the middle of the combat, lifting my eyes up to heaven, I saw an eagle soaring above our troops, chasing the vultures to the side of the English. If Bonaparte had been there, what a thought would have animated his great soul at the sight of this omen, this good fortune foretold.

"The enemy's boats passed through a canal they had dug to join the Villeroy canal to the river. We feared an attack on the other bank; only an unfinished line, not a battery, opposed them on the other side, and we had grave concerns. General Morgan, a former surveyor, commanded that line of 1,200 poorly armed Kentuckians, vigorous farmers as tall as Patagonians, 200 New Orleans Militiamen, and some planters from the Acadian coast. He was hastily informed that the enemy had landed a league further away and was marching toward him. He responded only:

'Let him come'. It was beautiful, and the name 'let him come' stayed with him.

"Here came the English, advancing, sounding the charge. Their trumpets could not destroy our walls—we did not have any—but produced in our soldiers the effect of Medusa's head: one after another they took flight. The Orleans Militiamen wanted to use their cannon, but the barrel fell off the carriage, and they barely had time to spike it; it stayed with the enemy, as did the flag, still in its sheath, of the First Regiment of the Militia, whose commander rested tranquilly under a tent. 'Did you hear the "tromp-tromp"? said an Acadian, fleeing as fast as his legs would carry him, to his comrade, more dead than alive. 'What do you call that?' 'A hurricane!' My late father always spoke of them as frightful things on the sea, but on land, Almighty God, they are much worse!

"This disorder should have led to the loss of our city, but once more Providence protected us and delivered us from our enemies. They believed that this flight was nothing but a ruse, and that our Acadians were running to rally further away, to come back and charge. Now, in their turn, the English took off in full flight, carrying along the flag of the First Regiment, still in its sheath. During this time, all those in the city moved out hastily, looking for a retreat in the cypress trees, and so ended the memorable day of the eighth of January, which we celebrate every year with a ball and public merrymaking.

"The intense cold, which we had to suffer ourselves, surprised the English so much it became the principal cause of our success. By an unheard-of chance, it did not thaw for fourteen days. Moreover, it rendered several regiments of Negroes brought from Jamaica completely useless to the enemy. Join to that their small knowledge of the place, the loss of their general in charge, and the miscalculation of the troops, who believed they were disembarking in a land torn by dissension and expecting to see a part of its citizens passing over to their side—that is crazy! They did not know that all private hatreds disappear in front of a common danger, and that liberty is the most basic need! Alas! Some traitors can be found, however; more than once, native deserters, whose names are no longer pronounced in the colony, guided the English.

"We did not follow the English at all as they got away on their ships, evacuating the lakes, in their haste abandoning 80 wounded to the generosity of the Americans. That night the Militia from the Red River arrived.

"How great was our joy and what intoxication among an entire population whose courage prevented an invasion; when, lacking everything—no arms or clothing (to clothe the Tennesseeans, 10,000 piasters were collected)—our poor militias marched, more confident in the holiness of their cause than in their strength against an army so handsome, so seasoned, and so disciplined."

"What became of Savary, the leader of the Mulattos?[54]

"Savary lived a long time, esteemed and respected, as much as his color permitted, and finally, he died . . . without having obtained his citizenship which he claimed as the price of his services rendered to the Republic!"

Here the story of the veteran ended.

May I be pardoned these details, for I am closely tied to the one who told them to me, this soldier of two worlds, this ancient midshipman aboard the *Vengeance*, who became a citizen of the United States, and the venerable priest who blessed the twenty-six stars on a field of blue with his seventy-year-old hand and joined his prayers to the arms of his brothers, this priest remembered throughout Louisiana from the humblest hut to the plaza where an army assembled, was my grandfather's brother!

La Balise

Any foreigner who begins to suffer from the heat will do well to flee Louisiana, especially its capital. What a sad sight he sees: a quay, formerly lively, now long dead and deserted, abandoned hotels, and lugubrious and mournful voices around a casket! And yet, many ambitious merchants, needy travelers, and imprudent Americans from the North dare face the terrible summer season—one escapes, eighty succumb! I confess that I too, might have desired to attempt the adventure, to see this powerful nature in all its phases, but fear, or perhaps reason, won over adven-

54. Santo Domingan refugee Joseph Savary was commissioned Second Major by Andrew Jackson; he led the Second Battalion of Free Men of Color. A skilled sharpshooter, Savary was reputed to have killed Lord Pakenham, brother-in-law of Wellington. Later, Humbert and Savary joined Laffite.

ture, and I booked passage on board the *Henri Astor* setting sail for Bordeaux.

In truth, we travelers are quite a peculiar people. I had a passionate desire for France and its cool shade; the Mississippi, inordinately wide, reflecting a fiery sun, made me miss the limpid waves of the Loire with its slender poplars, green minarets above sparkling domes of willows and young elms, the old Gothic towers in ruins, with their ivy and their memories. All that comes to mind, a thousand times enhanced; nonetheless, I felt myself stopped, idling on these American shores. I cast a last loving glance over this very lively city, illuminated as if for a festival by the rays of the evening sun, and as the shadows invaded the horizon, I felt increasingly sad. But once on board, I no longer clung to America! The anchor raised, the cannon boomed, I felt violently moved. I do not know why the departure cannon, solemn and brusque at the same time, has something that hurts the traveler and separates the land from the Ocean.

The towboat *Waverly* took our ship on the right, and a three-masted freighter bound for le Havre on the left, gravely conducting us toward the Gulf of Mexico, as one takes the arm of two friends. We communicated from one boat to another across the towboat, and the passengers on the two decks joined in gazing one last time at the port. Some among them were crying, those were the young people going to France to seek an education—eight years schooling to learn Latin, even though a Creole has a pressing need to speak English and Spanish. Others said nothing and smoked; I could easily recognize among them Spaniards forced by Mexican law to abandon their homes in Vera Cruz, their rich dwellings in Mexico, their mountains where they had cherished families. Still others made a conspicuous noise arranging their mattresses, trunks, and utensils in the narrow cabin; those were travelers—businessmen for whom the countryside is no longer of any interest when the merchandise is gone—donning their nightcaps, beginning the boring life on board the ship, which they brighten in their own way.

When night fell, I had to sleep, but first the dreadful ruckus of the tug, then the gnats, made it impossible. Like any such torture, it would have been a thousand times better to be on horseback at daybreak in the frost, tormented by seasickness, walking all day long in the prairie without finding a stream for refreshment, or rolling in a stagecoach four or five nights in a row in the snowy Appalachian Mountains when the north wind moans in the pines! One must spend twenty-four hours in Balise without mosquito netting to understand all the horror of a similar position: devoured relentlessly by imperceptible insects that buzz in the ears, unable to close one's eyes for an instant, suffering from head to foot, to be no more than stings and pustules, and feel a million needles enter one's body. Cuban pirates take no greater pleasure than to stake a naked prisoner in full sun in the middle of the marshes; one half hour later, he no longer has a human form! An unfortunate young man who shared my cabin suffered so from the gnats that, despite being a Creole, twenty days later, when we had obtained more temperate latitudes, he was still covered with poisonous and potentially dangerous bites.

After crossing the parish of Plaquemine and the English point where the Mississippi forms a detour that sailors used to dread because, before towboats, one needed all four winds to get around it, and after passing Fort Philip, one encounters the moving prairies, as far as the eye can see. A sad sight, this wretched landscape offers sailors who cast anchor on the low and marshy coast no other entertainment than lassoing some stray head of cattle to augment their provisions.

On the edge of the forest there is a barely visible cabin. Passengers on a French boat, lost on a hunting expedition across the prairies, once stayed for a while at a barely visible cabin on the edge of the forest, seeing no one, only two men who fled at their approach. Those frightened beings crept back with arms and frankly confessed to the foreigners that they had escaped two years before from the penitentiary at Brest. They lived so unhappily in this uninhabited wilderness as almost to miss the chain and the galleys; subsisting only by hunting, this was the first time the miserable brigands had dared to communicate with human beings. Whatever they might be, I believe they have paid the price of their freedom, if indeed what they have is freedom, and that it belongs to them if not by law, at least by right.

Ships going upstream without the help of a towboat may pick up a pilot stationed at La Balise. The river empties into the Gulf of Mexico by four branches or principal passages, without counting the Otter Pass to the east of the others; the southeast is the deepest, even though no more than sixteen feet of water cover a sandbar that crosses the channel. We brushed it lightly with our keel, but the other boat rammed it more seriously; a completely loaded three-masted English schooner went aground, its length blocking a part of the passage. A weak northwest breeze favored us, and with the help of the current from the Mississippi, which flows twelve more leagues across the ocean without losing its color, in spite of the wind and tide, we quickly headed toward the open seas.

Nothing is more terrible, more distressing, or more sublimely horrible than the mouth of the Mississippi. I know more than one Frenchman, attracted to the banks of the "Father of Rivers" by the descriptions of Chateaubriand, who cried from disappointment at the sight of La Balise, a landscape of nothing but moving prairies, withered reeds, polluted marshes as far as the eye can see. Uncountable vultures flock there among the pelicans, flamingos, and cranes, and hideous alligators, monstrous turtles, and black serpents mottled with ghastly spots float near the riverbanks. Nothing that meets the eye could give you an inkling of the admirable forest of the interior. Where to disembark, where to place one's foot on this mud that would swallow up an entire army? When the Spanish tried to descend the river toward the Tampico area, the eighty soldiers hurled themselves ashore and disappeared with arms and baggage! At two leagues from the sea, one can barely distinguish the outline of the coast, because it lies so low. At the entrance of the southwest passage, the top of a shipwrecked schooner sticks up; further along, one can see the broken booms of a brig, with reptiles that come to sleep on the end of the mast.

Such is my last sight of the magnificent Mississippi, closing its twelve hundred leagues of forests, habitations, villages, and cities in a disastrous tableau, frightening, but grandiose in its ugliness. Man can do nothing about it, since the ocean itself is compressed by its own power. We no longer saw its banks, but its influence still made itself felt; the smoke of the towboat returning to New Orleans rose up in the distance toward the horizon, a little cloud of land reminded us of the presence of America, present but less and less perceptible, a vapor, an imprecise line, a dot, then nothing more. But all of the feelings a man experiences, all of the memories he amasses, engrave themselves on his soul in pictures that cannot be erased. Oh, beautiful America! Land of liberty, mother republic of twenty-six other republics, refuge to all who suffer, asylum of the oppressed, homeland of melancholy hearts, farewell. I loved you—me, a capricious child seeking the wilderness and peace—and you were good for me. I will never forget your lakes whose limpid waves I heard murmuring, your rivers without headwaters, your proud cities, and especially, the nocturnal sojourns beside a stream when all nature slumbers, from the hummingbird, deep in a flower, to an Indian, happy on a buffalo skin. Today when all that is finished for me, you give me sweet dreams still, and I love to speak of you as an absent friend.

CONCLUSION

Barely out to sea, we saw three waterspouts shoot their columns up to the clouds, then collapse and bubble like the lava of a volcano; in a flat calm, the frightening masses, parading gravely on the horizon, passed among three ships without touching them. In the middle of the night, a gust of wind came along so suddenly that it was impossible to take in the sails; it would have taken little more to carry them away. Thus the fickle weather of the Gulf announced itself. At sunrise, four ships passed at full sail, pushed along by occasional breezes we could not feel. For ten days a deadly calm exposed us unmercifully to the heat of a tropical sun; thunder rumbled at night, and lightning bolts followed one another continuously. What a bewitching tableau—the heavens on fire, the sea illuminated by phosphorescent vapors, each drop on the guy wires glistening like a pearl! As the storm coming upon us covered the cannons, pumps, and anchors with a dazzling brightness, and a plume of fire exploded at the end of the lightning rod, yet we detected not the slightest wind, not an oscillation on this vast liquid plain, not the least noise, except the painful aspiration of a dolphin, the leap of the porpoise, and the wheezing of a shark sniffing its prey.

Thirty leagues from the western tip of Cuba, the nights seemed perfumed, perhaps only through the power of suggestion, still each passenger took pleasure in a dreamy stroll on the deck, catching an unexpected breeze blowing in off the land, cooling the boiling atmosphere, and losing itself in the capricious studding sails with a murmur like the cooing of a wood pigeon. Sometimes we gathered under the tent in torchlight, the ladies blended their voices with our somewhat hoarse ones, and the resulting songs were, if not melodious, at least in tune, spontaneous, and marked with an original melancholy produced when pleasure and pain, enjoyment and danger, are all experienced in common, when one must share everything, life and death.

We passed through the Bahaman Canal slowly for we had to sound it, recognize the islands of the strait, and tack under low sails. One evening we discovered the tip of the Floridas,[55] approaching closely enough to distinguish, without glasses, the forest on the shore, and the marshes with the magnolias behind them. Several little sails passed close to the land, and the crew set our cannons in firing position because fewer fishermen than pirates sail in this part of the world. Then some mild breezes reached us; the listing boat with its light cloud of sails, its sharp keel, and its sea-way white with froth made a beautiful spectacle. Bream gave us the pleasure of fishing, and the crew spent its leisure hours harpooning sharks. Flying fish jumped above the waves in front of the bowsprit like a flock of starlings; nothing is more fantastic than these inhabitants of the waters, with their fins waving like fans. Chased from their element by bream, shunted back into the water by the seagulls, falling on the decks with dry fins, they remain in perpetual flight, and everywhere find enemies. A seagull came to rest on the dinghy, but when I grabbed it by the feet, it flapped me vigorously with his wing—that made me let go!

Upon our arrival at Cape Hatteras, a terrible storm struck us, carrying off the two main sails, and shredding the jibs to pieces. We could barely flee in front of the swell that struck us from behind and flooded the deck, washing the chicken coops away, and St. Elmo's fire rolled in luminous fireballs over the mast. It was impossible to calculate the speed of the ship, we covered nearly a hundred leagues in twenty-four hours. An American schooner—one of several tacking on the horizon—passed so near we almost collided, but traveling at such speeds we could not even exchange greetings; when she drew up alongside, a wave snatched off part of her load of oranges and bananas. A sad spectacle presented itself the next day: a mast, some sails, and some rigging floated in the distance, and an entire cargo of casks of oil and staves announced the recent loss of a ship. Our sailors became silent, we barely had strength to cheer each

55. Notice that "the Floridas," once extending from the Atlantic coast to the Mississippi River, had become one Spanish Florida when Spain retroceded much territory to France in 1802, just prior to the Louisiana Purchase. At that time Spain kept Florida, which it sold to the United States in 1819.

other; it was a terrible warning about the sea, where so many lives depend on a single false turn of the rudder, a failed maneuver, a split plank, a rat hole in the keel!

After forty-two days at sea, only twenty-two days since we left the tip of Florida, we entered the Gulf of Gascony. I spent the whole night watching the pilots, and the next day we sighted the coast of France, promised to us for two days by the red sails of the fisherman, the heavy sails of the chasse-marées and of the luggers. After a long exile, France, the fatherland, lay in front of us, two miles away, coasts covered with vines, fields of wheat, the noise of the flails chopping the harvest—all of my childhood could be rediscovered on that shore!

We narrowly avoided perishing on the protruding rocks. In the sloop, the crew doubled its efforts to tow us, as the tide dragged us violently; the pilot no longer knew what to do. To be shipwrecked at the port, in view of your native land, would be cruel after escaping so many perils, when you have so many things to say and are so happy, and when your friend's eye can see you from the shore! A change of wind wrested us from danger, and in the evening we anchored in the Bay of Verdun in the middle of a flotilla of foreign boats. We arrived on St. Peter's Day [June 29, 1830], while the fishermen were celebrating their patron saint in their way with a multitude of fires burning on the beach.

Two days of quarantine were required—another torture—to gaze at cherry trees laden with fruit and see at every moment small boats loaded with passengers traveling freely while we remained at anchor after forty-four days at sea, unable to run down those fresh paths picking the fruits of France, or even tread upon the soil of France! Nonetheless, the last night I spent on board was a little sad; if you could know how much a boat on which one has crossed an Ocean becomes dear to a traveler! I had trouble, in spite of everything, renouncing the sea forever. It seemed that I could no longer sleep without its waves, without its swell, without its rocking breezes. I lost it all: fantastic dreams of storms, long reveries of calm times, rejoicing in the adventurous and independent life of a sailor who had finished his voyage so well. I was so happy on my mattress of moss, my head on a plank, when the ship seemed to be swallowed up under the waves; this poor ship which found its way so valiantly, which kept its course so well, which suffered a broken mast so violently, like a blade of grass cut by the plow, whose elegant masts cried out in the night,

whose shrouds groaned in the wind, this infernal music of a storm coming on, pulling back, returning, with its crescendos, its pianos, its harmonies that Hoffman knew how to produce.[56] Where to find that again
under my peaceful roof, at the corner of my fire? Do you believe, people
of the land who have never set foot on deck, do you believe all that can
be forgotten with ease, and that your sleep, so profoundly heavy, is worth
the perpetual series of dangers that you would brave on a voyage? My
good-byes to France had been grievous, and painful good-byes to
America, that land so beautiful; how could I leave without sorrow this
ocean, my first love?

Once at Bordeaux, I felt myself become French again in a single
stroke, and that is easy to imagine. During the year of travel in America,
no event worth mentioning had taken place there. Hardly disembarked,
I was applauding *Hernani* at the Grand Théâtre; the stage had had its
revolution, and a week later, Algiers fell like the walls of Jericho in front
of the French army! Another week later, an ancient dynasty collapsed,
and all of the kings of Europe trembled on their thrones! Who would not
have been awakened at the noise of a whole world shaken loose from its
foundations!

56. Novelist and musician Ernst Theodore Wilhelm Hoffman, known as E.T.A., was
highly esteemed in French and German Romantic circles. Pavie shared with him the belief
that the holy mission of the arts was to express nature in a manner that raises all beings
toward a more sublime life. See Honour, *Romanticism*, 118, 318.

APPENDIX A
Other Pavies

Louis Joseph François Marie Pavie and his wife, Marie-Jeanne Couasse, were married October 5, 1733, at Notre-Dame de La Rochelle. Over the next twenty-two years, they had these children baptized at the Church of St. Barthélémy, whose archives are housed at the Bibliothèque de la Ville de La Rochelle. This list, graciously provided by Mary Anne Bernard in 1976 for Gary B. Mills and Elizabeth Shown Mills, who graciously forwarded it to me, has been expanded with information from interviews with Victor Pavie's descendants Geneviève Chouan's, Pascale Voisin, and Gilles, Serge, and Yves Pavie. Family tradition says that there were twenty children instead of eighteen, although I suspect the suggestion came from a poem in which the poet found it easier to create a rhyme by rounding the number up to "vingt."

1. Marie-Rose (born 14 September 1734).
2. Renée-Jeanne (11 September 1735).
3. Joseph (23 August 1736), the first-born son, apparently did not live, because the name returns in 1746.
4. Louis-Joseph, born on Christmas Day (25 December 1737), was the second son who did not survive.
5. Guillaume (15 January 1739), the first surviving son, remained in La Rochelle and worked with his father in the Temple de Minerve all of his adult life. Their business is indirectly described by Robert Darnton in a chapter entitled "Readers Respond to Rousseau" in his book *The Great*

Cat Massacre. Guillaume bought out the business interests of the other heirs upon the death of the patriarch in 1790 but was the proprietor only until 1793. Guillaume's unmarried sisters, nuns turned out of their convents by the Revolution, lived in the family home with him. Because his brother Pierre had been declared civilly dead by the revolutionary government and his share of the estate would have been seized by the state, there exists a lengthy public inventory of Guillaume's household at the time of his death.

6. Étienne (12 April 1740) immigrated to the post in Natchitoches, Louisiana, to establish trade with the Indians of Texas and Louisiana in the mid-1760s. "Étienne Pavie" became "Esteban Pavia" in 1766 when the Spanish took control of western Louisiana, where he was murdered in 1787.

7. Pierre (15 June 1741), crossed the Atlantic as a political-spiritual refugee during the Revolution. He became a devout, but tolerant, parish priest in Natchitoches, and served his parish and the Spanish crown faithfully until he officially lost his position at the time of the Louisiana Purchase. He lived for a few years with his brother Joseph in New Orleans, where he blessed the pirates and militiamen at the Battle of New Orleans. At the time of his death, he was canon at the cathedral in La Rochelle.

8. Jean-Baptiste (16 September 1742) was a fur trader who operated a trans-Atlantic trade from Bordeaux. He married and had ten children, two of whom went to Natchitoches: Antoine, who died there young, suddenly, and Charles, who married a Creole, Marianne Rouquier. They received their "nephew" Théodore in the winter of 1829–1830.

9. Nicolas-Pierre (6 December 1743).

10. Jeanne-Thérèse (15 January 1745) became a nun.

11. Joseph (27 February 1746) went to the Louisiana colony as a trader. After a stint in Natchitoches, he moved to New Orleans. Spanish officials issued a warrant for his arrest for embezzling customs fees, but after the Louisiana Purchase, he was the alcalde of his New Orleans district. Unmarried and without legal heirs, he apparently fathered two daughters with his quadroon companion, all three of whom are mentioned in his will.

12. Augustin (14 November 1747).

13. Charles (7 April 1749), not to be confused with his nephew Charles Roque Pavie. This Charles did not go to Louisiana.

14. Louis (2 June 1750).

15. Louis-Victor (10 May 1752), grandfather of Théodore and Victor. He stayed in France to assist his father and brother. Later he established his own press in Angers, married (around 1776) Marie Fabre, and had two children, but the daughter died young. Their son, Louis Pavie, married another Mademoiselle Fabre, who bore two sons, Théodore and Victor. She died suddenly when Théodore was two. At seventeen, he sailed to America and spent the winter in Natchitoches with his Uncle Charles. His travel journals, of course, became *Souvenirs atlantiques;* some drawings from his sketchbooks are published for the first time in this book.

16. Marie-Madeleine (17 July 1753).

17. Anne (20 September 1754).

18. Marie-Anne Claire (23 February 1756).

In 1761 Marie-Jeanne Couasse Pavie died after having given birth to twenty children in twenty-eight years of marriage. Joseph Pavie survived his wife nearly thirty years without remarrying. He died in 1790.

OTHER WELL-KNOWN LOUISIANA PAVIES

In 1828 a certain P. J. Pavy arrived in New Orleans, where he became a very successful commission merchant. But the provenance of this man, whose descendants would have a decisive historic impact on Louisiana, has not been ascertained for the period prior to 1828, when "he arrived from France." One of his grandsons, Dr. Felix Octave Pavy, perished on the ill-fated Greeley polar expedition. Another of P. J. Pavy's grandsons, Judge Benjamin Pavy, had a daughter who married Carl Weiss, the accused killer of Louisiana Governor Huey P. Long, who died with him in a shower of ricocheting bullets. Long had gerrymandered his political opponent Judge Pavy out of a voting district and was threatening to "reveal" that Pavy had African-American blood. Because Judge Pavy's ancestor was named Pierre-Joseph, the very names of Théodore's great uncles Pierre and Joseph, who lived together in New Orleans during certain years, the question arises whether Long's "henchmen," in their zeal to uncover scandal in the virtuous judge's past, somehow found documents relating to the quadroon companion of Joseph Pavie mentioned in his will. Many of P. J. Pavy's descendants live in Louisiana today, where they are among the state's leading citizens.

APPENDIX B
John Murel's Published Account of a
Murder Discussed by Théodore Pavie

In his autobiography, the brigand John Murel (Murrell) bragged about murdering free people of color whom he had lured to Texas with promises of land. This published account suggests that it was at his cabin that Théodore and Charles Pavie stopped. Some historians of East Texas—Archie McDonald of Nacogdoches, Jack Jackson of Austin, and Jean Epperson of Dayton—find many traces of the Yoakum gang in the Pavie description. Murel's account below is from a 1994 reprint by Dogwood Press of Woodville, Texas, of *A History of the Detection, Conviction, Life and Designs of John A. Murel, the Great Western Land Pirate: Together with His System of Villany, and Plan of Exciting a Negro Rebellion . . . by Augustus Q. Walton, Esq.*

My next speculation was in the Choctaw nation. Myself and my brother stole two fine horses, and made our way into the Choctaw nation. We got in with an old Negro man and his wife and three sons to go off with us to Texas, and promised them that if they would work with us for one year after we got there, we would let them go free; and they told many fine stories. We got into the Mississippi swamp, and was badly bothered to reach the bank of the river. We had turned our horses loose at the edge of the swamp, and let them go to hell. After we reached the bank of the river we were in a bad condition, as we had no craft to convey us down the river, and our provisions gave out, and our only means for support was killing varmints and eating them. Eventually we found an Indian trail through the bottom, and followed it to a bayou that made into the river, and we had the pleasure of finding a large canoe locked to the bank; we broke it loose and rowed it into the main river, and were soon descending the river for New Orleans.

The old negro man became suspicious that we were going to sell them, and became quite contrary. We saw it would not do to have him with us; so we landed one day by the side of an island, and I requested him to go with me around the point of the island, to hunt a good place to catch some fish: after we were obscured from our company I shot him through the head, and then ripped open his belly and tumbled him into the river! I returned to my company and told them the old Negro had fallen into the river, and that he never came up after he went under. We landed fifty miles above New Orleans, and went into the country and sold our Negroes to a Frenchman for nineteen hundred dollars.

We went from where we sold the Negroes to New Orleans, and dressed ourselves like young lords. I mixed with the loose characters at the swamp every night.

APPENDIX C

Athanase de Mézières
and Madame de Genlis

GENEALOGY[1]

Marie Josephte Minard (1697–1754) married first (1717)

1. Claude Christophe Mauguet de Mézières (1689–1734); (2 offspring)
   Marie Françoise Félicité de Mézières Ducrest (1717–1790); (2 offspring)
      Caroline Stéphanie Félicité ("Mme de Genlis") (1746–1830)
      Charles Louis, Marquis du Crest (1747–?)
   Athanase Christophe Fortunat Mauguet de Mézières (1719–1779)
2. Louis, Marquis de la Haie de Riou
   Charlotte Jeanne (1738–1806), who married twice:
   1. 1757 M. de Montesson (1687–1769); (no offspring)
   2. April 1773, secretly and morganatically (without inheritance),
      Louis Philippe Joseph, duc d'Orléans (1725–1793), aka Philippe Égalité (1792–1793), who had no offspring with his secret
      wife, though he had legitimate children with his legitimate wife
      and, perhaps, illegitimate children with their tutor, the niece
      (Mme de Genlis) of his morganatic wife (Charlotte Jeanne,
      Mme de Montesson).

Athanase Christophe Fortunat Mauguet de Mézières was the uncle of
Madame de Genlis, a writer-pedagogue unknown in America today ex-

1. Only relevant offspring are listed. This genealogy is compiled from information in
Herbert Eugene Bolton, *Athanase de Mézières and the Louisiana-Texas Frontier, 1768–
1780*, vol. 1 (1914; reprint, New York: Kraus Reprint, 1970), 83–84, and Elizabeth Shown

cept in academic circles, where accounts of her scandals usually over-shadow her pedagogical contributions. Genlis admired her uncle, who visited her in Paris circa 1773, about the time Madame de Montesson (her aunt and the half-sister of Athanase de Mézières) secretly married Philippe, duc d'Orléans. De Mézières's visit took place not at the Louvre or Versailles, the homes of the ruling Bourbons, but at the Palais Royal, the seat of their cousins the Orléans family, whose patriarch later took the name "Philippe Égalité" and then voted to behead his Bourbon cousin King Louis XVI shortly before his own rendezvous with the guillotine. Madame de Genlis probably had two daughters by the regicide duc d'Orléans, her uncle by marriage, whose legitimate children she tutored during the Ancien Régime, when she exerted much influence. During the Terror, she rescued the children, then lived to see one of them become France's last king in 1830.

In 1825, Ladvocat (the Bonapartist bookseller in the Palais Royal) published the *Mémoires* of Madame de Genlis. There she explains her family relationship to Athanase de Mézières and praises his service as commandant of the French post at Natchitoches, lieutenant-governor of Louisiana, and acting governor of Texas. Although she tends to misname his appointments, she does not exaggerate his significance in Louisiana-Texas history. Like the legacy of his niece Madame de Genlis, Athanase de Mézières' historic legacy will turn out to be his detailed empirical descriptions of the time and place in which he lived.

Madam the Marquise (Marchioness) de la Haie, my grand-mother, had first married M. de Mézières, who owned land in Burgundy, near Avallon. My grandmother became a widow, still quite young and beautiful. She had two children by M. de Mézières, a son and a daughter—who was my mother—one age eight or nine and the other six. She put the girl in the convent in Malnoue Abbey, near Paris, and the boy in *collège,* and she remarried even before her one year of widow's mourning had passed. For her second husband she married the Marquis de la Haie, known as the handsome La Haie; he had been the page, then the lover of the

Mills, "(de) Mézières-Trichel-Grappe: A Study of a Tri-Caste Lineage in the Old South," *Genealogist* 6 (1985): 36–80.

Duchess of Berry, daughter of the Regent [the founder of New Orleans and the protector of John Law]; he was very rich. Madam de la Haie developed an aversion to the children of her first marriage and informed the Abbess of Malnoue that she intended for her daughter to become a nun and that she expected her to be reared with that idea. As soon as her son M. de Mézières was thirteen, she had him deported to America as an undesirable subject. This child was the most distinguished man and the most surprising due to his mind, his imagination, his courage, and his virtues. He arrived in the southern portion of North America, but left and took refuge in Canada among the savages; he wasn't even fourteen yet. He made them understand that he had been abandoned by his parents and that he wanted to live with them; they consented, on the condition that he submit to tattooing, that is that he allow them to paint his whole body their way with dye from herbs—a very painful operation that he tolerated with a courage that won over the savages. He had a prodigious memory and the most robust health; soon he learned their language and excelled at all of their sports. In order not to forget what he already knew (he had been an excellent student and brought home all of the prizes in his classes), every day he scrawled Latin and French passages and geometric figures on pieces of bark. He made a prodigious collection of his bark tablets that he saved with the greatest care; he acquired the highest respect among the savages, and before the age of twenty, he became their chief by a unanimous proclamation.

It is unknown whether the beautiful but wicked mother sent her son Athanase to America because he reminded her of his father (who went broke in the colonies before he died) or because the child's presence betrayed her age, not apparent from her appearance. Athanase most likely landed at the Balize, then proceeded to New Orleans and joined a Canadian trader on his return trip north. The deceased father of Athanase had a strong reputation as a geometrician but apparently little interest in wider fields of knowledge, so it is the son's resourcefulness in maintaining his knowledge, not his outstanding intellectual faculties, that is impressive.

In the continuation of the story, the basic history of the French cession of Louisiana to the Spanish is recognizable despite minor distortions in Madame de Genlis' retelling. De Mézières drifted down the Mississippi River to the Louisiana-Texas borderlands where the "savages" were from different tribes. The banishment of Athanase de Mézières was annulled by the French king on June 29, 1742, although no evidence has surfaced that he was ever informed of the annulment. It is probable that he was not informed because his service among the Indians was useful to the colonial government. These "savages" were Comanches, constantly at war with the Apaches. The Spanish were fortunate to secure subsequently the excellent services of de Mézières for a task to which they had never been equal. Madame de Genlis does not distinguish between Louisiana and Texas in her account: de Mézières served as lieutenant-governor of Louisiana and acting governor of Texas, and would have become governor of Texas had he lived.

In New Orleans and Natchitoches, imported European furnishings and a superb library were not uncommon in the plantations of the well-educated and wealthy planters. Most libraries were dispersed by succeeding generations that were either illiterate, failed to learn French, or simply needed money more than books. According to Madame de Genlis, de Mézières learned the trick of his mentor-predecessor and father-in-law, St. Denis, who had also astonished the Spanish by dealing with them in Latin.

> The savages declared war on the Spanish. My uncle taught the savages to fight more intelligently; commanding them, he achieved advantages that surprised the Spanish, who discovered that the young chief of the savages had extraordinary talents. They discussed peace, my uncle was sent to negotiate it, and he topped off the astonishment of the Spaniards by not talking to them except in Latin. They questioned this singular savage; and, touched by the account that he gave them, charmed by the mind, even the genius that he displayed to them, they offered to attach him to the service of the Spanish; he consented on the condition that they make peace with the savages. When this peace was made, he left, and went over to the Spanish where he conducted himself in such a perfect manner that he made a rich marriage [to the daughter of St. Denis], and, at the end of ten or twelve years, he was named governor of Louisiana. He acquired beautiful plantations, collected a superb library, and lived there perfectly happy.

The sagas of the Pavie and de Mézières families intersect and overlap at several junctures. Athanase père was the commandment of the post when Étienne and Joseph were militiamen and traders. From the available documents, their generation seems to have worked well together. Later, however, when Father Pierre Pavie arrived, two of de Mézières's sons, Antonio and Zosime, were involved in a Jacobin revolt led by the cleric Jean Delvaux, whom Pavie was destined to replace. Their group of *Revenants* wanted to overthrow the Spanish crown and reinstate French rule in Louisiana. Zosime apparently got escorted to the Cabildo in New Orleans in custody of his oldest brother, Athanase fils.

Fortunately the Natchitoches parish united within a year or two behind their new priest, one who knew firsthand the risks of revolution. Father Pavie's niece Hélène, the daughter of his late brother Étienne, would marry one of de Mézières's grandsons, Athanase Poissot. After Charles Pavie arrived in Natchitoches and married a Creole (whose brother had also been an active *Revenant*), he developed a close friendship with de Mézières's oldest son, whose plantation was next to that of the Pavies. When de Mézières fils died in 1827, he left his entire estate to Charles Pavie, including any eventual inheritance coming from his father's half-sister Charlotte de la Haie, wife of Philippe Égalité. De Mézières was probably entrusting the care of his estate and his beloved companion Marie-Jeanne, sister of Marie-Thérèse-Coincoin, to his friend Pavie instead of trusting legal channels, which would not have permitted the African American to inherit his property.[2]

As fascinating as we find these stories of colonial jacobinism, friendship, and inheritance, they must remain tantalizingly incomplete. Many of the records have vanished from the archives in Natchitoches, and as Mills points out, even the documents detailing this revolutionary epilogue to the tale of de Mézières no longer exist. The records of the colonial post at Rapides, where de Mézières's younger sons lived at the time, were destroyed on May 1, 1864, when the Federal troops burned down the town of Alexandria.[3]

2. Gilbert C. Din, "Father Jean Delvaux and the Natchitoches Revolt of 1795," *Louisiana History* 40 (1999): 5–33; Mills, "(de) Mézières-Trichel-Grappe," 85, 36–38.

3. Mills, "(de) Mézières-Trichel-Grappe," 38.

BIBLIOGRAPHY

d'Abrantès, la Duchesse (Laure Junot). *At the Court of Napoleon: Memoirs de la Duchesse d'Abrantès.* New York: Doubleday, 1989.

Agnew, Janet Margaret. "A Southern Bibliography: Fiction, 1929–1930." Louisiana State University *Bulletin* 31:7, 32:8,11 (1939). (N.B.: does not include Texas.)

Allen, Winnie. "The History of Nacogdoches, 1691–1830." Master's thesis, University of Texas at Austin, 1925. Special Collections, Steen Library, Stephen F. Austin University; Nacogdoches, Texas.

Bancroft, Hubert Howe. *The Works of Hubert Howe Bancroft.* Vol. 13, *History of Mexico: Vol. V, 1824–1861.* 1885. Reprint: Arno Press for McGraw-Hill, n.d.

Bannon, John Francis. *Bolton and the Spanish Borderlands: A Chronicle of Old Florida and the Southwest.* Norman: Oklahoma University Press, 1964.

Barbé de Marbois, François, Marquis de. *L'Histoire de la Louisiane et de la Cession de cette colonie par la France aux États-Unis de l'Amérique septentrionale.* Paris: Firmin-Didot, 1829.

Barker, Eugene C. *A Comprehensive, Readable History of Texas.* Dallas: Southwest Press, 1929.

Barker, Nancy Nichols. *The French Legation in Texas.* 2 vols. Austin: Texas State Historical Association, 1973.

Bâtard, T. M. *Essai sur la flore du Département de Maine et Loire.* Angers, France: Veuve Pavie et Fils, 1809.

Bazin, René. "Un Voyageur" (obituary of Théodore Pavie), *Feuilleton du Journal des Débats,* May 31, 1896.

Beaumont de la Bonninière, Gustave de. *Lettres d'Amérique, 1831–1832.* Paris: Presses Universitaires de France, 1973.

Bédé, Jean Albert. "L'Itinéraire spirituel de Chateaubriand en Amérique," *French Review* 49 (1976): 985–1000.

Benavides, Adán, Jr. *Bexar Archives (1717–1836): A Name Guide.* Austin: University of Texas Press, 1989.

Berlandier, Jean Louis. *Journey to Mexico During the Years 1826 to 1834.* 2 vols. Trans. Sheila Ohlendorf et al. Austin: Texas State Historical Association, 1980.

Bertrand, Louis [Aloysius]. *Oeuvres poétiques: La Volupté et pièces diverses.* Ed. Cargill Sprietsma. Paris: Librairie ancienne Honoré Champion, 1926. Preface.

Binkley, William C. *The Expansionist Movement in Texas, 1836–1850.* Berkeley: University of California Press, 1970.

Biré, Edmond. *Victor Hugo avant 1830.* Paris: Jules Gervais, 1883.

Blake, Robert Bruce. Robert Bruce Blake Papers. Bexar Archives, Barker Center for American History, University of Texas at Austin.

Bolton, Herbert Eugene. *Athanase de Mézières and the Louisiana-Texas Frontier, 1768–1780.* . . . 2 vols. 1914. Reprint, New York: Kraus Reprint, 1970.

———. *Texas in the Middle Eighteenth Century: Studies in Spanish Colonial History and Administration.* Vol. 3 of *University of California Publications in History.* 1915. Reprint, Austin: University of Texas Press & Texas State Historical Association, 1970.

Boorstin, Daniel J. *The Exploring Spirit: America and the World, Then and Now.* New York: Random House, 1976.

———. "From Traveler to Tourist." In *Hidden History.* Ed. Daniel J. Boorstin and Ruth F. Boorstin. New York: Harper & Row, 1987.

Bournouf, Eugène. *Choix de Lettres d'Eugène Bournouf: 1825–1852.* Paris: Honore Champion, 1894.

———. *Papiers d'Eugène Burnouf conservés à la Bibliothèque nationale.* Ed. Léon Feer. Paris: H. Champion, 1899.

Brooks, Philip Coolidge. *Diplomacy and the Borderlands: The Adams-Onís Treaty of 1819.* University of California Publications in History 24. Berkeley: University of California Press, 1939.

Carr, Philip. *Days with the French Romantics in the Paris of 1830.* London: Methuen, 1932.

Carter, Clarence E., ed. *The Territorial Papers of the United States.* Vol. 9, *The Territory of Orleans, 1803–1812.* Washington, D.C.: U.S. Government Printing Office, 1940.

Castañeda, Carlos E. *Our Catholic Heritage in Texas, 1519–1936.* 7 vols. Austin: Von Boeckmann-Jones Co., 1936–1958.

Chabot, Frederick C. *With the Makers of San Antonio: Genealogies of the Early*

Latin, AngloAmerican, and German Families. . . . San Antonio: privately published, 1937.

Chase, Mary Katherine. *Négociations de la République du Texas en Europe, 1837–1845.* Paris: Honoré Champion, 1932.

Chateaubriand, François Auguste René, vicomte de. *Atala.* Critical edition with introduction by Armand Weil. Paris: Corti, 1950.

———. *Atala, René, Les Abencérages, suivis du Voyage en Amérique.* Paris: Librarie de Firmin-Didot frères, 1853.

———. *Les Natchez, livres I et II: Contribution à l'étude des sources de Chateaubriand, par Gilbert Chinard.* Berkeley: University of California Press, 1919.

———. *Mémoires d'outre-tombe (1814–1815).* 2 vols. Ed. Pierre Clarac. Paris: Gallimard, 1946.

———. *Itinéraire de Paris à Jerusalem.* Paris: Éditions Juliard, 1964.

Chipman, Donald E. *Spanish Texas, 1519–1821.* Austin: University of Texas Press, 1992.

Clark, Patricia Parkhurst. *Literary France: The Making of a Culture.* Berkeley and Los Angeles: University of California Press, 1987.

Clark, Thomas D. *The Ante Bellum South, 1825–1860: Cotton, Slavery, and Conflict.* Vol. 3 of *Travels in the Old South, a Bibliography.* Norman: Oklahoma University Press, 1959.

Coifard, Jean-Luc. *Pierre-Jean David d'Angers, "Sculpteur d'histoire": L'Angevin, le républican (1788–1856).* Angers: Serge Malgogne, 1985.

Collins, Christopher. *The Poetics of the Mind's Eye: Literature and the Psychology of Imagination.* Philadelphia: University of Pennsylvania Press, 1991.

Colombier, Pierre du. *Decamps.* Paris: Éditions Rieder, 1928.

Cooper, James Fenimore. *The Last of the Mohicans.* London: Blackie & Son, n.d.

Cox, Isaac J. "The Southwest Boundary of Texas." *TSHA Quarterly* 6 (1902): 81–102.

———. "The Louisiana-Texas Frontier." Part 1, *TSHA Quarterly* (1906): 1–75. Part 2, *Southwestern Historical Quarterly* 17 (1913): 1–42 and 140–87.

Crete, Liliane. *Daily Life in Louisiana, 1815–1830.* Translated by Patrick Gregory. Baton Rouge: Louisiana State University Press, 1981.

Crisp, James E. "Sam Houston's Speechwriters: The Grad Student, the Teenager, the Editors, and the Historians." *Southwestern Historical Quarterly* 97 (1993): 202–37.

Crocket, George L. *Two Centuries in East Texas: A History of San Augustine County and Surrounding Territory.* Dallas: Southwest Press, 1932.

Crosnier, Alexis. *Théodore Pavie, le voyageur, le professeur, l'écrivain, l'homme et le chrétien.* Angers: Lachèse et Cie, 1897.

Darnton, Robert. "Readers Respond to Rousseau: The Fabrication of Romantic Sensitivity." In *The Great Cat Massacre and Other Episodes in French Cultural History*, 215–56. New York: Vintage Books, 1984.

David d'Angers, Pierre-Jean. *Les Carnets de David d'Angers*. Vol. 1, *1828–1837*. Ed. André Bruel. Paris: Librairie Plon, 1958.

———. *David d'Angers et ses relations littéraires: correspondance du maître*. Ed. Henry Jouin. Paris: Plon-Nourrit, 1890.

deBlieux, Robert D. *Natchitoches: A Walking Tour of the Historic District*. Natchitoches, La.: *Natchitoches Times*, 1989.

d'Eckstein, le Baron. *Lettres inédites du baron d'Eckstein: Société et Littérature à Paris en 1838–1840*. Paris: Presses Universitaires de France, 1984.

DeConde, Alexander. *This Affair of Louisiana*. New York: Charles Scribner's Sons, 1976.

Deiler, J. Hanno. *The Settlement of the German Coast of Louisiana and the Creoles of German Descent*. Baltimore: Genealogical Publishing Co., 1969.

Deléry, Simone de la Souchère. *Napoleon's Soldiers in America*. Gretna, La.: Pelican Publishing Co., 1972.

Delteil, Loys. *Le Peintre-Graveur Illustré: Paul Huet*. Vol. 7. Paris: Loys Delteil, 1911.

De Ville, Winston. *Marriage Contracts of Natchitoches, 1739–1803*. Nashville: Benson Printing Co., 1961.

———. *Natchitoches Documents, 1732–1785: A Calendar of Civil Records from Fort St. Jean Baptiste in the French and Spanish Province of Louisiana*. Ville Platte, La.: Provincial Press, 1994.

Din, Gilbert C. "Father Jean Delvaux and the Natchitoches Revolt of 1795," *Louisiana History* 40 (1999): 5–33.

———. "Protecting the 'Barrera': Spain's Defenses in Louisiana, 1763–1779," *Louisiana History* 19 (1978): 183–211.

Dobie, J. Frank. *The Mustangs*. Boston: Little, Brown & Co., 1934.

Dorsey, Florence C. *Master of the Mississippi: Henry Shreve and the Conquest of the Mississippi*. Boston: Houghton Mifflin Co., 1941.

Dumur, Guy. *Delacroix et le Maroc*. Paris: Éditions Herscher, 1988.

Ehrenberg, Herman. *With Milam and Fannin: Adventures of a German Boy in Texas' Revolution*. Austin: Pemberton Press, 1968.

Encyclopedia of Forts, Posts, Named Camps and Other Military Installations in Louisiana, 1700–1981. Ed. Powell A. Casey. Baton Rouge: Claitor's Publishing Division, 1983.

Encyclopedia of Southern History. Ed. David C. Roller and Robert W. Twyman. Baton Rouge: Louisiana State University Press, 1991.

Ericson, Carolyn. *Natchitoches Neighbors in the Neutral Strip: Land Claims Between the Rio Hondo and the Sabine.* Reprint, Nacogdoches, Tex.: Ericson Books, 1993.

Escholier, Raymond. *Victor Hugo.* Trans. Lewis Galantière. New York: Payson & Clark, 1930.

Evans, David Owen. *Social Romanticism in France.* Oxford: Clarendon Press, 1951.

Flores, Dan. *Jefferson and Southwestern Exploration: The Freeman and Custis Accounts of the Red River of 1806.* Norman: Oklahoma University Press, 1984.

Garrett, Kathryn Julia, ed. "Dr. John Sibley and the Louisiana-Texas Frontier, 1803–1814." *Southwestern Historical Quarterly* 45–49 (1942–1946).

Gaudon, Jean, Sheila Gaudon, and Bernard Leuilliot, eds. *Victor Hugo Correspondance Familiale et écrits intimes.* Vol. 2, *1828–1839,* 233. Paris: R. Laffont, 1988–91.

Gaulmier, Jean. *L'Idéologue Volney.* Geneva: Slatkine Reprints, 1980.

Geertz, Clifford. *The Interpretation of Cultures.* New York: Basic Books, 1973.

Genlis, Madame la Comtesse de. *Mémoires . . . sur le dixhuitième siècle et la Révolution française depuis 1756 jusqu'à nos jours.* Paris: Ladvocat, 1825.

Gibson, Charles. *Spain in America.* New York: Harper & Row, 1966.

Giraud, Marcel. *The Reign of Louis XIV, 1698–1715.* Vol. 1 of *A History of French Louisiana.* Trans. Joseph C. Lambert. Baton Rouge: Louisiana State University Press, 1974. Published in France by Presses Universitaires de France, 1953.

Goetzmann, William. *New Lands, New Men: America and the Second Age of Discovery.* New York: Penguin, 1986.

Hamilton, James F. "The Ideology of Exoticism in Chateaubriand's *Atala,* an Eighteenth-Century Perspective." *French Literature Series* 13 (1986): 28–37.

Hamon, Philippe. *Introduction à l'analyse du descriptif.* Paris: Hachette, 1981.

Hartmann, L. (of Strasbourg) and Millard. *Le Texas, ou Notice historique sur le Champ d'Asile.* Paris: Beguin, 1819.

———. *The Story of Champs d'Asile.* Trans. Donald Joseph. Dallas: Book Club of Texas, 1937.

Hoese, H. Dickson. "On the Correct Landfall of La Salle in Texas, 1685." *Louisiana History* 19 (1978): 5–32.

Hogan, William Ransom. " 'Tall Talk' and Cultural Ferment." In *The Texas Republic: A Social and Economic History,* 160–90. Austin: University of Texas Press, 1969.

Holderbaum, Jagmes. "Portrait Sculpture" and "Pierre-Jean David d'Angers." In

The Romantics to Rodin: French Nineteenth-Century Sculpture from North American Collections Organized and Collected by Peter Fusco and H. W. Janson, 36–51 and 211–25. Los Angeles: Los Angeles County Museum of Art and George Brazillier, Inc., 1980.

Holley, Mary Austin. Texas. 1836. Reprint, Austin: Texas State Historical Association, 1990.

Honour, Hugh. Romanticism. New York: Harper & Row, 1979.

Houck, Louis. The Boundaries of the Louisiana Purchase. St. Louis: Phillip Roeder's Book Store, 1901. Reprint, North Stratford, New Hampshire: Ayer Co., 1995.

Hugo, Adèle. Victor Hugo Raconté par un Témoin de sa Vie. Paris: Plon, 1985.

Hugo, Victor Marie. Bug Jargal. Vol. 5 of The Works of Victor Hugo. New York: The Nottingham Society, n.d.

———. Choses Vues. Ottawa: Le Cercle du Livre de France, ca. 1951.

———. Lettres à la fiancée/Correspondance. Ed. La Librarie Ollendorff. Paris: Albin Michel, 1947.

Jackson, Jack, Robert S. Weddle, and Winston de Ville. Mapping Texas and the Gulf Coast. College Station: Texas A&M University Press, 1990.

Jacquin, Philippe. Vers l'Ouest: Un Nouveau Monde. Paris: Gallimard, 1987.

John, Elizabeth A. H. "Inside the Comancheria, 1785: The Diary of Pedro Vial and Francisco Xavier Chaves. . . ." Southwestern Historical Quarterly 98 (1994): 27–56. Note on Ybarvo is n. 14, pp. 31–32.

———. Storms Brewed in Other Men's Worlds: The confrontation of Indians, Spanish, and French in the Southwest, 1540–1795. Lincoln: University of Nebraska Press, 1981.

Kieffer, Jean-Luc. Anquetil-Duperron: L'Inde en France au XVIIIième Siècle. Paris: Les Belles Lettres, 1983.

Klier, Betje B. "Pesta, Tempestad, & Pâtisserie: The 'Pastry War,' France's Contribution to the Maintenance of Texas Independence." Gulf Coast Historical Review 12 (1997): 58–73.

———. Tales of the Sabine Borderlands: Early Louisiana and Texas Literature by Théodore Pavie. College Station: Texas A&M University Press, 1998.

Lagarde, André, and Laurent Michard. XVIIIième siecle. Paris: Bordas, 1960.

Lally, Frank Edward. French Opposition to the Mexican Policy of the Second Empire. Johns Hopkins University Studies in Historical and Political Science. Baltimore: Johns Hopkins Press, 1931.

Langlois, Anatole. "Théodore Pavie," Revue de l'Anjou nouvelle 2 (1896): 44–61.

Launois, Pierre. "La vie inquiète et laborieuse de Théodore Pavie, grand voyageur et orientaliste." Mémoires Académie Angers (1983–84): 209–26.

Leeper, Clare d'Artois. *Louisiana Places: A Collection of the Columns from the Baton Rouge Sunday Advocate, 1964–1974.* Baton Rouge: Legacy Publishing Co., 1976.

Le Page du Pratz. *The History of Louisiana or of the Western Parts of Virginia and Carolina.* London: T. Becket, 1774. Reprint, Baton Rouge: Claitor's Publishing Division, 1974.

Lowrey, George. *Louisiana Birds.* 2nd ed. Baton Rouge: Louisiana State University Press, 1960.

Lucas, Edith E. *La Littérature anti-esclavagiste au dix-neuvième siècle: Étude sur Madame Beecher-Stowe et son influence en France.* Paris: Boccard, 1930.

Lyon, E. Wilson. *Louisiana in French Diplomacy, 1759–1804.* Norman: Oklahoma University Press, 1934.

Margry, Pierre. *Découverts et Établissements des Français.* Paris: D. Jouast, n.d.

Marrinan, Michael. *Painting Politics for Louis-Philippe: Art and Ideology in Orléanist France, 1830–1848.* New Haven: Yale University Press, 1988.

Marshall, Thomas Maitland. *A History of the Western Boundary of the Louisiana Purchase, 1819–1841.* Berkeley: University of California Press, 1970.

———. "The Southwestern Boundary of Texas, 1821–1840." *Southwestern Historical Quarterly* 14 (1911): 277–93.

Martin, Andrew. "The Occidental Orient." In *French Prose and Criticism, 1790 to World War II.* Ed. Harold Bloom. New York: Chelsea House, 1990.

Martin, Henri-Jean and Roger Chartier, eds. *Histoire de l'Edition Française.* 2 vols. Paris: Promodis, 1984.

McDonald, Archie P. *Nacogdoches: Wilderness Outpost to Modern City, 1779–1979.* Burnet, Tex.: Eakin Press, 1980.

McGraw, A. Joachim et al. *A Texas Legacy the Old San Antonio Road and the Caminos Reales: A Tricentennial History, 1691–1991.* Austin: Texas State Dept. of Highways & Public Transportation, 1991.

Mémoires de l'Institut Royal de France: Académie des Inscriptions et Belles Lettres 40 (1845): 30–31.

Meyrieux-Smith, Jacqueline. "Les Français au Texas." Ph.D. diss., University of Texas at Austin, 1978.

Mills, Dona Rachal. *Biographical and Historical Memoirs of Natchitoches Parish, Louisiana.* Tuscaloosa: Mills Historical Press, 1985.

Mills, Elizabeth Shown. "Family and Social Patterns of the Colonial Louisiana Frontier: A Quantitative Analysis, 1714–1803." Master's thesis, University of Alabama, 1981.

———. "(de) Mézières-Trichel-Grappe: A Study of a Tri-Caste Lineage in the Old South." *Genealogist* 6 (1985): 4–84.

―――. *Natchitoches: Abstracts of the Catholic Church Registers of the French and Spanish Post of St. Jean-Baptiste des Natchitoches in Louisiana, 1729–1803.* Vol. 2 of the Cane River Creole Series. New Orleans: Polyanthos, 1977.

―――. *Natchitoches Church Marriages, 1818–1850: Translated Abstracts from the Registers of St. François des Natchitoches, Louisiana.* Vol. 6 of the Cane River Creole Series. Tuscaloosa: Mills Historical Press, 1985.

―――. *Natchitoches: Translated Abstracts of Register Number Five of the Catholic Church Parish of St. François des Natchitoches in Louisiana, 1800–1826.* Vol. 4 of the Cane River Creole Series. New Orleans: Polyanthos, 1980.

Mills, Gary B. *The Forgotten People: Cane River's Creoles of Color.* Baton Rouge: Louisiana State University Press, 1977.

Molyneux, Peter. *The Romantic Story of Texas.* New York: Cordova Press, 1936.

Monaghan, Frank. *French Travellers in the United States, 1762–1832.* New York: New York Public Library, 1933.

Moraud, Marcel. "French Explorers, Pioneers, and Social Reformers in Texas, 1682–1860." *The Magazine of the French Legion of Honor* (n.d.) in the Moraud collection at the Sam Houston Regional Library and Research Center, Liberty, Tex.

Nackman, Mark E. *A Nation Within a Nation: The Rise of Texas Nationalism.* Port Washington, N.Y.: Kennikat Press, 1975.

Noon, Patrick. *Richard Parkes Bonington—On the Pleasure of Painting.* New Haven: Yale University Press, 1991.

Nouvel-Kammerer, Odile. *Papiers Peints Panoramiques.* Paris: Flammarion, 1990.

Nouvelle Biographie générale depuis les temps les plus reculés jusqu'à nos jours, avec les renseignements bibliographiques et l'indication des sources à consulter. Paris: Firmin-Didot, 1852–77. 46 vols.

Ornish, Natalie. *Pioneer Jewish Texans.* Dallas: Texas Heritage Press, 1989.

Osterweis, Rollin G. *Romanticism and Nationalism in the Old South.* New Haven: Yale University Press, 1949.

Partin, James Gallway. "A History of Nacogdoches and Nacogdoches County, Texas, to 1877." Master's thesis, University of Texas at Austin, 1968. Housed in Special Collections, Steen Library, Stephen F. Austin University; Nacogdoches, Texas.

Pavie, André. *Médaillons Romantiques.* Paris: Émile Paul, 1909.

Pavie, Théodore. *Contes et Nouvelles.* Paris: Benjamin Duprat, 1839.

―――. *Fragments du Mahâbhârata traduits en français sur le texte sanskrit de Calcutta.* Paris: Benjamin Duprat, 1841.

―――. "Passage des Andes en hiver." *Revue des deux mondes,* August 15, 1835.

———. *Victor Pavie: sa jeunesse, ses relations littéraires*. Angers: Lachèse et Dolbeau, 1887.

———. "Lointains souvenirs: Lettre aux neveux et à la nièce [de TP]." 1876. Private collection.

———. *Souvenirs atlantiques*. 1st ed., Angers: L. Pavie, 1832; 2nd ed., Paris: Roret, 1833.

Pavie, Victor. "Goëthe et David: Souvenirs d'un voyage à Weimar." In *Mémoires de la Société d'Agriculture, Sciences et Arts d'Angers*. Angers: Lachèse, Belleuvre et Dolbeau, 1874.

———. *Oeuvres choisis*. Preface [biographical notice] by René Bazin. Paris: Perrin, 1887.

Pratt, Mary Louise. "Conventions of Representation: Where Discourse and Ideology Meet." In *Contemporary Perceptions of Language: Interdisciplinary Dimensions*. Georgetown University Round Table on Languages and Linguistics, 1982. Ed. Heidi Byrnes. Washington D.C.: Georgetown University Press, 1982.

———. *Imperial Eyes: Travel Writing and Transculturation*. London: Routledge, 1992.

———. "Fieldwork in Uncommon Places." In *Writing Culture: the Poetics and Politics of Ethnography*. Ed. James Clifford and George E. Marcus. Berkeley and Los Angeles: University of California Press, 1986.

Prud'homme, Lucille Keater and Fern B. Christensen. *The Natchitoches Cemeteries: Transcriptions of Gravestones from the Eighteenth, Nineteenth and Twentieth Centuries in Northwest Louisiana*. New Orleans: Polyanthos, 1977.

Puelles, José Maria de Jesus. "Puelles' Report of 1827 on the Texas-Louisiana Boundary." Trans. Benedict Leutenegger; notes by Marion A. Habig. *Louisiana History* 19 (1978):133–82.

Raines, Cadwell Walton. *A Bibliography of Texas*. Austin: Gammel Book Co., 1896. (N.B.: Raines missed Pavie.)

Ramón, Don Domingo. "Diary of His Expedition into Texas in 1716." Trans. Paul J. Foik. *Preliminary Studies of the Texas Catholic Historical Society* 1 (1930): 1–24.

Ramsden, Maureen Anne. "Literary Manifestations of the Self: Their Forms and Functions in Modern French Factual and Fictional Documentary Works." *Forum for Modern Language Studies* 24 (1990): 193–203.

Read, William A. "Louisiana Place-Names of Indian Origin." Louisiana State University *Bulletin* 19 (1927).

Regard, Maurice. *Chateaubriand: Oeuvres Romanesques et voyages*. Paris: Gallimard, 1969.

Remak, Henry H. H. "Exoticism in Romanticism." *Comparative Literature Studies* 15 (1978): 53–66.

Rémond, René. *Les Etats-Unis devant l'opinion française, 1815–1852.* 2 vols. Paris: Lib. Armand Colin, 1962.

Said, Edward. *Orientalism.* New York: Vintage Books, 1979.

Sainte-Beuve, C.A. *Correspondance générale.* Ed. Jean Bonnerot. 19 vols. Paris: Lib. Stock, 1935.

Sealsfield, Charles. *The Americans As They Are.* (Later known as *The Cabin Book: Sketches of Life in Texas.*) 1871. Reprint, Austin: Eakin Press for the German-Texan Heritage Society, 1985.

Seznec, Jean. *John Martin en France.* London: Faber & Faber, 1964.

Shattuck, Roger. *The Innocent Eye: On Modern Literature and the Arts.* New York: Farrar Straus Giroux, 1984.

Sheehan, Sister Mary Agatha. "A Study of the First Four Novels of Texas." Master's thesis, Catholic University of America, 1939.

Sibley, John. *A Report from Natchitoches in 1807.* Edited and with an introduction by Annie Heloise Able. Indians and Monographs: A Series of Publications Relating to the American Aborigines. New York: Museum of the American Indians, 1922.

Sibley, Marilyn McAdams. *Travelers in Texas, 1761–1860.* Austin: University of Texas Press, 1967.

Smith, F. Todd. *The Caddo Indians: Tribes at the Convergence of Empires, 1542–1854.* College Station: Texas A&M University Press, 1996.

Smith, Francis J. *A Brief History of Ile Brevelle and St. Augustine Church.* Natchitoches, Louisiana: n.p., ca. 1981.

Spitzer, Alan B. *The French Generation of 1820.* Princeton: Princeton University Press, 1987.

Stafford, Barbara. *Voyage into Substance: Art, Science, Nature, and the Illustrated Travel Account, 1760–1840.* Cambridge, Massachusetts: MIT Press, 1984.

Stewart, Philip. *Engraven Desire.* Durham, N.C.: Duke University Press, 1992.

Streeter, Thomas Winthrop. *Bibliography of Texas, 1795–1845.* Cambridge: Harvard University Press, 1955–1960. 5 vols. (N.B.: Streeter also missed Pavie.)

Teja, Frank de la and John Wheat. "Bexar: Profile of a Tejano Community, 1820–1832." *Southwestern Historical Quarterly* 89 (1985): 7–34.

Thorgold, Algar. *Six Masters of Disillusion.* Port Washington, New York: Kennikat Press, 1909, 1971.

Tinker, Edward Laroque. *Les Écrits de Langue française en Louisiane au*

XIXième siècle. Bibliothèque de la revue de la littérature comparée. Vol. 85, 1932.

Tixier, Victor. *Voyage aux prairies Osages, Louisiane et Misouri, 1839–1840*. Clermont-Ferrand: Chez Perol, 1844, 1845.

Trollope, Frances. *Domestic Manners of the Americans*. Barre, Mass.: Imprint Society, 1969.

Tyler, Ron. *Visions of America: Pioneer Artists in a New Land*. New York: Thames & Hudson, 1983.

Tyler, Ron, ed. *Alfred Jacob Miller: Artist on the Oregon Trail*. Fort Worth, Tex.: Amon Carter Museum, 1982.

———. *The New Handbook of Texas*. 6 vols. Austin: Texas State Historical Association, 1996.

Tyson, Carl N. *The Red River in Southwestern History*. Norman: Oklahoma University Press, 1981.

Vanloo, Carle and Jean Restout. *Les Lithographies de Paysages en France à l'époque romantique*. Paris: Armand Colin, 1938.

Vaïsse, Léon. *Essai sur l'Histoire de la Philologie Orientale*. Paris: Firmin-Didot, 1844.

Vercoutter, Jean. *A la recherche de l'Egypte oubliée*. Paris: Gallimard, ca. 1993.

Villiers, Marc de. *Histoire de la Fondation de la Nouvelle-Orléans (1717–1722)*. Paris: Imprimerie Nationale, 1917.

Wallace, Ernest, David M. Vigness, and George B. Ward, eds. *Documents of Texas History*. 2nd ed. Austin: State House Press, 1994.

Waller, Margaret. *The Male Malady: Fictions of Impotence in the French Romantic Novel*. New Brunswick, N.J.: Rutgers University Press, 1993.

Walton, Augustus Q. *A History of the Detection, Conviction, Life and Designs of John A. Murel, the Great Western Land Pirate*. Reprint: Woodville, Texas: Dogwood Press, 1984.

Warren, Harris G. *The Sword Was Their Passport: A History of American Filibustering in the Mexican Revolution*. Baton Rouge: Louisiana State University Press, 1943.

Weddle, Robert S. *The French Thorn: Rival Explorers in the Spanish Sea, 1682–1762*. College Station: Texas A&M Press, 1968; paperback reprint, 1991.

Wells, Carol, ed. *Cane River Country Louisiana*. Natchitoches, La.: North Western State University Press, 1979.

Whittington, G. P. "Dr. John Sibley of Natchitoches, 1757–1832." *Louisiana Historical Quarterly* 20 (1927): 467–512.

Wise, Marie Norris. *Norris-Jones-Crockett-Payne-Blanchard: The Heritage of Marie Norris Wise*. Sulphur, Louisiana: Wise Publications, 1994.

Williams, T. Harry. *Huey Long.* New York: Alfred A. Knopf, 1969.

Worcester, Don. *The Chisolm Trail: High Road of the Cattle Kingdom.* Lincoln: University of Nebraska Press, 1980.

Zimra, Clarisse. "La Vision du Nouveau Monde de Chateaubriand à Beaumont." *French Review* 49 (1976): 1001–24.

INDEX

NOTE: Because the text primarily deals with Théodore Pavie's life and travels, references to him are found throughout the index. Please refer to specific entries (e.g., birth date, parents, travels, Romanticism, etc.). Entries that do not specifically refer to another person should be assumed to refer to Théodore Pavie.

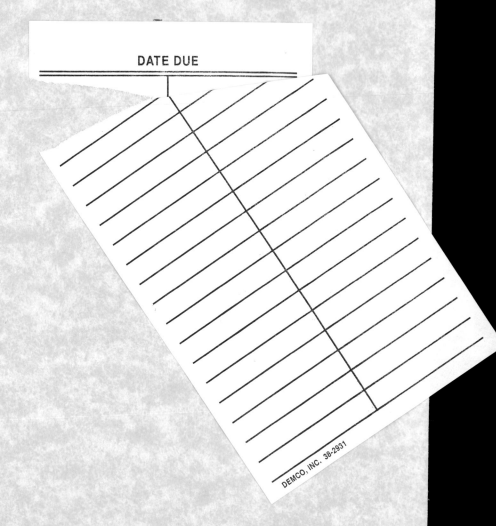

DATE DUE